DAVID BOYLE is the a
Tyranny of Numbers and
Economics Foundation. H

Praise for *Authenticity*:

'Ranging over the past, present and the future, Boyle lines up some heavy-duty referrals for his claims . . . There is a lightness of touch about many of the arguments put forward.' *Irish Examiner*

'As an analysis of the growing demand for "authentic" experiences and products in modern society, this entertaining book illustrates both the complexity of these demands and authenticity as a concept . . . The tone throughout is optimistic and realistic . . . Boyle succeeds in crafting a comprehensive, entertaining, evocative and engaging comfort blanket for those who want to eat their fair trade ice-cream with a clear conscience whilst watching *The Hulk*.' *New Consumer*

'An authentically original hypothesis.' *Times Higher Education Supplement*

'A spirited diatribe . . . This is an insightful, ambitious argument' *Independent*

'A highly thought-provoking book . . . Through his optimistic and witty writing, Boyle has put the notion of authenticity firmly on the map – showing the reader an unexpected force that could change our lives.' *Ecologist*

By the same author

Funny Money:
In Search of Alternative Cash

The Tyranny of Numbers:
Why Counting Can't Make Us Happy

AUTHENTICITY

Brands, Fakes, Spin
and the Lust for Real Life

DAVID BOYLE

HARPER PERENNIAL

Harper Perennial
An imprint of HarperCollins*Publishers*
77–85 Fulham Palace Road,
Hammersmith, London W6 8JB

www.harpercollins.co.uk/harperperennial

This edition published by Harper Perennial 2004
9 8 7 6 5 4 3 2 1

First published by Flamingo 2003

A catalogue record for this book
is available from the British Library

ISBN 0 00 717964 2

Set in Postscript Monotype Photina by
Rowland Phototypesetting Ltd, Bury St Edmunds, Suffolk

Printed and bound in Great Britain by
Clays Ltd, St Ives plc

To Sarah

CONTENTS

Acknowledgements ix
Introduction: Getting Real xiii

1 · Living in an Artificial World 1
2 · Real Business 26
3 · FAKE REAL #1: Fake Real and Virtual Real 56
4 · Real Food 74
5 · FAKE REAL #2: Out-Counter-Culturing 104
6 · Real Culture 123
7 · FAKE REAL #3: Living Real 154
8 · Real Relationships 177
9 · FAKE REAL #4: Pinning it Down 204
10 · Real Politics 226
11 · Authenticity Wars 259
12 · The New Renaissance 286

Index 297

ACKNOWLEDGEMENTS

I live in Crystal Palace – a suburb of London without palaces and almost completely free of crystal – so maybe that's what makes me interested in authenticity. The trouble is that I've got so fascinated during the writing of this book that nobody around me has been able to escape. For that reason, anyone who has had even a short conversation with me over the last year or so is partly responsible for what's in it. They may not see themselves there, but my obsession with the subject has meant I've been blown this way and that by everyone I've talked to – and I'm very grateful to them all for putting up with me.

I have found myself referring over and over again to a number of pioneering titles. Anyone who would like to follow some of the reading paths that brought me where I am now should have a look at Richard DeGrandpre's *Digitopia*, Jean Gimpel's *The End of the Future*, John Grant's *The New Marketing Manifesto*, Naomi Klein's *No Logo*, Kalle Lasn's *Culture Jam*, David Lewis's *The Soul of the New Consumer*, John Naisbitt's *High Tech High Touch*, Theodore Roszak's *The Cult of Information*, and of course Charlene Spretnak's *The Resurgence of the Real*.

I am particularly grateful to Judith Hodge, who helped me with the research and without whose ideas and suggestions I would never have finished writing. Also to my editors, first Lucinda McNeile and then Georgina Laycock, Philip Gwyn-Jones and Louise Tucker who have brought their imagination and good sense to the project and made an enormous difference to the book. And to Andrew Simms and Matthew Thomson who read great chunks of various drafts and whose comments have been absolutely invaluable. And to my agent Julian Alexander and his assistant Lucinda Cooke without whom I never would have started writing.

I'm also especially grateful to the following people for reading chapters for me or coming up with other vital ideas, guidance and advice: my father Richard Boyle who supplied many of the best anecdotes, Carol Cornish, Kate Cutler, Leonie Greene, Lesley Harding, Sue Holliday, Brian Jenner, Daphne Luchtenberg, Ed Mayo, Gill Paul, Chris Seeley, Perry Walker, Leila Zaghari, everyone at the New Economics Foundation and others too numerous to list here. The mistakes are all mine, but without all these friends and allies I wouldn't have managed at all.

And finally to Sarah, who was endlessly patient and supportive while I was writing and generally obsessive about the project, to whom I dedicate this book.

David Boyle
Crystal Palace

'Understand this clearly: you can teach a man to draw a straight line; to strike a curved line, and to carve it; and to copy and carve any number of given lines or forms, with admirable speed and precise precision; and you will find his work perfect of its kind: but if you ask him to think about any of those forms, to consider if he cannot find any better in his own head, he stops; his execution becomes hesitating; he thinks, and ten to one he thinks wrong; ten to one he makes a mistake in the first touch he gives to his work as a thinking being. But you have made a man of him for all that, he was only a machine before, an animated tool.'

John Ruskin, *The Stones of Venice*

'Primroses and landscapes, he pointed out, have one grave defect: they are gratuitous. A love of nature keeps no factories busy. It was decided to abolish the love of nature, at any rate among the lower classes; to abolish the love of nature, but not the tendency to consume transport. For of course it was essential that they should keep on going to the country, even though they hated it. The problem was to find an economically sounder reason for consuming transport than a mere affection for primroses and landscapes. It was duly found . . .'

Aldous Huxley, *Brave New World*

INTRODUCTION

Getting Real

> **'We keep coming back and coming back**
> **To the real . . .'**
>
> Wallace Stevens, 'An ordinary evening in New Haven', 1950

Imagine for a moment that, once Spectre had been safely defeated by Sean Connery, they turned the set of *You Only Live Twice* into a theme park – with a sliding roof over an artificial beach. Imagine they also put in a wave machine and heated the whole thing up to a steady 30 degrees centigrade. You will then have some idea of what the Japanese theme park Ocean Dome is like (motto: 'Paradise within a paradise').

In the course of thinking about this book, I've been to some of the most artificial places on earth. I've been to the wonderfully tacky Camp Snoopy in the middle of the Mall of America outside Minneapolis, the biggest shopping mall in the USA – the same size as the City of London's financial centre. I've been to the small Colorado town of Black Hawk, leached of all reality by legalized gambling – which has driven everything else away, leaving only some fearsome-looking men in dark glasses offering to park your car. I've even been to a Centreparc. But there is something special about Ocean Dome.

It's partly because it's bigger than anything like it in the world, bigger than many ocean liners – over one thousand feet long, it stretches along the coast highway, part of Myazaki's struggling Seagaia resort. But it's also partly because Ocean Dome is actually positioned right next to rolling waves – the Pacific coast is just on the other side of the road.

There is the artificial beach, a few hundred yards from the real beach, with similar waves lapping it – though Ocean Dome waves can be produced ten foot high for surfing at the press of a button, each precisely the same as the last. Nor does Ocean Dome, with its 13,500 tons of water and space for 10,000 people, have the mild inconveniences of salt water, crabs, seaweed or fish. 'This is a place where we can feel that we are part of nature,' says Phoenix Resorts, which invested $1 billion to build it. I don't think they're right.

The Japanese are masters of theme parks. There is a reproduction of Hans Andersen's house in Hokkaido, robots of American movie stars at Tochigi-ken, a whole British-style village at Shizuoka and a reproduction of the *Santa Maria* in Osaka – bizarrely, twice the size of the original (*better* than real, perhaps), in case the smallness of the ship that discovered America should disappoint. There is a theme park in the Tokyo suburbs devoted to Hello Kitty, the kitten with a red hair ribbon, a cartoon character which is said to live in London, created by the company Sanrio. There is even an 'authentic' reproduction of Christ's tomb in Aomori prefecture.

But it was Ocean Dome I had to see, because there was something about building a virtual version of a beach just over a fence, through a small wood and across a motorway from a real one which made my head spin. After all, when we are constantly told that the future of the world is global and virtual, Ocean Dome ought to represent the future. But there are other unrecorded forces at work in the opposite direction, and to pinpoint exactly *why* people are beginning to turn away from an entirely unreal future, I thought I ought to go there myself.

I went by bus, after a ruinously expensive flight to Myazaki – following in the path of the foreign ministers of the G8, who held their summit there in 2000. The bus had blurred window glass, which did nothing for my jet-lag, but it was all too obvious when I got there that Ocean Dome is no longer the most exciting holiday prospect for the average Japanese holiday-maker. I was almost the only punter to go near the place all day, and the staff seemed delighted to see me.

I shouldn't have read quite so much into that, perhaps. Japan is, after all, a country where security women at the airport X-ray machines smile at you charmingly, bow and say: 'Excuse please. Do you have a knife?'

I spent ages choosing a pair of swimming trunks, having left mine behind in London, and eventually fastened on a bright orange design with yachts – much to the concern of the staff. It turned out I was only expected to hire them, and would have to give them back at the end of the day. But having made the transaction, and wearing the orange yachts, I finally walked out into the fake beach.

It was a beautiful day, with a light breeze, but the sliding translucent roof stayed firmly in place in case the real world should tempt us outside. The beach itself was made of small white pebbles, a smaller version of the kind used on graves in English country churchyards. But once you got into the water in the surf, it was more like the surface of a very worn ski-slope. I crunched down towards the waves, with the sense of being inside the school gymnasium on a beautiful summer's day. The only other bathers were a small child, an elderly lady in a long T-shirt, a lifeguard and a man with a hoover – and a woman behind the counter who sold me something called Oolong tea, which I don't recommend.

The palm trees were too perfect to be real. The fruit behind the counter turned out to be plastic, and the backdrop where the horizon should have been was painted with small clouds and a deep blue sky as the Pacific view outside probably should have been. There was the sound of a waterfall at one end, and the piped sound of 'Swing Low Sweet Chariot' – which you wouldn't, let's face it, get on a real beach.

The other end was a small replica volcano, complete with water slides, called Bali Ha'i. I wondered if it had ever occurred to James Michener or Oscar Hammerstein, writing *Tales of the South Pacific* just after VJ Day, that their imaginary island would one day become a Japanese theme park (spelled 'Bari Hai'). A big picture of Eric the Juggler behind me – wearing a bowtie and looking like a CNN newsreader – implied that there was often more going on here than there was today. But it was Friday afternoon: you would have expected a little more activity, even taking into account Japan's parlous economic state.

After an hour or so writing postcards on the beach, I gave up. The real sunshine filtering through the glass at either end of the monstrous auditorium was just too tempting. There was something fascinating about Ocean Dome, but something unnerving too. I suppose the fear in the back of the mind is that this may soon be the only kind of beaches we've got left – having abandoned the rest to chemical jetties or oil slicks.

And I realized that this is exactly what I've been told throughout my life – either by those who were excited about this brave new artificial future or by those who felt powerless to stop it. We have lived through more than half a century of being constantly told that the future of food was artificial, the future of books, newspapers, medicine and schools was virtual. And that we would soon deal entirely with computerized teachers and doctors through screens.

For most of that time, the predictions seemed only too true. But if you look around today, despite Ocean Dome and McDonald's and Microsoft, the real world has been fighting back. The idea of artificial beaches and holidays by holodeck – the virtual reality holidays enjoyed by *Star Trek: The Next Generation* – do not look likely to satisfy us after all.

In fact, everywhere we look, there is a barely recorded struggle happening between real and artificial, with the word 'authentic' cropping up again and again in advertisements. The word was once used in marketing to mean 'genuine copy', but now 'authentic' seems to have a deeper meaning which is hard to pin down. This book is my attempt to pinpoint it, investigate it and see what's going on – and decide who is winning. Because far from experiencing the last twitches of the real world, I believe this struggle may be a clue to the way the future is going to be.

What do I mean by 'real'? This book is a kind of definition, so I won't pre-empt myself here – except to say that I believe people increasingly mean something very specific, even if they haven't actually sat down and defined it themselves. And except to say that this isn't intended to be an addition to the growing literature which says that we are living at a unique period and technology is either about to ruin us or transform us. I don't believe either of those things: I want to be optimistic about it – I believe we will adapt and cope, but primarily by demanding authenticity.

It isn't so much that I *want* the world to be more authentic – though I do. I'm arguing that this process is happening already, and is a direct result of people's fears that what they consider real is endangered – a fear that every experience they are offered in the modern world is trying to persuade them, shape them or cajole them.

No, this is intended to be a book about the future that's excited about it – without forgetting what might go wrong, and without falling for the myth that it's going to be so high-tech that we won't recognize ourselves as human.

I am only too aware that there may seem to be contradictions in this. Trying to pin down authenticity is fiendishly paradoxical. On the one hand I'm saying that people are demanding authenticity because they are fed up with being foisted off with fake. On the other hand, I'm saying that many of the predictions of a virtual future we have been brought up with have failed – and without us quite noticing, all that plastic and formica has given way to a tiptoed return of cotton, brick and real ceramics. But as I hope you will agree with me, by the book's end, these are parallel processes. In practice they don't contradict. People are simultaneously reacting against the artificial world they are forced to live in – much as they may enjoy some of it – and re-discovering the importance of authenticity. There is a struggle going on.

The paragraphs at the end of each chapter entitled *It never happened* are predictions of a virtual or a downright fake future which haven't happened – at least so far. They are intended not so much as a comment on the futility of making predictions – I am making some of my own, after all – but to make it clear how the artificial futures predicted for us for the past half century simply haven't come to pass.

They may still, of course. But I hope what I've written here will arm us a little more for a debate about whether or not we want them.

It never happened . . .

'Someday, perhaps, office workers need not even abandon their desks. They will simply watch a destination tape and swallow a vacation tablet. In the meantime, we will just have to struggle along with the next best thing; re-creations of the Great Outdoors, set inside sanitized domes. With sand.'

Ron Gluckman on Ocean Dome,
Korean Airlines magazine *Morning Calm*, 1999

1

Living in an Artificial World

'Come, bombs, and blow to smithereens
Those air-conditioned, bright canteens,
Tinned fruit, tinned meat, tinned milk, tinned beans
Tinned minds, tinned breath . . .'

John Betjeman, *Slough*, 1937

'Better authentic Mammon than bogus god.'

Louis MacNeice, *Autumn Journal*, 1937

There we were, a serendipitous assortment of people, on top of King's Tor in Dartmoor, not too far from the maximum security prison. Laden with picnics and umbrellas, we chatted idly about marriage and making bread, as we waited for the long anticipated total eclipse of the sun over Britain's far south-western corner in the summer of 1999.

Other groups had brought along their picnic chairs, portable tables and toys for the kids, and were busily unwrapping sandwiches. One man had even brought a hand-held TV and was watching footage of the still un-eclipsed sun, listening to a BBC commentator on the Lizard peninsula describing the scene.

He was calling some of this out, because – Dartmoor being what it is – the sky was entirely overcast. The sun had already been covered by what looked like a large wet grey duvet in the sky, which seemed likely to keep any eclipse entirely secret.

So we couldn't actually see what the BBC was broadcasting so clearly: the moon edging its way over the sun, two discs that – through some bizarre astronomical coincidence – look exactly the same size when seen from Earth. 'It's covering fifteen per cent,' shouted the man, his eye fixed to the television. 'It's covering thirty per cent.'

But then suddenly, the shadow of the moon passed over Dartmoor, and everyone stopped talking. It was an extraordinary upside-down experience, as the whole world went dark at 11 in the morning. The sheep lay down, the street lights in the nearest village in the distance across the moor came on automatically. It was a moment of almost spiritual doubt. As if God had unilaterally torn up his contract with the Earth, and darkness once more covered the face of the deep. Although it was only three minutes, it seemed such an impossible change that the return of light didn't seem so certain any more.

So, having been a little cynical about the whole expedition, I clambered back across the boulders thinking that nothing would ever be the same again. It was, of course – it usually is – but that doesn't take away from the feeling of having the world plunged into night during elevenses.

As the moon's shadow had shot over us, and all conversation suddenly ceased in mid-sentence, there was just one voice remaining. It was the wife of the man with the hand-held TV, shouting at him: 'Turn it off! Turn it off! *Experience it!*'

Of course, it feels a little dangerous to experience the eclipse without having it mediated through a TV commentator – what are we supposed to think about it, after all? But the man reluctantly flicked the switch and then watched spellbound with the rest of us.

Over the years that have followed, I've realized that many people have been making that same demand for the authentic in many areas of life. The picture on the television might have been better and clearer. It might have included the expert opinions of scientists and even, maybe, background mood music. It might have told us the correct things to feel at the right moments. The point is that many of us – and an increasing proportion of the Western world – want to experience it ourselves. We want it real.

On the face of it, the world is accelerating in the opposite direction. We live in a world dominated by spin-doctors, advertising, virtual goods and services. We are surrounded by the shoddy and the unreal, and by a global economy determined to foist it on us, even if we weren't prepared to embrace it enthusiastically ourselves – which we so often are.

We have come through a period of unprecedented prosperity and aggressive certainty, ushered in by the end of the Cold War and the internet revolution. We have been told endlessly that the future is going to be overwhelmingly global and gloriously virtual, and that the two strands are intricately related. We have seen the pictures of rabbis in black robes and ringlets, putting their mobile phones up to Jerusalem's Wailing Wall so that relatives in New York could pray. We have read about the call centre staff in India who are given detailed lessons about *EastEnders*, so they can exchange chitchat with callers ringing about gas leaks in Weybridge. We've probably talked to them ourselves without knowing it. The recession may have slowed down the 'inevitable' progress towards a virtual world, but most of us accept that globalization is with us for good.

Yet that trend has begun to spawn its opposite, and – although the demand for the real is barely showing itself above the horizon yet – it has already made itself felt in many different areas of cultural life, from poetry to politics and from food to fashion. It is beginning to be clear that the dominant cultural force of the century ahead won't just be global and virtual, but a powerful interweaving of opposites – globalization *and* localization, virtual *and* real, with an advance guard constantly undermining what is packaged and drawing much of society along behind them.

Despite the accepted wisdom about the future of business and the planet – that anything local and real is hopelessly old-fashioned or economically impractical, or both – people's demands for the authentic are increasingly felt. A revolution is starting that is going to mean trouble for businesspeople and marketeers alike, as their most conscious consumers suddenly launch a determined rejection of the fake, the virtual, the spun and the mass-produced.

These same people are also going to carry on wanting the benefits of the virtual world. They're not going to give up email or MTV or mobile phones or microwaves. This isn't a phenomenon where people long for the past, just one that tries to learn from it about what they want. And they aren't necessarily going to conform to a technological future mapped out for them by a strange alliance of big telecom corporations, American libertarian theorists, futuristic IT magazines like *Wired* and people who see economics as just a brutal extension of Darwin's evolution theory.

No, they increasingly want 'real' food – maybe organic – that tastes of something, doesn't involve fish genes for temperature control, and comes from a real place somewhere on the map. They don't want the kind of consumables in the form of pills or tubes that experts used to tell us represented the future of food because the Apollo and Gemini astronauts used them.

They want the real sound of people working, not the recorded muttering that the BBC paid £2,300 for in 2000 when they worried that their accounts department was too quiet. Or the fake smells that London Underground tried in their tunnels the same year.

Or the fake places that all look the same, with the same global storefronts in every town and city around the world, in the cheapest international style of glass and concrete.

Or fake politicians whose slightest utterance is tested before focus groups and scripted, and who – like George W. Bush – even have the word 'Wow!' on the teleprompter.

Or the fake relationships people create online, never having to meet, using fake names – sometimes even breaking up real flesh-and-blood relationships in the process.

Or fake community activity, like the Holiday Bowling Lanes in New London, Connecticut, which social theorist Robert Putnam describes in his book *Bowling Alone*, with giant TV screens above each lane, where the players never talk to each other between turns, but just stare sadly upwards.

Or the kind of world where, except for the very rich, most will have to rely on virtual bankers, virtual doctors, virtual pharmacists, virtual carers and virtual teachers.

That's not to say that there's no market for internet chat rooms, Pot Noodle, NHS Online – or George W. Bush for that matter. There clearly is. But there's also a growing suspicion of a world where we don't have to see people or touch anything, and a longing for something we can't quite put our fingers on. Just how big that market is, I'll discuss later – but what large numbers of people in the Western economy want, they tend to get.

Their problem is that the world seems geared up to give them something else. Remote controls now outnumber people in the USA, after all. New York marketing expert David Alpert has fifty-five in his home in Long Island. He doesn't have to sully his hands at all. There is a concerted attempt going on to define humanity in such a way that no distinction is possible between real and virtual – because human beings *are* just glorified computers. It is the justification for the millions being pumped into the idea of replacing biological human life with a mixture of genetic engineering, cryogenics, artificial intelligence and nano-technology.

Nor is this an idea that's confined to weird Montana militia-men or crazy scientists. Francis Fukuyama, influential author of *The End of History*, could talk about 'abolishing human beings as such' within a couple of generations, so that 'a new post-human history will begin'. MIT's Marvin Minsky talked about the advent of 'artificial scientists, artists, composers and personal compan-ions'. Even the head of BT's laboratory Peter Cochrane looked forward to a 'creeping evolution towards a cyborg world of partially artificial people'. 'So what separates us and our noisy neurons from those in the latest machines?' he asked in 1999. 'Only scale and sensors. Our awareness comes from sight, sound, touch, smell and taste. We can now give all of this to a machine in a form that could be superior to ours.'

As the philosopher Theodore Roszak points out, these are views expressed by corporations, like IBM or AT&T, with a stake in it being so: 'Whenever I hear vested interests like these speak-ing of information as if it was *all* the human mind needs to think with, I begin to feel as if I had strayed into some strange sect where all about me I find people worshipping light bulbs. No question but that light bulbs are useful devices; I would not want to live without them. But I never would have thought of them as objects of veneration.'

However, the tide is turning. The co-founder of Sun Micro-systems, Bill Joy, recently warned that 'the future may not need us', when systems get so complex that the computers are effectively in control of them. The pioneer of virtual reality, Jaron Lanier, also attacked what he called 'cybernetic totalism' and the idea that 'biology and physics will merge with computer science . . . resulting in life and the physical universe becoming mercurial, achieving the supposed nature of computer software'.

The totally virtual world on offer frightens many of us, but in some ways we are already part of it. Bill Joy's 'uncontrollably complex systems' is actually rather a good description of the way the current world stock markets are organized. The realism of some children's computer games is out of all proportion to what it was even five years ago – and often wildly violent. To reach the most advanced stage of the Sony Playstation 2 game *Carmageddon*, a child has to have successfully run over and killed a total of 33,000 virtual pedestrians.

And of course there is a steady stream of modern prophets drawing attention to the dangers. The American psychologist Richard DeGrandpre warns of a virtual world that's 'emptying of reality', causing hyperactivity, depression and violence. There are modern Luddites like Kirkpatrick Sale, philosophers like Theodore Roszak, social critics like Jean Baudrillard, but it's strange how few are business writers. What is so powerful about the new search for authenticity is that people are doing it without the phenomenon being fed back to them incessantly by the media – quite the reverse. Many of them actually feel they are swimming against the tide – flying in the face of the technological prophets who tell them constantly that they are trapped, and the business writers who tell them they are perverse.

Still, there are exceptions that prove the rule. 'In a virtual world, we'll long for reality even more,' said the philosopher Robert Nozick, and that could be a motto for this book. And right back in 1982, the business guru and author of *Megatrends* John Naisbitt predicted a phenomenon he called 'high tech/high touch' that seems to lift the curtain on the demand for authenticity. 'The more our lives are steeped in technology, the more people want to be with other people (at movies, museums, book cubs, kids' soccer games),' he wrote later. 'The more high-tech medicine becomes, the greater the interest in alternative healing practices; the more we toil on computers using our brains not our bodies, the more high touch and sensual our leisure activities become (gardening, cooking, carpentry, bird watching).'

He's absolutely right, and twenty years on we can see it emerging. Even so, the trenchant California cyber-critic Paulina Borsook put her finger on the real issue when she described an afternoon of videos about the future by AT&T, Apple and Sun Microsystems at the San Francisco Exploratorium in 1994. She came away feeling sick.

'Strangely enough it was a *boring* world,' she wrote afterwards. 'A world where technology in general and software in particular has taken over all higher brain functions . . . is one where people don't get to be creative, act on hunches, or, ultimately, get to use their instrumental intelligence. At best, people were reduced to cyber-kindergartners, cutting and pasting bits of information, collage-like, with their computers supplying the virtual equivalent of library paste.'

It's the key reason that so many people are starting, in the media equivalent of a dim light, to feel around them for something firm to grasp.

Just outside Disney World, in Florida, you will find the spankingly ever-so-wired, futuristic new town of Celebration – the one satirized in the film *Shrek*. Celebration was the brainchild of Walt Disney himself. He wanted to create a town with a sense of community and cleanliness, but it was put on hold the moment he died in 1966, and it had to wait to be turned into bricks and mortar by Disney's extremely well-paid CEO, Michael Eisner, three decades later.

One clue that there is something a little peculiar about Celebration is that it looks scarily like the suburb that imprisoned Jim Carrey in *The Truman Show*, which was actually filmed in nearby Seaside. Another is the constant repetition in the corporate hype that Celebration is 'real'.

Why might there be any doubt about the reality of Celebration? Well, in the first place, it is probably the first town in the world to have the internet planned in from the start. Celebration is designed specifically as a wired and virtual town – a virtual community, in fact. There are online bulletin boards for everything and an amazing array of online interactivity, delivered by fibre-optic network. There is even constant closed-circuit TV coverage of what's going on at school which you can watch on the internet.

But what really casts doubt on the reality of the place is the way that it pretends to some kind of permanence. Most of the homes are designed in turn-of-the-century style, like almost every Disney film you've ever seen. The shops have signs with bogus foundation dates like 'since 1905' when actually everything is less than five years old. It is designed to give a timeless sense of what smalltown America used to be like – or should have been like – in the days of *It's a Wonderful Life*. Muzak is piped from speakers built into the roots of the palm trees in the streets. There's a particularly disturbing corner of the town called the 'Preview Center' which consists simply of full-size pictures of the houses on sale, mounted on billboards – real cardboard cut-outs.

Disney's brochures call it a 'hopscotch-and-tag neighborhood to be viewed from a front porch swing' and a 'special place for families . . . in a time of innocence'. While we might gag on that kind of saccharine, something in this fake place actually smacks of a new search for something real. There's no Burger King, McDonald's or Walmart, as there is in every other town in the USA. It's the only place in the vicinity of Orlando where you can't buy Disney World sweatshirts.

But what really marks Celebration out as worryingly unreal is the involvement of Disney itself, the great reality-manager. And in this, there is another very important aspect of the new search for authenticity.

Celebration is a corporate town, there entirely for the greater glory of Disney, and that has some peculiar and unreal implications. When some of the families complained about standards in the Disney-run Celebration school, the company ignored them and promptly hired a light plane to encourage the principal, Bobbi Vogel, whom they were afraid had been disheartened by the dispute. It towed a big banner across the town centre bearing the enthusiastic slogan 'Great Job Bobbi!' on Celebration's rapidly organized Teacher Appreciation Day.

When some of the families involved decided to pack up and leave, Disney offered to waive the rule that they couldn't profit from the sale if they left in less than a year – but only on condition they signed a contract promising never to reveal their reasons for wanting to go.

There are whole phone directories full of rules for residents – including one that denies them the right to park pick-up trucks in the street. These can't be changed, even by the elected Homeowners' Association, without the written approval of the company. All power remains behind the scenes with Disney for as long as they want it. Even more peculiar is the attitude of some of the residents to all this. 'It's definitely a democracy,' one couple told the *New York Times Magazine*, 'because we can go to the town hall and express our feelings.' That isn't the conventional definition, but then this is ersatz consumer democracy rather than the old-fashioned voting kind – and people there don't always seem to be able to tell the difference.

Many people enjoy living like that, but increasingly there are many who don't – those who fear that their lives and experiences are being repackaged and fed back to them by corporate communicators interested only in short-term profit. It's the fear not just that every town from Dover to Des Moines will soon look the same, but that every corner of our mental lives will be populated by the same logos.

This is the fear of the power over reality that modern marketing has – when a product like Jell-O, made by tobacco giant Phillip Morris, gets designated Utah's official state snack after a po-faced debate in the Utah senate. Or when a leading star in Aussie rules football gets paid to change his name to that of a prominent cat food, so that the commentators have to exclaim that 'Whiskas' has scored a goal.

Or when pupils find themselves doing problems – as they do increasingly in North America – where they compare the viscosity of Prego sauce to Ragu, because Campbell's Soup has sponsored the teaching materials. Or about how long it will take to save up for a pair of trainers, because they've been sponsored by Nike. Or when children are herded into the classroom to watch sponsored television from the US Channel One, on the condition that they don't speak during the ads, in return for corporate sponsorship of their school.

Or when over 130 everyday phrases like 'Hey, it could happen' or 'Have you had your break today?' turn out to be 'owned' by McDonald's, and when a word like 'Enjoy!' claims to have been officially sponsored by Coca-Cola. Or where Microsoft lays legal claim to the phrase 'Where do you want to go today?'

Or when the local church in Munster, Indiana, now sports a Starbucks in the lobby (not to mention the McDonald's in the Brentwood Baptist Church in Houston). Or when the human gene for obesity is leased to Swiss drugs giant Hoffman LaRoche.

In this kind of branded reality, people are afraid that their grip on what is authentic is somehow slipping from them. Worse, that they may be starting to live out the world of the 1999 film *The Matrix*, where everyone's brains exist in a vat, but are programmed into a wonderful hyper-real virtual world by a giant corporation. The roots of the new demand for authenticity lie in this kind of excess – a sense that reality itself is up for sale. In this sense, and others too, both globalization and the internet contain within them the seeds of their own antithesis.

The effect of an increasingly virtual world, where nothing is quite what it seems, has led to a growing clamour for what is genuine and human. 'Human relations are declining in the selling game,' says the legendary former General Electric chief executive Jack Welch. But when everything is available online, then a bit of real humanity may be the only thing that gives you an edge over your rivals. The equally legendary virtual share-trader E*Trade has opened its first real branch, in New York's Madison Avenue. 'The two biggest markets in the $8 trillion-a-year economy of the United States,' said John Naisbitt, 'are 1) consumer technology and 2) the escape from consumer technology.'

But the same paradox is also true of globalization. Its whole logic is that every price and wage advantage will eventually be filled and everywhere in the world – from Manhattan to Manila – will cost much the same (rather like London house prices that have expanded to take in almost every corner of the capital, however unpleasant). At that point, you might as well produce your stuff locally – at least you don't have to pay transport costs, and local roots give you something to market.

Globalization is not suddenly going to disappear, sending us all back to a cottage economy. Nor are we going to un-invent the internet and beat our computers into ploughshares. It's not going to happen. But simply because globalization is so powerful, there's an equally strong opposite reaction going on.

That's why a *Business Week* survey of the seventy-four top brands in the world in 2001 found that forty-one had lost value in the previous year, with the biggest brands – Coca-Cola, Gillette, Nike and McDonald's – taking the biggest hit. The trend has continued since. That's why the top ten brands in China have squeezed out anything made by Coke or Procter & Gamble – they're all local. That's why the big corporations have been buying up homegrown, homespun brands like Ben & Jerry's (Unilever) or Aroma coffee houses (McDonald's).

'Mass marketing has become a very hard thing to do because people don't like to be seen as "normal" any more – they all want to be seen as individuals,' says Martin Hayward, chairman of the forecasters Henley Centre. 'The bigger you become, the less appealing you become. It's a dilemma: somehow, you have to find a way of exploiting the behind-the-scenes benefits of being big, yet at the point at which you touch the consumer, you have to be seen to be small.'

That's the tough new world business has to operate in. It's also the first glimmering of the demand for authenticity.

'By reality, I mean shops like Selfridges, and motor buses, and the *Daily Express*,' said Lawrence of Arabia, complaining about expatriate writers who had lost touch with real life at home – and, at the same time, proving that all this talk about realism and authenticity isn't really very new.

We have, after all, just lived through a century when the followers of Freud defined authenticity as meaning a close understanding of one's unconscious, while the followers of Marx defined it as a close understanding of the proletariat and ordinary life. T. E. Lawrence meant pretty much the same, but defined it in terms of a middle-class life of shopping, department stores and the excesses of the Beaverbrook Press. He meant ordinary everyday reality.

We have lived through a generation when architects believed 'real' life was so appalling that they really ought to make that awfulness more visible. The result: the tenants of their imagination had to live in brutally monstrous housing estates – a kind of self-fulfilling prophecy if ever there was one. We've also lived through a generation that used the term 'realism' to hit the middle classes over the head with – as if suburban life wasn't nearly brutal enough to be realistic.

There's another problem too. When people today talk about the real thing – when they are not referring to the worn-out slogan owned by Coca-Cola, that is – they often mean something old-fashioned. They mean 'real' linen sheets or 'real' country villages with thatched roofs, or 'real' meals of roast beef cooked slowly and lovingly without the aid of modern appliances, and by somebody else. Or a 'real' community where the women took cold soup round to elderly people every Tuesday afternoon.

The trouble with that kind of real is that it harks back to days where authenticity was bought, either at great expense, or by misusing women or black people or poor people, to provide these so-called 'real' things – people we didn't pay properly, and sometimes didn't pay at all. Microwaves and washing machines brought freedom from that kind of authenticity, and we don't want to go back there even if we could.

There's a worrying extreme conservatism that lurks behind

this. There are those who believe that an 'authentic' English town means that only people of Anglo-Saxon descent live there – and that authenticity means a rigorous stamping out of the modern world, with the aid of birches and detention centres. In this unpleasant sense, immigrants are somehow not authentic citizens and disabled people somehow aren't authentic humans.

The current demand for authenticity is something different and, although there are sometimes echoes of these in the meaning of the word, much more coherent. It does hark backwards, but it's more than that. It derives from the so-called 'cultural creatives' in the USA and the so-called 'inner-directeds' in Europe – those people identified by the sociologists who put education, individuality and authenticity at the heart of their ambitions for themselves. For the sake of argument, let's distinguish them from the old kind by calling them New Realists.

When fashion designer Stella McCartney adopted a look involving jeans and a second-hand corset, launching a vogue for vintage clothes that now sells through charity shops, dress agencies and Christie's, she was recreating a sense of authenticity in the past. But she was doing it in a very contemporary way. Vintage fashions are absolutely individual and you won't find an expensive brand label anywhere.

So there's a danger that too much talk of the wrong kind of authenticity gives strength to ethnic cleansing, but this is something modern. The modern real – New Realism – includes different elements: it would be difficult to buy a product that displayed all of these following strands at once. But they relate to each other, and taken together, they represent a revolution in the way many people want to live. I've tried to pinpoint ten.

Authenticity element #1: *Real means ethical*

I remember explaining the concept of ethical investment – that you concentrate your investments in companies whose activities you approve of – to someone who had never come across the idea before. 'I don't believe you,' she laughed, which made me sound even more pompous than I had been before. 'You're joking!'

The fact is that making those kind of demands on companies makes no sense at all to people with a different world view. But £4 billion is now ethically 'screened' in the UK, and at least $100 billion in the USA – mainly because some people are reacting against the way their lives seemed morally fragmented. They may disapprove of selling weapons to impoverished countries. They may be members of conservation groups or environmental organizations – and yet their pension money is invested in arms companies or multinationals extracting oil from the Arctic or chopping down rainforests. Their breakfast cereal may be owned by a tobacco multinational that is pressing the riskiest cigarettes on teenagers in Vietnam. It isn't enough for people just to pray or give money to charity – they want real moral coherence.

They don't expect moral purity. They know that, however much they buy recycled toilet paper, they still stamp on creepy-crawlies every time they go into the shop. But they do want that sense that their lives are not, through their actions, undermining people or planet.

Authenticity element #2: *Real means natural*

Employees of the semiconductor giant Intel now receive an average of 300 emails a day, part of the company's total daily average of 3,000,000. This overload can swamp normal human communication, and any of us who work in an office in the Western world can testify to something along the same lines. It isn't just

Intel's people who could spend their entire working lives answering emails.

Unfortunately, this kind of set-up is also a charter for the worst kind of managers – those who prefer to have no face-to-face dealings at all. Businesses are increasingly aware of this problem, because face-to-face management – what the business guru Tom Peters calls MBWA (Management By Walking Around) – is considerably more effective. Virtual management can take no account of individual foibles, can't respond to the kind of human feedback people give, and it's a disaster.

Human contact is important. It's also natural and authentic, and it chimes with the growing feeling some people have – the reverse of a generation or so back – that natural processes are more effective than unnatural ones. Hence the suspicion of 'unnatural' developments like genetically modified food, and burgeoning interest in 'natural' childbirth, 'natural' death, 'natural' pest control, even 'natural' yoghurt – and 'natural' health. More than half the population of the UK and USA have already used alternative health practitioners. This also explains the way that fake soft drinks like Coke and Pepsi have been losing out to natural ones like mineral water and fruit juices.

There is a growing sense, rightly or wrongly, that working *with* natural processes is safe, while working against them – managing the weather, suppressing immune systems – is best avoided except in serious emergencies. Half a century ago, this attitude would have been dismissed as quaint or downright Luddite.

Authenticity element #3: *Real means honest*

It's a peculiar paradox that we believe our politicians less than ever, but are ever more intolerant of their failings. Surveys show that we think they lie the whole time, but we are less prepared to endure it. We obsess about very narrow but blatant lies – 'I have not had sexual relations with that woman, Miss Lewinsky' – while forgetting the half-truths we are fed the rest of the time.

The search for authenticity is making people impatient with our passive acceptance. We are increasingly losing our tolerance for the subtle Big Lies. When Disney sells high-priced T-shirts decorated with a happy character like Winnie the Pooh, and the people who make them in Bangladesh are paid the equivalent of 20 cents for each shirt – well below a living wage – then that is a kind of lie. So are other smiling logos that conceal something darker.

When the British establishment invests as Lloyds 'names' in the insurance market believing in 'unlimited liability' – an impossibility – then it isn't surprising that this lie caused penury and despair for many of them. When the so-called New Economy could inflate the value of a website like Yahoo beyond that of American Airlines, then somebody was always going to get hurt. It's the same when the UK government declared that BSE in cows was no risk to humans, while secretly suppressing any research that might contradict them. Big Lies – the self-delusions of parliaments or corporations – do the most terrible damage because they're unreal. Especially the biggest lie of all: about 97 per cent of the $2 trillion that changes hands through the world's computers every day actually has nothing to do with goods, services or trade. It's all speculative froth.

Authenticity element #4: *Real means simple*

It isn't just the success of the Slow Food movement, the Campaign for Real Ale, organic food and O'Hagan's sausages. They are all symptoms of the demand for authenticity, but they are also all simple – simple recipes, simple traditional ingredients, no E numbers, no obscure chemicals.

Nor is it just food. Somewhere between 70 and 80 per cent of the population of both Britain and America say they want to take steps to simplify their lives. Those who fail to do so are usually the ones who are locked into highly complex lives by mortgage repayments. Many succeed, flying in the face of the ideologues who believe entrepreneurs have a sacred calling to carry on until they drop. There is more on this in Chapter 7.

Authenticity element #5: *Real means unspun*

When the ABC television network in the USA became the first to broadcast more than fifteen minutes of advertisements every hour, it set a disturbing precedent – quickly copied by its rivals – and the accusation that they were causing depression.

Most of us see images urging us to buy every few minutes, and in the process feel a little discontented. Most of us have found ways to counteract them – otherwise we'd be very poor indeed. But there's still a suspicion that advertisers are purchasing reality and twisting it around, possibly in the hope that we might catch 'logophilia' – defined by *Elle* as 'I am who I wear'.

It's a suspicion that is leading many back to poetry, to reading, to painting, to adventure holidays – anything that can keep us independent of the spinners.

Authenticity element #6: *Real means sustainable:*

Whenever you hear about a disastrous earthquake – be it in Turkey or Mexico – when the buildings fall down because of inadequate foundations, it's because the people who built them were living on a fantasy timescale. Buildings have often got to last centuries, and our life-support systems for the planet for millennia and more. Anything that undermines the way we live or upsets the planet's systems is not authentic.

The earthquake example was one of the inspirations for the

Long Now Foundation, who are planning a gigantic 10,000 year clock under the American desert, that – in the words of super-computer designer Daniel Hillis – 'ticks once a year, bongs once a century, and the cuckoo comes out every millennium.' That's real.

Authenticity element #7: *Real means beautiful*

'Beauty makes our public servants nervous,' wrote architect Richard Rogers after chairing the British government's Urban Task Force. He was repeatedly and strongly advised to remove words like 'beauty', 'harmony' and 'aesthetic', and replace them with bland alternatives like 'good design'. 'A building without beauty is not architecture but a construction, much as music without beauty is just noise,' he wrote.

Governments avoid the concept of beauty partly because it sounds so expensive and partly because they can't measure it. But it is an important aspect of authenticity because it implies both a sense of place and an antidote to identikit non-places. It's also an antidote to the standardized concrete landscaping where people are only permitted to walk on paths – what the landscape gardener Jurgen Albrecht calls 'the annihilation of human traces through perfect gardening'.

Authenticity element #8: *Real means rooted*

Sometimes that means rooted in tradition, one of the reasons why natural fibres, trams, bicycles and bricks have been making such a quiet comeback. But more often it means rooted locally, with a place of origin – rather than the merely manufactured, that appears to come from deep in the countryside but doesn't. Often it doesn't matter where that somewhere is. It could be the local farm or a small Vietnamese village; what matters is that it is somewhere specific, made by someone specific.

And to a certain extent this is a guarantee of ethics. If a

manufacturer tells you about where their product is made, or the person who made it, it is more likely that it is the result of an equal exchange. If the real story of the product is that it's made by twelve year olds, paid a pittance for working an eighteen-hour day in a sweatshop patrolled by guards who beat them if they slow down, then it is much more likely to appear on the retailer's shelf without any indication of where it comes from. Anonymity is suspect if you're looking for authenticity.

Then there is the new phenomenon known as 'back-shifting', or moving back 'home'. Half the UK population now lives within half an hour of where they were brought up. This isn't exactly globalization.

Authenticity element #9: *Real means three-dimensional*

Of course, in one sense, eating in McDonald's is perfectly solid – if not actually real. But in another sense, the experience is a shiny, manufactured one, designed to be absolutely ubiquitous, when real experience has depth. It is more than just a superficial engagement with a brand, delivered with the help of software by a human being whose actions are all managed by time-and-motion analysis.

People increasingly want their experiences to be multi-dimensional, complex and slightly less than perfect, because that is what real life is all about – and what it feels like to interact with a human being.

Authenticity element #10: *Real means human*

Although I've come to this last, it is actually the most important – the aspect of authenticity that weaves its way through all the rest. It means rooted in humanity, tolerant and human-scale, rather than based on some factory version of what mass-produced people ought to be like. And if it's human, it has to be diverse.

There is no place in authenticity for single, top-down solutions, because these are just not human. But more of this towards the end of the book.

It isn't that these New Realists want to plunge back into the past or give up the benefits virtual technology has given them – or that they are fully aware of exactly what they do want. There will still be arguments about different kinds of authenticity, such as: is royalty fake because it seems archaic, or authentic because it's traditional in an age where everything else seems to require corporate sponsorship? I tend to think the latter. The point is that people seem increasingly to have a sense that the word sums up a quality that can balance the extreme dislocation of the rest of their lives, when place and time just slip through all our fingers. 'In the time of my childhood, Monday was wash day, Tuesday was market day, and Sunday was worship and a day for rest,' said Hillis. 'In this age of twenty-four-hours-a-day, seven-days-a-week convenience, I have begun to lose my bearings.'

Of course there are quite enough of us out there who don't get a disturbing shiver at what is blatantly unreal – who will happily behave like an Accidental Tourist abroad. 'There's nothing here to remind you that you are in Switzerland,' said a McDonald's spokesman proudly about two hotels they opened there, complete with golden arch chairs. Many people wouldn't yet find anything odd about that statement.

But even the most fervent globalization enthusiasts hanker for the real. *New York Times* writer Thomas Friedman – author of that hymn to globalization *The Lexus and the Olive Tree* – wrote about his brother-in-law's delight in locally grown Jersey Beefsteak tomatoes, and how much better they tasted than laboratory ones. And when he suggested that his brother-in-law get straight on the internet, find someone offering Jersey Beefsteak online, and have them Fedexed to him overnight – he wasn't so much missing the point, as looking for ways that something local and real could be available more widely. It's an important paradox that I'll come back to in Chapter 4.

'The future of globalization may depend on it,' he said, and – as a compromise between what's virtual and what's real – it might indeed.

I once heard about a gardener in Mexico City whose principal job was painting chickens a healthy yellow colour. Most of the chickens in the market were kept in filthy conditions, and as a result were pale, scrawny, white things. A lick of paint and they looked considerably more edible. My father used to tell a similar story about a Frenchman he knew in Bolivia, who ran a travel agency catering for tourists who came, mainly, to see the Inca ruins. He had discovered plenty of Inca ruins for a full day's tour, and several for an overnight stay, but absolutely nothing ruinous suitable for a half-day tour. So he built one, and wrote the guide-book to it.

It's tougher to behave in this way these days. Once the New Realists start sniffing out what's authentic, the fakery they've put up with over the years seems almost as blatant as the paint – which is not so very different from E numbers and additives after all. And it isn't just because of globalization's all-seeing eyes. It's because of society's increasing obsession with what is fake and what is real. Does it count if you climb Everest using oxygen, or do you have to do it the hardest way, on your own, and without crampons? Is the Jerry Springer Show staged? Is that a real Ralph Lauren? Do exam results count when children are force-fed on Ritalin? And, even in the USA when a quarter of all cosmetic surgery is on under thirty-nines, is that face and body *really* yours?

When the TV show *Survivor* arrived in the USA, NBC booked a soap star who had played a character on a desert island to comment. *Time* magazine didn't let them get away with it. 'A fake person analysing a fake event,' they said. And when former Spice Girl Victoria Beckham greeted her fans in Birmingham in 2001 wearing a fake lip ring – and had the misfortune to drop her microphone during her performance, so the audience could hear her mysteriously carry on singing – she made the front pages even of the serious papers. So did Coca-Cola when their 'pure' Dasani water was revealed to come out of the tap.

So don't be taken in if the home-grown, home-spun attributes of this New Realism sound too bloodless and gentle. The truth is the debate can sometimes seem pretty brutal, even hypocritical. It isn't the companies with the worst record on the environment that come under the full media spotlight – it's those like the Body Shop that have made claims or tried to make a difference. Hypocrisy – failures in authenticity – are often the only story the media wants to cover. When a company like Monsanto tried to peddle GM food that could be portrayed as 'fake', it did them serious damage. Their share price was sent falling, undermining the career of their shiny new chief executive and in the process cutting US corn imports to Europe by 96 per cent in one year.

Of course, the vogue for authenticity isn't going to embrace the whole world. For those more steeped than most in cyberspace, the whole idea probably seems incoherent. But those who haven't yet grasped that people's ideas of reality are going to be stricter may have problems.

Take Denny Wilkinson, of Princeton Video Image (PVI). PVI

is responsible for new kinds of advertising. For instance, it is now possible to put virtual adverts on TV sporting events, making them seem as if they are on the pitch, but aren't really. 'No. Why should they?' he replied when the Canadian magazine *Adbusters* asked him whether people might not feel nostalgia for the days when people could tell editorial from ads on TV. 'That's reality. That's how the world has evolved.'

I disagree. The world is evolving differently to all expectations. It may be ambiguous or paradoxical or hypocritical, but authenticity is going to take an increasingly strong grip on the way we live our lives.

It didn't happen . . .

'In from three to eight years, we will have a machine with the general intelligence of any human being. I mean a machine that will be able to read Shakespeare, grease a car, play office politics, tell a joke, have a fight. At that point, the machine will begin to educate itself with fantastic speed. In a few months, it will be at genius level, and a few months after that its power will be incalculable.'

Marvin Minsky, *Life* magazine, 20 November 1970

2

Real Business

'Nothing is so galling to people . . . as a paternalistic or, in other words, a meddling government which tells them what to read and see and eat and drink and wear.'

Thomas Macaulay

'Authenticity is the benchmark against which all brands are now judged.'

John Grant, *The New Marketing Manifesto*

When parents start calling their children after their favourite brands, an air of unreality is swooshing through the home life of Western civilization.

It isn't just Aussie rules football stars who name themselves after brands like Coke, McDonald's or Whiskas. In the summer of 2000, scores of American families called their new babies 'Iuma', to win $5,000 each in prize money offered by a new website of the same name – or, to be precise, called Internet Underground Music Archive. 'We're proud to bring open-minded people the opportunity to name their children after a website that stands for new and creative expression,' said Iuma founder Jeff Patterson. Though not quite so creative that they could actually name their child for themselves.

Calling humans after brands is the ultimate takeover of reality. Brands are our new traditions, our values to live by, our ideals in a shapeless and shifting world, they say. But the idea of transforming a child into a walking, talking advert is downright disturbing. At least robots have their own names.

The odd thing is that it isn't actually very unusual. A recent poll of American parents found that 21 per cent would name their child after a brand for half a million dollars. Another 28 per cent said they'd consider it.

I got the story of Iuma from the Canadian 'culture-jamming' magazine *Adbusters*, one of the strangest symptoms of the movement that has grown up battling mass advertising. *Adbusters* is published by the Vancouver-based Media Foundation, and it's peculiar not just because of its insight into the new demand for authenticity – but because it is beautifully designed and photographed, including spoof adverts that are created by real advertising executives, working at night. Like their 'Joe Camel' poster, with the cigarette Camel in a hospital bed, under the slogan 'Joe Chemo'. Or the Absolut vodka ad 'Absolut Nonsense', with the bottle displaying the unmistakable symptoms of brewer's droop, which led to legal action from Absolut. Or the Obsession ad with an ultra-thin bulimic model, puking into a toilet.

Adbusters owes its existence to an advertising campaign for the controversial British Columbia logging industry. In 1989, they launched a multi-million campaign of TV spots and posters on bus stops, explaining the wonderful job they were doing of managing Canada's forests, all under the slogan 'Forests Forever'. The ads so enraged two documentary film-makers, Kalle Lasn and Bill Schmalz, that they assembled a small team of creative people and made their own advertisements, called *Mystical Forests*, to tell the other side of the story. But when they tried to buy airtime, the broadcaster CBC refused to take their money. The result was a widespread public campaign of people phoning CBC, demanding to know why they were showing *Forests Forever* – paid for by rich corporations – but refusing to air *Mystical Forests*. A few weeks later, CBC partially succumbed: they pulled *Forests Forever*.

Lasn's Media Foundation grew out of the forests experience. They started making more television ads about overconsumption, including one of a rampaging dinosaur made of scrap cars. Almost no TV station in North America would air it. They then turned to organizing international campaigns like Buy Nothing Day and TV Turn-off Week, and then to the spoof magazine advertisements.

Adbusters is not for purists, who object to the way they advertise their own T-shirts and calendars. But they have also spawned a whole industry of culture-jammers – borrowing the term from a San Francisco band called Negativland – many of them renegade survivors from the advertising industry, who work on brands by day and subversive poster displays by night, and battling what they see as the increasing fakeness dominating our inner and outer environments.

Lasn was born and brought up in Estonia, under Soviet rule – and draws parallels between there and corporate USA. There's a similar lack of public discourse in the USA, he says – not about government assault on reality, but about the assault from business. Advertising is bound to influence people – that's what it's for, after all. But there is something about the triumph of marketing, in all its subtle modern forms, that threatens mental crowding, even a mental invasion – a re-construction of the world into a battlefield of competing brands. We can either respond by mounting a vigilant resistance to marketing messages, or by giving in completely and *wanting*.

In 1999, graphic designer Fiona Jack got an Auckland billboard company to sponsor an advertising campaign called Nothing™, with a series of posters which did nothing more than carry slogans like 'What you've been looking for' or 'Wonderful just the way you are'. By the end of the project, brand recognition in Auckland had leapt to about a third of the population, and a number of people had phoned – demanding to know where they could buy whatever it was.

Some people are so hungry for the fake authenticity of a brand name that they seem particularly vulnerable to mental takeover. We have such a tenuous hold on reality sometimes, that deep down we are often aware of – and frightened by it. Because if we submitted entirely to the siren voices of the billboards – and we see at least 100 just between getting up and arriving at work according to the Henley Centre – we would fall victim to the insidious marketing messages: that it is because we are inadequate, unattractive, peculiar, that we need, need, need. We have to build up defences against the reality takeover, because otherwise we might just go crazy.

Still, some of the extreme examples of marketing mind control ought to disturb us. Not just the way that IBM beams their logo onto clouds above San Francisco with a laser – or the even more worrying plans of Pepsi-Cola to project their logo onto the moon – but the way Sydney schoolboy David Bentley rents his head to advertisers, shaving a new logo in his hair every week. Or how the Nike swoosh is now the most popular item people ask for in tattoo parlours across America. Or when Coca-Cola identifies thirty-two 'possible beverage occasions' in an average day and plans to dominate them all.

And even if the brands don't reach our minds when we look up in the night sky or at our children's hair, they are chatting away happily to us on video screens on our supermarket trolleys

– thanks to the new VideoCarte interactive screens. Or they are being ever so careful about what scientific research about their products sees the light of day. Or they are pressurizing editors where they advertise to keep news coverage safe and happy. Or if they're really ambitious, they are remaking the local environment in their unreal image – Liberty Orchard sweets, for example, threatened to withdraw from their home town of Cashmere, Washington, in 1997, unless all road signs and city correspondence were changed to bear the slogan 'Home of Aplets and Cotlets'.

It makes you wonder a little at the obsession educators have about children's 'attention spans'. It's important, of course, and we do have an idea why some children are more unmanageable than others. But the North American trend is now to pack the more obstreperous off to the doctor, get them diagnosed with 'attention deficit disorder', and pump them full of the drug Ritalin. The USA and Canada now account for 95 per cent of the world's consumption of Ritalin.

This would be all very well, if it was just about lessons, but marketeers are obsessed about children's attention too. The US TV network Channel One provides schools with computer equipment on condition children are made to watch their programmes – including two minutes of advertisements a day. Teachers are not allowed to turn off or adjust the volume of the adverts, and the children must sit there. Teachers' organizations have embraced the idea because it gives them a few moments peace. 'The advertiser gets a group of kids who cannot go to the bathroom, who cannot change the station, who cannot listen to their mother yell in the background, who cannot be playing Nintendo, who cannot have their headsets on,' said Channel One's former president Joel Babbit.

But Channel One is just the tip of the iceberg. There are

Burger King and McDonald's kiosks in US schools. There are Coke and Pepsi sponsorship deals that include a contractual obligation for schools, not just to provide drinks dispenser machines, but to 'maximize sale opportunities for Pepsi-Cola products'. UK schools are following rapidly in the same direction, with their resource packs for teachers from companies like Cadbury, Shell or the meat industry. As many as 85 per cent of British schools have already allowed some kind of corporate promotion on their walls.

The kids don't mind in general, of course, but there are examples of children who just won't play. Mike Cameron of Greenbrier High School in Evans, Georgia, wore a Pepsi T-shirt to the school's 'Coke Day' and was suspended. Jennifer Beatty from Morain Valley Community College in Palos Hills, Illinois, locked herself to the metal mesh curtains of the McDonald's Student Center at her school in protest, and was arrested and expelled.

Children have a fascination for brands. We all know children as young as six who refuse to wear anything without a logo. *No Logo* author Naomi Klein describes herself as growing up with 'a deep longing for the seductions of fake'. 'I wanted to disappear into shiny, perfect, unreal objects,' she said, and I remember just what she means. This is what the novelist Umberto Eco called 'hyper-real': products and experiences intended to be even more real than real. Children want to be able to hold onto cartoon characters – and now they can. They can collect them with their burgers, be given expensive versions of them for Christmas, and as the various corporations merge into gigantic multi-media providers this kind of crossover is increasingly possible.

Advertising to children increased by 50 per cent just between 1993 and 1996, with movies, sneakers and hamburger wrappers all linked together as part of the elaborate child marketing system.

By 1997, partly thanks to *Batman*, *Hercules* and *Star Wars*, up to half the spending on toys went on those licensed for TV or films. Since the French phone company Vivendi now owns Universal Studios, they are able to offer answerphone messages to European customers in the 'authentic' voice of the mummy in *The Mummy Returns*.

It all appears as a wonderful contrast with the dusty reality of life at home, but children lose something too. 'If you have read Elisabeth Kubler-Ross, you will recognize that the stages your kids are going through – denial, anger, depression, bargaining – closely mimic the stages of grief, as if they are adjusting to a loss,' writes Kalle Lasn. 'Which in a real way they are: the loss of their selves. Or rather, the loss of the selves that feel most authentic to them.'

That's the fear of our current branded world. It sometimes seems that we are being threatened with the colonization of reality and ourselves by the highest bidder, and it frightens us.

'The great thing about them [children] is that their memory banks are relatively empty,' said Peter Mead of the advertising agency Abbott Mead Vickers. 'Any message that goes in gets retained.'

Quite so. And while we live in this strange netherworld of brand and image – half loving the experience, half looking for new ways to inoculate ourselves against it – the strange thing is that even hard-nosed business seems also to be becoming unreal. It isn't just the bizarre interrelationships between brands so that so many of those competing packages, shouting at us from the supermarket shelves, are actually owned by the same companies. Nor is it just the hyper-real pay-packets of the corporate bosses. It's the way the whole basis for raising money and valuing companies left Planet Real and hurtled off into space.

It may be that we will look back in a few years and see the terrorist attack on the World Trade Center as the moment the markets came back to earth. Even so, that implies there is some underlying reality to them, and it's not clear that there is. What Keynes used to call 'plain men' talk obsessively about getting back to the economic fundamentals, as if these were a port of reality in a fantasy world. The Washington correspondent of a major British newspaper once assured me that our money is waiting for us in a bank vault and that the pound is underpinned by gold held in the Bank of England – it hasn't been since 1931.

The truth is that we now live in a financial system run by twenty-somethings with an interest in keeping it mildly unstable. It's a system where the derivatives market can be described by one writer as a 'phantasmagoric world' dealing in over 47,000 different options but no touchable products at all. By 1994, the New York Mercantile Exchange was trading 200 million barrels of oil a year – four times the real amount produced in the world: 'like trading ether,' said Nick Leeson, whose efforts in this unreal world led to the collapse of Barings Bank.

Far from being based on gold, currencies are now based on heavy national debts, the most spectacular of which is the unpayable American budget deficit, running at over $60,000 per household. 'In God we trust', say the notes. In fact, they're underpinned not by gold or even banknotes in the vault, but by the world's collective belief in the US government's promise to pay its gigantic debt. The tech stocks phenomenon of the late 1990s had us believing for a moment that a website like @Home was worth the same as Lockheed Martin, or the internet share-trader E*Trade was worth the same as the giant American Airlines.

One scapegoat for the whole dreaming unreality of the internet bubble looks like being the so-called Queen of the Net, Mary Meeker. Meeker was paid $15 million by Morgan Stanley in her top year, 1999, for giving advice to their investors. The trouble was that the Chinese walls that are supposed to divide investor advice and some of the other banking operations in Wall Street banks had long disappeared. Modern analysts like Meeker were supposed to help the other teams look out for promising companies, sit in on strategy sessions, take new companies public, and – at least by implication – provide favourable advice that helps sell their shares. Most Wall Street analysts' pay was linked to the number of banking deals they are involved with.

It was, at the very least, bolstering the unreality. People were loading up with tech stocks partly because their analysts were simultaneously advising them impartially to do so, while selling the shares with the other hand. This was Mary Meeker's advice on Amazon in 1997: 'We have one general response to the word "valuation" these days: "Bull market" . . . we believe we have entered a new valuation zone.'

The problem was, for so many people in Wall Street and the City of London, that advice couched in the right way seemed to *create* reality. That's what the herd instinct of the financial world was all about. In those circumstances, the whole idea of impartial advice about objective valuations goes out of the window. If you say something is under-valued, and people believe you, then it is. If they don't, it isn't.

It's rather like Peter Pan and Tinkerbell. 'Every time a child says "I don't believe in fairies" there is a little fairy somewhere that falls down dead,' said Peter Pan. If you believe in fairies in the unreal financial world, they exist. Which is why so many investors are responding to the dot.com collapse and the Enron scandal with a demand for reliable, authentic information on which to base investment decisions. The answer is that it isn't there – but then, if it was, we probably wouldn't need expert services anyway.

Faced with this constructed world of shifting unreality, it isn't surprising that so many people are demanding something more authentic. The marketeers believe that this is the force behind brand – a search for some kind of reality – and to some extent they are right. 'Brands are the stamp of authenticity,' said Stephen Colegrave of Saatchi & Saatchi in a BBC documentary about reaching young minds. Brands seem to give us a flicker of reality in a virtual world, and it does give them authority.

The 'new' marketeers think brand are our new traditions, even – according to the advertising agency Young & Rubicam – our new religions. 'In a way, the media have become surrogate tribal elders,' says John Grant, co-founder of the influential and innovative London advertising agency St Luke's. 'A brand is a popular set of ideas that people live by.' In his book *The New Marketing Manifesto*, Grant talks about the 'luminosity' of modern branding, how it taps into primal emotional instincts, and gives people a sense of what's real.

But this isn't enough for the New Realists. The great guru of the virtual world, Nicholas Negroponte of MIT, talks enthusiastically about a future he describes as 'nothing, never, nowhere'. But many people – maybe even most people – actually want something rooted. The new brands can't carry that kind of weight of expectation. If brands are a way for corporations to find their soul and express it, then it won't be long before more people rumble them – and they do.

This is where the 'new' marketeers get it wrong: they argue that nothing is real in business anyway. But people aren't satisfied by the flickering hint of reality: they want the real thing. The world of brands can satisfy as long as they are, for example, simply a guarantee against counterfeit or second-rate goods, but beyond that they always disappoint. The children grow up. We grow out of our love affair. The handsome prince turns back into a frog, and the illusion shatters. We wake up and look for reality somewhere real.

'Fake it!' said a Body Shop advert for tanning lotion, showing a man looking sadly down into his pants. Postmodern ads have become notorious for having layer upon layer of meaning and irony, and this was no exception. It was at once a joke advert urging people to fake a tan, but while using real products in an ethical way. No wonder it took America by surprise. One shopper in a New Hampshire mall fainted when she saw it.

The Body Shop doesn't go in for mass advertising, a principle that left it in serious trouble at the limits of its North American expansion, fighting off competitors who didn't have to carry the costs of its ethical baggage. So the posters it has created have always been tongue in cheek, usually commenting in some way or other on the great divide between appearance and reality.

Take 'Ruby', for example. Ruby was the star attraction in a twenty-eight-page Body Shop booklet called *Body and Self-Esteem* – almost the first time a cosmetics company had taken such a wild ethical step in the dark. She was a real-sized woman mannequin. 'There are three billion women who don't look like supermodels and only eight who do,' it said, tackling head on the terrible fact that 80 per cent of all American ten-year-old girls are on a diet.

But Ruby, unexpectedly, got the company into trouble. Mattel threatened legal action because they said it defamed their doll Barbie. Ruby posters were banned by the Hong Kong mass transit authority because they would offend passengers. The resistance to reality by big industry can be pretty extreme.

I mention all this because two parallel British companies, the Body Shop and Lush, exemplify the problems for business in a world where people are demanding authenticity. What is a real business, after all? One that uses traditional recipes or manufacturing methods? One that insists on scouring for local raw materials? One that behaves ethically to its stakeholders? One that respects the environment? In practice, all of those have been invoked, and both these companies have demonstrated most of these things – but they still have a problem. As multinational retailers, with franchises all over the world, they are worldwide brands carrying authentic products – thus they are real and unreal at the same time.

The Body Shop sources many of its ingredients deep in the Amazonian rainforests, persuading people in villages in the bush to mix shea butter for face masks – and paying them a fair wage. It even started off by selling its shampoos in urine sample bottles from the local hospital in Brighton, because it was all founder Anita Roddick could lay her hands on at the time – but it gave the products a simple realism people responded to.

Lush sets great store by making its soaps from fresh fruit and vegetables, sourced locally where possible, and made up in its local shops. A series of ethical principles are prominently featured on its website. But there clearly is a tension. 'We love all that sort of thing,' said one of the two men behind Lush, the former property investor Andrew Gerrie. 'There is a real desire for people now to have certain products from specific places – like champagne or cigars. But there is a contradiction too, because we are also taking the shops to other countries.'

Both retailers have different strategies. Lush tries to present itself as a local brand. Its Japanese company is called Lush-Japan, and the products there have Japanese names and 85 per cent are made in Japan – though Gerrie points out that Brazilians actually *want* the Englishness. The company in Brazil is called Lush-London, but perhaps that's simply a different kind of authenticity.

The Body Shop has traditionally tried to emphasize its internationalism with Anita Roddick's high-profile ethical campaigns – notably against Shell after the Nigerian government's execution of playwright Ken Saro-Wiwa. In doing so, she has tried to present a different kind of version about what real business might look like. 'I have no interest in being the biggest, the most profitable or the largest retailer,' she says in her book *Business as Unusual*. 'I just want the Body Shop to be the best, most breathlessly exciting company.'

In practice, that has meant working with small communities around the world, providing them with a fair income – setting up its soap factory in the notorious Glasgow Easterhouse estate – and just being noisy about global issues. The campaigning has never helped Body Shop's sales in the short term, which drop when a campaign is at its height – but it certainly made them talked about. And seriously disliked by the mainstream business world, ever since Roddick used her platform at a business awards ceremony to attack what she called 'dinosaurs in pin-stripes' – inspiring Robert Maxwell, of all people, to walk out in protest.

'People are responding to a redefinition of business, where the human spirit comes into play,' she says, and I believe that's true. People instinctively know when a company is really wearing its heart on its sleeve, or whether they are going in for a sophisticated ethical greenwash. That isn't to do with achievements – even the most authentic company can get things wrong, and is hauled into the public spotlight. It's more to do with its intention and the direction the company is travelling in. If Shell publishes a Values Report, but is still undermining the lives of the embattled Ogoni people on their oil fields in Nigeria, it's going to be vulnerable. Just as much as Dixons is when it calls its own brand Asai, simply because Japanese names sound more authentic for electrical goods.

The point is that, whatever the marketeers say about brands being the new soul, no brand or company is going to be able to survive in this climate unless the gap between image and reality closes a little. Reputation just doesn't work unless it's real.

'More often than not, image leads reality by the nose,' says John Smythe, whose company Smythe Dorward Lambert pioneered many of the internal communications techniques in the 1990s. 'And image, like perfumes and sex, often disappoints.' It became clear over the past decade that companies without real values wouldn't just lose their customers, they were in danger of losing their staff too. The textbooks might say that business has to stay amoral – above the ordinary day-to-day issues of right and wrong – but in practice most people far prefer devoting their energies to a company with an ambition to improve the world than one that slashes, burns and doesn't give a damn.

But it's harder than that for business, because authenticity is a moving target. Corporate donations to disabled charities might have satisfied the New Realists a few years ago – now they want the company's ethics to be reflected in every financial transaction. Soon they will want production to be localized too. The desire for authenticity is like a drug: more and more is needed until every hint of fake and every implied lie is slung out. There is a progression that lies behind the spread of authenticity: what seemed real a few months ago suddenly starts grating for the New Realists. And the agenda moves on.

So how do you make your values and reputation real? You make them arise from your employees, while encouraging them to create and buy into these values and reputation at the same time, according to Smythe Dorward Lambert. And I'm not exaggerating. I was once commissioned to write an environmental ethics statement for a major building materials company which they could adopt – they gave me no information about what they actually felt, no background discussion with employees and other stakeholders. It's amazing that they felt they could get away with instant tick-box values – tick here if you refuse bribes – but they did.

But even 'real reputations' have a habit of turning round and biting you. Some companies who represent their values as being deeply embedded in their employees have staff who mouth the mantras like automatons – and that isn't real either.

It's always the way. The closer you get to the ideal – be it freedom or values or authenticity – the more likely you are to veer off suddenly in the opposite direction.

You only have to look around the average high street, at the fashion victims and the brand labels, to realize that not everybody is demanding authenticity, so it's worth asking how many people are driving the trend.

It seems like an impossible question, but there is some evidence that it's about half of us in the UK. That's the proportion of the British population categorized as 'inner-directed' – people whose prime motivation is no longer conspicuous consumption or keeping up with their neighbours, but autonomy, self-expression, health and independence. These are people who are suspicious of mass production, who want things customized or tailor-made, who may or may not be excited by information technology and computers – but who are definitely part of the world of self-actualization, and maybe self-employment, tracked by modern prophets like Charles Handy.

'Inner-directedness' isn't a new discovery. The idea goes back to a book called *The Lonely Crowd*, published in 1950 by the sociologist David Riesman. It was a revolutionary way of categorizing the public, when most sociologists were used to categorizing people according to their class rather than their attitudes. Instead, he divided consumers into three. There was *sustenance*-driven: people motivated primarily by getting by, or where the next meal would come from. Then there were the *outer-directeds*, the vast majority of the population, who were in control of their insecurity about the next meal, but who were busily consuming conspicuously – the marketing dream. *Inner-directeds* were then a small, barely visible third group, in control of their insecurity about what the neighbours might think, and moving on to something else.

It was thought that their interest in independence made many of them Thatcher voters in the 1980s, though they are probably more natural Liberal Democrats or Greens. These are the people who leave the cities for the countryside – or who want to – who downshift, who experiment with new ideas and sometimes new technology. They are deeply suspicious of marketing and serious enthusiasts for health and education. They are the shock troops of authenticity.

By the end of the 1980s, about 37 per cent of British people were classified as inner-directed – only the Netherlands had a higher proportion – and there was speculation about what would happen if they suddenly became the majority. Would those outer-directeds, so busily keeping up with the Joneses, suddenly start copying them?

The British, Dutch and Scandinavians now lead the world in inner-directedness, where anything up to half of their population are inner-directed, and that has indeed been something of a shock to the system. One of the reasons British advertising is so far ahead of the rest of the world is that it's had to cope before most countries with consumers who hopped happily from product to product, and whose brand loyalty seemed to dissolve every time they had a bath.

It was also a shock to the old structures of bureaucracy and social control. The futurist Francis Kinsman described explaining the concept to a conference of senior managers from the old Central Electricity Generating Board, a model of old-fashioned corporate hierarchy if ever there was one. The first question came from a senior personnel officer who said: 'What I want to know is: how can we identify these inner-directed people in our organization and stamp them out?'

'Inner-directed' is echoed in other concepts, like the 'i-Society', coined by the London-based Future Foundation to describe the emerging group of conspicuous non-consumers interested in individuality, self-expression, independence and authenticity. Or the 'New Consumers' described by marketing guru David Lewis, who are independent, individualist and overwhelmingly fascinated by what's 'real'.

Or in America, the idea of 'Cultural Creatives' which are identified by Paul Ray, of the Institute of Noetic Sciences, believing they make up a quarter of the American population. It is no coincidence that the inner-directed category makes up a similar quarter of all Americans. His figures put what he calls Modernists, those primarily motivated by material wealth, at 47 per cent of the US population. Cultural Creatives, at 24 per cent, are those he sees as reinventing culture, interested in health and spirituality, and searching for integrity, quality in what they buy – and, of course, authenticity.

Many Cultural Creatives think they're alone in their beliefs, says Ray – or maybe just them and their ten closest friends. It's a strange phenomenon: because the demand for authenticity isn't really reflected in the media, they don't feel they are part of anything widespread or new. In some ways, the demand for what's real is even more powerful than it seems.

That's the bottom line. A little less than half the British population, and just under a quarter of the American population, are driving the demand for authenticity. And as if to confirm it, exactly 47 per cent of Britons are interested enough in education and self-improvement – central characteristics of inner-directedness – to tell one pollster that they were 'studying on my own using books and other materials'.

That, in itself, suggests a reason for the sudden interest in slightly obscure academic works of popular science or philosophy – from Stephen Hawking's *A Brief History of Time* to Alain de Botton's *The Consolations of Philosophy*. It's also probably why as many as 79 per cent of Brits say they would rather be cleverer than more good-looking. And it's why *Viewpoint* magazine coined the phrase 'consumenism' – defined as a human quality combined with consumerism – to describe the rise in ethical spending.

New Realists come from all classes and ages. Many of them are burned-out baby-boomers, immune to the blandishments of advertisers. One of the reasons so much effort is concentrated on marketing to the young people is that their parents have grown out of adverts. They've learned how to switch them off. But some New Realists are also probably convention-breaking Generation X types, dedicated to self-reliance and self-discovery. And that raises rather an interesting paradox. How come these people are breaking conventions and searching for traditional roots, both at the same time?

Anita Roddick points to traditional wisdom and ritual as the basis for authenticity, and that's half the story. This is a paradox that the whole search for authenticity rests on, because I don't think the new drive towards authenticity is anything to do with harking back to the past – though racists and fundamentalists might use the same kind of language sometimes. New consumers, inner-directeds – call them what you will – exemplify the kind of sturdy independence that has turned its back on old-fashioned authority, whether it's the authority of politicians, religious leaders or advertisers. They may still be searching for roots when every other value seems to be disintegrating, but often these are old roots, now understood in new ways.

Take the new trend towards 'vintage' clothing, for example. The idea has spread far beyond Stella McCartney and Ralph Lauren. 'Style is not about extravagance any more. It's about showing how creative you are,' says Tiffany Dubin, the founder of Sotheby's new fashion department which deals entirely in vintage clothes. Fashion retailers like DKNY sell a mixture of new and second-hand clothes, including the kind of battered ex-army stuff that used to be reserved for disaffected youth.

Authenticity doesn't just mean reliving the past: it means using it to find new ways of living – maybe even new kinds of progress. The most authentic isn't necessarily the most true to the past; it could be the most creative or the most human.

A friend of mine was explaining to me recently why he decided to buy a tiny flat in Paris. Apart from the illicit thrill of Paris – which has infected the British since the days of the Impressionists and the *fin-de-siécle* – he said it was 'because they've still got real shops'.

Like everyone else in the room, I knew immediately what he meant – and why the shops in his home town of Oxford are not correspondingly 'real'. We knew that Paris is full of tiny, colourful, family-owned stores, full of evocative smells and baguettes and croissants baked on the premises in the early hours of the morning – in neighbourhoods where the customers might well be known by name to the shopkeeper. Although they might stock brand names, the shops themselves are much more than a local purveyor of international logos. There is something beyond the brand – real shopkeepers, real local roots. The occasional seedy family-owned tobacconist in Oxford hardly offers competition to the Parisian shops.

Although, of course, it wasn't just supermarket bullying that drove the total of 222,000 grocers in Britain in 1950 down to just 37,000 in 1997 – it was customer choice. Once the supermarkets were able to offer customers self-service from the 1960s, they were able to provide them with a new independence and breezy efficiency that those long waits behind the counter hadn't given them. Then they offered them choice, standards, international cuisine. It isn't surprising, in those circumstances, that the so-called 'real shops' took a battering.

But something is changing. In August 2001, *Time* magazine devoted most of one edition to a rediscovery of European crafts, just when the whole idea of craftsmanship was supposed to have been banished by the shiny virtual world.

There was Waterford Crystal. They might still have a master cutter who keeps 400 different designs in his head and cuts them all from memory, but they also made record profits the previous year of $88.6 million. There were a range of other thriving crafts companies, making Scotch whisky or champagne, or Herend porcelain from Hungary or Berthillon's ice cream from Paris. Even more peculiar, two of the most successful European crafts 'brands' – Morgan sports cars and Aga stoves – are using updated versions of designs that left the drawing board around seventy years ago.

These are exclusive brands for the wealthy, but you can see why people want things that are handmade by 'master cutters' or their equivalent, partly because it means that every piece has an individual touch – in a world where everything else seems mass-produced. It was made by somebody particular and it's probably ever so slightly different from the others. 'A wine that's constantly identical from year to year bothers me,' said champagne grower Anselme Selosse – and while it doesn't bother everyone, the idea that it is ever so slightly different in every bottle is extremely appealing if you're searching for what's real.

And strangest of all has been the revival of one of the medieval crafts traditions, the so-called Walz of Saxony. The Walz sends young artisans, carpenters and craftspeople on a wandering journey around Europe for about three years, learning new tools and methods and passing them on, and – incidentally – meeting the demand for short-term workers. They wear strange traditional costumes, including flared corduroy trousers and a wide-brimmed hat. As many as 500 people are currently doing a Walz, and 10 per cent of them are women. With those hats, you should be able to see them coming from some distance away.

A recession may temporarily dampen the revival of crafts in Europe – many of them are catering for a very exclusive market after all – but even before the economic clouds were gathering, while crafts were booming, the hidebound unreal brands were taking a battering.

The brands are attempting to fight back, with the help of 'new marketeers' like John Grant. They are all too aware that the old idea that brands and labels supply proof of authenticity in themselves doesn't hold water any more. Yes, a Ralph Lauren or Polo label might prove that it isn't a cheap imitation – but does that matter? All too often, these days, 'real' designer shirts are often made in the same garment factories in Bangladesh as the fakes – and sold for about a fifth of the price in big warehouses in the Middle East.

The new brands are seeking an authentic ring whether like the Body Shop and Lush using fresh produce or ethical methods, or trying to link themselves to intense emotions and direct experiences, like the erotic black-and-white photos used to sell Haagen Dazs ice cream, or the human closeness used to sell One-2-One or BT ('It's good to talk').

There is a corresponding dash to turn shopping and eating out into experiences, blurring the distinctions between art galleries, theme parks and shopping. Mandarina Duck has opened a shop-cum-theme park in Paris designed by the Dutch collective Droog. Helmut Lang commissioned conceptual artist Jenny Holzer to jazz up their new parfumerie. New Prada stores in New York, San Francisco and Los Angeles deliberately 'fuse consumption and culture', using curvy walls, light shows and theatre, as designed by experimental architect Rem Koolhaas.

The success of theme restaurants – including the new prison-style restaurant Alcatraz Brewing Co in Indianapolis – has led the way to a merging of nearly all public activity into one single whole. And although it's a move designed to make shopping more 'authentic', it threatens us with something completely opposite – the nightmare of the continuous sale in airports and museums alike.

We are also getting the new Japanese 'anti-brands', like Muji (short for Mujirushi Ryohin, 'no-brand quality goods') or the cut-price clothes chain Uniqlo, shunning brand labels and using the 'authentic' slogan 'You are not what you wear'. Oki-ni in London's Savile Row has no cash desks or changing rooms, and sends your purchases on to you in three days.

There is a new air of defensiveness about anything blatantly inauthentic. The Trafford Centre outside Manchester, which has a food hall that imitates Caesar's Palace in Las Vegas, with a fantasy Italian piazza where the ceiling turns from dawn to dusk every twenty minutes – goes to great lengths to emphasize what is real. It has real gold leaf, says the promotional material, and real trees.

Yes, real business is with us, and though it suffers from some strange contradictions, you can see it everywhere – from the localization of brands like the Latin American Inca-Cola to the way that local content now dominates Murdoch's Star TV in the Far East or MTV or Disney's Chinese website. Or indeed the growth of micro-breweries in the USA, to the rise of unpackaged adventure holidays, to the explosion of niche crafts, home-made food, local workshops. All are symptoms of authenticity.

Take, for example, the recovery of local shops – now growing faster than supermarkets. Or the rapid growth of farmer's markets or Freedom Food eggs, or the 'real' products that have broken through the 1 per cent market share barrier like organic food or ethical investment – which is now running at over £4 billion in the UK. Other real products have built up a market share of over 20 per cent, like Fair Trade coffee or energy-saving bulbs, or even become the industry norm like recycled paper or unleaded petrol.

Then there's been the retreat of the new virtual banks into the real bricks and mortar world. In April 2001, E*trade opened a real bank in New York's Madison Avenue, announcing plans for thirty more across the USA – which was something of a *volte face* for a company that spent $390 million in 1999 belittling old-fashioned real competitors. It's all part of realizing that customers 'are human beings and not cyborgs', said *Fortune* columnist Geoffrey Colvin. And a similar phenomenon is probably behind the revival of the idea of local banks. Credit unions are booming in Britain, and London opened its first community bank in 2001 – the London Re-building Society, dedicated to lending to those social enterprises that ordinary banks prefer to fend off with a bargepole.

In the USA, the president of a small San Francisco bank network, the Bank of Santa Clara, reported that most of its small business customers poached by big banks with offers of unsecured credit were back after six months. They hadn't been able to find anyone real to help them the first time they had a problem. But perhaps that isn't surprising for a bank which boasts that its staff know about 18,000 of their 22,000 customers by their first name.

There's the explosion of interest among business people in learning and self-improvement, with companies like the Mind Gym or the range of educational websites on both sides of the Atlantic. Even Michael Milken – the 1980s junk bond king, rumoured to have earned $550 million in 1987 alone – believes that education is the future of business, setting up his own educational company the moment he got out of prison.

There's the business interest in nostalgia, with VW reviving the Beetle and Coke reviving their old hourglass bottles, and even the latest American ballparks are designed to look as if they were built in the 1950s. We have computerized versions of Fred Astaire selling vacuum cleaners, and James Brown's 'I Feel Good' selling laxatives. 'Consumers are not in a real experimental time now,' said Kraft Foods vice president Richard Helstein. 'They are looking for brands they can depend on – brands they grew up with.'

There is even talk of 'real' business leadership, like Procter & Gamble chairman John Pepper's PATER acronym. It stands for 'Passion, Authenticity, Truth, Enthusiasm and Respect', and it's likely to be considerably more effective than the kind of management by numbers, targets and statistics that has so signally failed Britain's public services.

In the light of the 'War on Terrorism', this return to what's real seems only understandable – and, understood like that, it might seem just a blip on the inevitable path towards the global, virtual future. But actually all these trends were well in place before Osama bin Laden aimed jets at the World Trade Center. They are an inevitable reaction to the slick marketing that dominates our brain space, and the growing sense that – by itself – big doesn't work very well.

It wasn't just the research project by KPMG that found that as many as 75 per cent of corporate mergers had failed. It was the realization that big corporate structures are sclerotic, that small teams do manage to tap into the imagination of staff – and that MBWA (Management By Walking Around) is considerably more effective than management by numerical targets, statistics and indicators.

Well, to be fair – these are not universally acknowledged quite yet. But when a leading Conservative peer, also chairman of Shandwick – then one of the biggest public relations agencies in the world – could use a slogan like 'Think global, act local', you know something is happening. Lord Chadlington may or may not have realized he was using the radical green slogan of a decade before, but he was certainly aware that acting locally was more effective than trying to act globally – ignorant of all these cultural differences that make the world what it is.

But it wasn't enough for HSBC just to rebrand itself as 'The World's Local Bank', because by now many communities are exploring what it means to act local, to hang onto what authenticity remains in their towns. Most small American towns have long since lost their last 'real restaurant'. A third of all fishmongers in the UK closed down between 1990 and 1995, and a large proportion of grocers, butchers, bakers and greengrocers are going the same way, leaving high streets dull, quiet places full of estate agents.

There's an economic problem with this too. If you've lost your network of small shops, the chances are that most of the spending power of the community will be siphoned off by supermarkets and utilities to headquarters that are miles away. A network of local businesses means that local money is used over and over again in the vicinity, creating wealth each time.

That's why the government of Western Australia is implementing a tough new 'buy local' policy. And it's why there are size caps on new stores in France and Ireland, and why local people in Cape Cod have used their veto over big shopping malls to see off Wal-mart more than once. Other towns, like Carmel in California – where Clint Eastwood was once mayor – have strict bylaws against formula restaurants. McDonald's can set up there; they're just not allowed to look like McDonald's.

Powers like these may not be available to local authorities in over-centralized Britain, but you can find similar trends emerging all over the world. Especially in France, where they famously described the coming of Disneyland Europe as a 'cultural Chernobyl', and where angry farmer José Bové became a national hero after his arson attack on McDonald's. Even in Britain, you have the strange spectacle of the respected business writer Hamish McRae urging readers to use their buying power to revive what's local and real. 'We should shop, wherever practical, at local stores rather than supermarket chains,' he wrote in the *Independent*. 'We should try to travel on smaller airlines. If our bank or building society is taken over by a larger one, we should leave the account, we should avoid going to chain restaurants . . .'

Many of us don't, of course. Many doubt whether the local can survive the spread of global monoculture – or whether any reaction to that can be in time. But there are inspirational examples proving that it can. The Italian region of Emilia-Romagna, for example, exemplifies what a modern local economy looks like when it works. The region has a network of over 90,000 small manufacturing companies – the legacy of massively downsized car factories – the vast majority of which have fewer than fifty employees. By joining together for big projects, then disbanding again when they are finished, the workshops have made Emilia-Romagna one of the most successful regions in Europe.

By coincidence, the very same region is picked out by the American sociologist Robert Putnam to explain how the most successful places are also the most authentic places in other ways. They don't necessarily have low taxes or low inflation, says Putnam, but they do have lots of 'civic activity' – describing Emila-Romagna as 'among the most modern, bustling, affluent, technologically advanced societies on the face of the earth'. 'It is,' he went on, 'the site of an unusual concentration of overlapping networks of social solidarity, peopled by citizens with an unusually well-developed public spirit – a web of civic communities.'

And, what's more, this has been going on there since the twelfth century. You can't get more real than that. It's more evidence of the progression towards greater and greater levels of authenticity demanded by the New Realists.

Putnam is invited to 10 Downing Street every time he visits the UK. His ideas about local roots, and how critical they are for economic and social success, are now almost mainstream. Of course, there will always be a demand for trendy brands, convenience stores and convenience food – the modern world still needs it. But we are already reacting against an unrooted, hyped and spun, virtual world – where nothing seems real. And we are doing so just as businesses move to differentiate themselves from the competition, through discovering and exploiting their unspun, authentic roots. The whole logic of globalization seems to point towards a more local business culture – in the end.

The shift to a service economy is also encouraging local roots, says the economist Paul Krugman. More and more people are employed teaching, or in legal work, or in massage or alternative health, that simply can't be provided using a computer and a phone line.

But that's hard for business. The more slick marketing becomes to persuade us that some products are somehow more authentic than others, the more unreal the whole thing looks. And however much the new marketeers use the language of authenticity, it still seems somehow to slip through their fingers. They use the fact that consumers flit from brand to brand to explain the need for their emotional, authentic branding. But if people want authenticity, marketeers can only supply some partial version of it – which drives the demand for authenticity even harder in response.

Yet companies can respond successfully to the demand for authenticity, helped by marketing experts who see further than most, like John Grant. Authentic sometimes means a bit rough around the edges, he says – if the product seems just made to please, then it doesn't seem real. Authentic means simple. 'Successful brands are simpler and simpler,' and of course the simpler your brand, the more you can shift its meaning in response to a changing world. That's not nearly so authentic a motive, but it is a business need which can't be ignored.

In the end, the main problem is that companies just aren't

real. They are legal fictions clawing their way to some kind of reality, yet undermining the process by behaving as if they only have two dimensions. So often they behave like corporate brontosauri, blundering along as Anita Roddick says, unable to feel anything more sophisticated than greed or fear. They can't because, like computer programmes, they can only demonstrate what's programmed in. 'People are desperate for human connection,' she says. 'If you strip back business to its basics, it's trading – the oldest form of human exchange.' But that's almost an impossibility for most businesses, certainly as they are organized now. 'A corporation cannot laugh or cry,' said David Loy of Tokyo's Bonkyo University. 'It cannot enjoy the world or suffer with it. Most of all, a corporation cannot love.'

That's the problem multinational brands have to face. In this new climate of authenticity, they can't just pretend to be comfortable and human – they have to be what they claim to be. And the vast majority won't be able to do that for the foreseeable future, if indeed ever. It's tough being a business in the Age of Authenticity.

It didn't happen . . .

'Newborn infants can be operated upon and the latest submicroelectronic equipment installed in the brain and at certain critical points in the spinal column so that they are almost certainly assured not only of the benefits of full non-radio communicative powers but also there is reason to believe that their scientific creative ability will be enhanced. Logically enough, this operation must be performed within two weeks of birth because if the infant is only slightly exposed to contact with its family who still have not completed their "unlearning" and

readjustment [to the new technology], he might never become a good subject for the modern system of communication.'

Dorman D. Israel, fellow of the Institute of Radio Engineers (USA), predictions for the year 2012, May 1962

3

FAKE REAL #1:
Fake Real and Virtual Real

'Oh, what a goodly outside falsehood hath!'
William Shakespeare, *The Merchant of Venice*

'Authenticity. If you can fake that, the rest will take care of itself.'
Seth Godin, *Permission Marketing*
(Sam Goldwyn said something similar about sincerity)

Doctors across the world share a similar, very modern problem. Over and over again the doctor, confronted with an elderly patient, knows perfectly well that what they need is a friend to visit them once a week, but all they have to dispense is pills. The patient may well have something physically wrong, but the *real* problem is that they are miserable, lonely or isolated. In our over-stretched, over-deferential health systems, it's a scenario that's repeated day after day. But one surgery in south London has come up with a partial solution.

Most doctors just shell out pills, of course, but at the Rushey Green Group Practice next to Lewisham hospital they can write a prescription instead for a friendly visit once a week, a lift to the shops, or for someone to come round and mend their door handles.

They are able to do so because Rushey Green has one of the

first so-called 'time banks' in the UK. Originally an American idea, it means that there's a time banker on the end of a phone, who you can contact if you need help – or a lift or a friendly face – and who will contact another patient who can provide that. The volunteers earn credits based on the time they spend helping out, and when they need help themselves they cash them in. The whole system is managed by special software that does the banking calculations in the time 'currency', matching up people's wants and needs.

There are about 200 time banks in the USA, earning 'time dollars' for supporting local people, helping out in schools, giving lifts or whatever is needed – and spending them on support for themselves. There are many more in Japan and China, with their rapidly ageing populations, where time banks are much more mainstream. In Japan, they earn and spend a currency called *fureai kippu* ('ticket for a caring relationship') which does just the same. The whole idea is to put people back in touch with each other where a sense of community has entirely disappeared. As Miami's time-dollar promoter and former banker Ana Miyares put it, time banks 'rebuild neighbourhoods relationship by relationship'.

They can be dramatically effective. 'I really feel like I've inherited a brother and sister,' said one participant in Brooklyn's time bank, Member to Member. 'They take me to the bank. They buy me my medicine. She [the time bank co-ordinator] sent me two angels from heaven in Lou and Pearl and I couldn't live without them.'

What's interesting about this is that these relationships are absolutely real, but they are made possible by information technology, software and telephones. They can change people's lives, but use a virtual delivery mechanism to do so. Because neighbourhood relationships are being driven out by the speed of modern society, you can't just jump start them with a mixture of hope and idealism. They have to be created using unreal methods. They need IT to rebuild them, and to take them to a wider market.

So, are time banks real or virtual? The answer is that they are both – they need to be if they're going to spread their benefits to a broad market.

The problem with reality is that it also tends to be pretty expensive. It's all very well for me to say how exciting it is that European craft brands are making a comeback. But with the exception of Lladro and Herend porcelain, all the successful craft 'brands' picked out by *Time* were just for the very rich.

Of course, there's always been a market in authenticity for the wealthy. Real diamonds. Real holidays on Caribbean islands. Real homes with riverside views. 'I went to this delightful island that hasn't been ruined by tourists,' they say. It's authentic and just for me. Even if it was just for reasons of snobbery, rich people have always been able to afford authenticity. Even writing about the subject can sound snobbish and I find myself apologizing for it. After all, can the poor afford Aga stoves or Morgan sports cars?

But it's even worse than that. Even if we could suddenly all afford Morgans, wore Swiss watches and quaffed the best Moët et Chandon every day, that kind of authenticity is going to stay exclusive. There simply aren't enough holidays on small Mediterranean islands or riverside apartments on the Thames to go round. There aren't enough of them for a mass market. That kind of exclusive authenticity is always going to be beyond the vast majority of the world's population.

Yet what makes the New Realist demand for reality so powerful is that it isn't just coming from the rich any more. And it isn't just a demand for exclusive experiences. It's a frustration that so much of what is served up to us as consumers is fake pap, perverting the way we see our lives. And it's a demand that everyday life should be authentic too – for real relationships, and real connection, as well as real champagne. That's the heart of the modern issue: how do you deliver authenticity to a mass market?

It isn't easy. You can't conjure up organic food from nowhere on that scale. You can't suddenly provide intimate places to meet in cities where there aren't any. You can't provide real neighbourliness when most people live behind seven mortice locks and are scared to go outside.

That's why so many of the big brands are trying to build a hint of authenticity into their products. Sometimes the authenticity is downright fake, like the pictures of happy chickens gambolling in the countryside on the boxes of eggs from battery farms. Sometimes it's pretty virtual, like the 'Seeds for a Change' label produced by Mars, which may well be organic but certainly won't produce the radical change it implies. Sometimes it's about creating a different relaxed atmosphere, like the American book chain Barnes & Noble, which encourages people to sit and read in comfortable armchairs.

But often, if you're going to reach a mass market, you need that authenticity to be helped along by something which doesn't seem real at all – either the internet, or computer technology, or the mass media. So it's real, but not in the way it's created. It's *virtual real.*

Internet chat rooms are clearly on the unreal end of the spectrum. But so is telephone polling, Playstation 2, NHS Direct, pot noodles and life on Prozac. They fulfil a series of important needs – there's nothing wrong with them, in themselves – but don't let's pretend this is real friendship, a real game, a real doctor or a real meal.

Farmers' markets, on the other hand, are pretty unambiguously real – ignoring the current bitter argument in the UK about what constitutes a 'real' farmers' market. They're local, and beautiful, and the vegetables are normally sold by the people who grew them. Reading groups are real too. So are acupuncture, free-range eggs, real ale, poetry and herbalism, to name but a few.

But then there's this other category of virtual real. It isn't that they are *half*-real, somehow, or that they come midway between the other extremes. But they do provide authentic experience by using modern delivery systems that look a little virtual. Take test-tube babies, for example. They are pretty self-evidently real, but the babies are made possible in a laboratory. An erection caused by Viagra is still a real erection, after all.

It's the same with computer dating. There isn't anything unreal about the quality of the relationship or what people feel about each other once they've met, but they were brought together using information technology – and attracted to it in the first place by an internet site, a newspaper ad or one of those strange thin adverts above your heads on the underground. That's virtual real.

Looking more closely, there are two different categories of virtual real. There are manifestations where the end product is absolutely real – like time banks or online poetry. But there are also manifestations where what is delivered is real experience, in some ways, but the final product seems somehow to be compromised by the whole process.

Like *Big Brother*, for instance, the 'reality' TV show where a group of ordinary people are locked for a month in a house filled with television cameras. There's no doubt that the emotions they are feeling are absolutely real – and that the TV show feeds a public which is demanding something more direct and emotional.

But somehow the situation is so ludicrous and contrived, and the strings are being pulled so vigorously by the TV executives, that the end result is more fake real than virtual real.

It's like pornography. You can argue about whether the couple is having real sex on a video, but even if they are, somehow the experience still isn't quite authentic. Just like *Big Brother* – itself a close relative of pornography – we're tempted more into real voyeurism than real life. It's all about real keyholes to peer through and that, in the end, isn't very real at all.

If you get lost in some of the great suburbs of north-west London, like Hendon or Cricklewood, you find yourself in a world of leafy, curving avenues which – unless you live there yourself – all look exactly the same. They are all laid out like a model village, mile upon mile of semi-detached houses with sloping roofs and front doors at extreme corners of each house, and strange semi-Elizabethan wood beam decorations, line upon line of little garden gates and garages with painted doors.

These suburbs became almost a byword for fake among the modernist architects, who were mainly excluded from their design in the 1920s and 1930s. Countless novels, works of art and pop songs of suburban angst have had their first seeds sown here. But in another sense, the semi-detached houses, produced in their hundreds of thousands between the world wars, are also – by some margin – Britain's most successful home design. They are also an early example of virtual real in action.

The designs are so common now, with their hints of Jacobean and Art Deco, their bay windows overlooking the front garden, that it's hard for us to see them objectively as what they seemed when they first appeared – as 'homes fit for heroes', immediately after the First World War. But at just £500, with mortgage payments of nine shillings a week (45p), they were a miraculous response to the housing crisis at a time when even railway carriages were being pressed into service as homes, and when most cities had urban cores of grimy, cramped, back-to-back hovels with whole families sharing the same room.

Semis catered for the new breed of white-collar workers that had been emerging in cities since the beginning of the century, and – for the vast majority of families who lived there – they were the first home they had ever owned. They also coincided with a sudden interest in homes and everything about them. *Homes and Gardens* magazine (1919) and *Ideal Home* magazine (1920) were suddenly flying off the station bookshelves, packed with articles about curtains, labour-saving kitchens and how to supplement your income by keeping chickens or breeding dogs in the back garden.

At the building peak in 1934, as many as 73,000 semi-detached homes were finished around London alone, many snaking into the further reaches of Middlesex along the new Metropolitan Line, and deep into the woods of Hertfordshire and Buckinghamshire. And each, inspired by the architects Raymond Unwin and Barry Parker – and their pioneering affordable rustic homes in Letchworth and Welwyn Garden City – was packed with symbols that tried to imply authenticity.

The front and back gardens were particularly important. They provided real grass and real nature to people who had been brought up in a very different kind of brick and concrete world, when the Music-Hall song used to boast that 'wiv a ladder an' some glasses/You can see the 'Ackney marshes/ If it wasn't for the 'ouses in between'.

The garden may have had a small winding path and a tiny gate, but it was in a small way – and really only symbolically –

a reflection of the paths and gates of country estates. It was the same with the tiled porches over the front doors. Symbolically at least, these were real country houses in the city – or as a John Laing & Son advertisement in Colindale in 1930 put it – 'a House, a Home, a little Palace, in a convenient healthy district, purchasable by anyone with a small capital and regular income'.

Builders found that the semis designed by architects were more difficult to sell, so they tended to be dropped from the projects – another reason for the profession to heap abuse on their whole concept right from the start. And it's true that in its most extreme manifestations, the suburban semi does seem unreal. For example, the old-fashioned leaded windows that were general issue were at once a response to the insecurity of modern times – and most importantly for selling purposes, to show this wasn't a council house.

Yet the builders increasingly took pains to make sure their new estates emphasized the genuinely authentic too. From 1930, John Laing laid out their estates to follow the natural contours of the land and to keep existing trees. A brochure for one estate in the grounds of the former Hendon Hall boasted: 'There is nothing new about it except the houses.' Another suburban semi architect, Blanden Shadbolt, went much further, using real timbers from demolished homes, with specially designed sagging rooflines and thatched roofs.

It was fashionable to say, as people were to say again two generations later about the new town of Milton Keynes, that the houses looked so much the same that you keep getting lost. But that was never an opinion shared by people who actually lived there, just as it isn't by the inhabitants of Milton Keynes. Many of the estate designers deliberately made every home different, some Tudor, some classical, some modernist, and for the locals the differences were plain.

Whatever the critics said – and there has been much snobbery about suburban semis ever since – these were real homes, provided with a great deal of inauthentic symbolism, but real nonetheless, as anyone brought up in them will confirm (yes, I was). They were real in a way that the alienated high-rise flats that followed them never could be, because they allowed people to have more authentic lives, with privacy, self-determination and a touch of nature around them. Suburban semis provided a kind of domestic authenticity for the mass market by using mass production and innovative financing techniques, and the marketing power of the new mass media. They are an early example of virtual real if ever there was one.

Now, moving half a century on to something completely different, but just as virtual real as the semi. Starbucks coffee shops, which over the last few years have become such a controversial and ubiquitous symbol of globalization, date back to a visit to Italy in 1984 by plastics salesman Howard Schultz.

He became fascinated by the authentic atmosphere of Milan's 1,500 expresso bars, with their beans grinding, their steaming milk, and theatrical barman at the heart of it all. At that time, Procter & Gamble and Nestlé controlled 90 per cent of the American coffee market, providing almost identical roasted and freeze-dried products in almost identical containers. Starbucks pioneered a different approach, with an authentic dash of Milan and the genuine experience of meeting friends that the coffee bars in the 1950s used to provide – and their profits were soon five times the industry average.

Pizza Express is another example of a brand, this time British, which is designed to deliver an 'authentic' Italian experience. It was founded in 1962 by the jazz and hockey enthusiast Peter Boizot – now owner of Peterborough Football Club. The pizzas are fresh and made on the premises. Like Starbucks, there's something theatrical about being able to watch your pizza being made in their open-plan kitchens. Pizza Express branches have real marble tables, real Italian beer, and often real jazz. The formula is successful enough, so it's said, to add 5 per cent to the value of your house when a Pizza Express opens locally.

But, of course, both Starbucks and Pizza Express are still brands and formulas. Real as the experience seems, it is constructed by marketing people and delivered by international boardrooms and bankers. It hasn't grown out of local life. 'It's a real trick to invent something that feels uninvented,' wrote John Grant in *The New Marketing Manifesto*.

Starbucks has now become such a symbol of globalization that its windows are vulnerable during demonstrations. And it's true that the Starbucks logo has become ubiquitous all over the world. But there are contradictions there too – because Schultz and Starbucks and Pizza Express are also, in their own way, attempting to meet the new mass demand for authenticity – just as suburban semis were in their own day. The Starbucks experience of sitting around in comfortable chairs listening to the hiss of coffee machines is real – though perhaps not quite as real as in Milan, or if the places were run by committed local owners who knew all their customers. This may be a mass-produced commodity, but it is still relaxing.

The argument continues whether there remains something missing, whether we have become infected by some of the emptiness at the heart of any big brand and take a little of it away with us when we leave. There is no doubt that Starbucks is – like time banks and computer dating – intended to provide a 'real' experience and deliver it to the mass market.

But it also perhaps adds a sub-category of virtual real – using the trappings of authenticity to deliver a product that is a strange mixture of the real and not quite real. This is real as seen through the lens of Steven Spielberg: not fake exactly, but mediated, sanitized and a little sickly sweet. It's an over-ripe reality, like the suburban semi with its black painted beams. Or Starbucks. Or, to take another example, organic chocolate.

Organic chocolate seems a contradiction in terms. Organic suggests that the food is unprocessed, but you can't get more processed than chocolate. Thus organic chocolate is a product that somehow manages to retain the best of both worlds: it doesn't use pesticides or artificial additives – one assumes – but it still tastes good.

Organic chocolate first appeared in the UK in the early 1990s. It took until 1998 to appear in the USA, when the Michigan-based Functional Foods Company produced a brand called SmartChocolate that catered for the authentic market so enthusiastically that – as was said of Julie Andrews in *The Sound of Music* – it felt like 'being hit over the head with a Valentine card'. SmartChocolate, to quote its website, uses 'organically grown chocolate from within the depths of the rainforest'. It deals with 'only those chocolate farmers who demonstrate their respect for the integrity and preservation of the rainforests'.

Now, providing a sustainable income to people in rainforests is an undeniable basis for conserving them, but you can't help wondering if they might be better off not being bludgeoned by this thoroughly Western view of authenticity. Admittedly, though, it is a better approach than driving down cocoa pay to slave-labour levels, spraying the fields with pesticides and packing the chocolate bars full of additives. So let's give organic chocolate its due. After all, it's almost real – using the trappings of authenticity to provide something real for the mass market.

We might say something similar about other Functional Foods products – organic fudge and organic coffee concentrate. Or indeed the organic chocolate almond cake, organic florentines and organic *pain au chocolat* produced by their British equivalent Green & Black. Products like that may not be strictly authentic, but do the virtual real trick the other way round. Time banks and computer dating provide a real experience delivered by virtual systems. Organic chocolate provides a virtual product delivered by real methods. Either way, it's virtual real.

Virtual/fake	Fake real	Virtual real	Authentic
Virtual holidays	*Big Brother*	Organic chocolate	Real ale
Loyalty cards	Designer books	Time banks	Live yoghurt
Benecol margarine	Motels	Computer dating	Raw-food restaurants
Online relationships	*Survivor*	Amazon.com	Back-packing
McDonald's	Ritalin	Dolly the Sheep	Reading groups
Plastic wrapping	Theme pubs	Friends Reunited	Brick homes
High-rise flats	Spice Girls	Starbucks	Organic free-range eggs
Web newspapers	*OK* magazine	*Changing Rooms*	Natural childbirth
Pot noodle	GM tomatoes	Gorillaz	Tate Modern
Playstation 2	Centreparcs	Viagra	Herbal medicine
Supermalls	NHS Direct	Martha Stewart	Ethical investment

I can't finish a chapter on virtual real without looking at virtual reality itself, because there's nothing – as you might expect – quite so virtual real as virtual reality. The idea goes back nearly half a century to flight simulators developed during the Second World War to train pilots quickly, built on platforms that tilt and wiggle like a real plane according to how the pilots manage the controls. The father of computer graphics, Ivan Sutherland, first proposed what he called a 'virtual world' in 1965, trying it out in 1968.

From there, virtual reality wandered through the ambitious byways of cinema, via the novels of William Gibson, until the appearance on the scene of the artist, mathematician and musician Jaron Lanier – complete with a Just William expression, a strange sense of humour and dreadlocks. It was Lanier, described at one stage in his career as 'like a kind of Rastafarian hobbit', who coined the phrase 'virtual reality'. He also, rather by accident, founded the main company involved in developing it, VPL Research. Asked what company he belonged to, he made up the name on the spur of the moment. It's an example of the unreal world of internet finance that, thus, the company existed and suddenly started earning investment money.

VPL Research developed the equipment needed for virtual reality, which – for the uninitiated – includes special helmets which allow you to see and hear the virtual world, and special gloves with sensors over the joints in your hands to measure the position of your fingers. Trackers then translate movements into co-ordinates, which are fed back to the computer so that the model of the virtual world changes accordingly.

Lanier talked his way into the mathematics department at New Mexico State University at the age of fourteen, and later was given a grant by the National Science Foundation to study mathematical notation and to see if all those mathematical symbols (+, − or ×) could be replaced. The result, what he called 'post-symbolic' visual programming language, a combination of maths symbols and interactive animated computer graphics, led directly to the development of virtual reality as one of the ways you could work with them.

VPL Research has long since disappeared, virtual reality has got stuck – nobody has managed to develop a headset that doesn't make you feel sick – and Jaron Lanier now concentrates on music.

He makes occasional sallies from his studio to attack the IT prophets who believe that computers and robots are going to replace human beings. He is, in short, a sensible fellow. But his invention is still a source of enormous controversy as those who believe in a wonderful virtual future slug it out with those who don't.

There is a fear that, as various forms of virtual reality spread increasingly through society, people won't be able to tell the difference between real and virtual – especially children. This is the scientist Stephen Jay Gould, writing about IMAX cinemas:

> In this different threat to the intrinsically higher status of 'real' objects, we can now make explicitly virtual representations so much bigger, so much scarier, so much more frenetic – in short so much more viscerally thrilling in a primal physiological sense – that many people (as our kids do already) might come to prefer the virtual to the real. Why spend thousands of bucks to visit a tropical rainforest, trek and sweat in the heat, endure leach bites and Delhi belly, and see very few animals from very far away, when you can practically get gargantuan-sized images on an IMAX screen for ten bucks?

The question is worth asking, but the answer is 'because it's real'. But it always seems to be other people, or children, who are the focus of this kind of fear. This is the technophobes succumbing to one of those fantasies they have been warning against – such as the one in which we would all soon be eating out of tubes, or having virtual reality holidays in the Antarctic. None of that was true, but nor was the fantasy that virtual illusion would be so brilliant that it would blur virtual and real permanently. For we cling to reality increasingly closely, and are ever better able to tell the difference – children too.

That isn't to say that the easy brutality of some computer

games isn't insidious, or that what John Naisbitt calls the Military-Nintendo Complex – the secret links between military trainers and computer-game designers – isn't worrying or brutalizing.

Nor is it that we can't be fooled sometimes. But human beings do learn from their mistakes. When the Lumière Brothers showed the first proper film, *Quitting Time at the Lumière Factory*, in 1895 at the Grand Café at the boulevard des Capucines in Paris – scene of the first Impressionist exhibitions – the audience flinched in terror at the now famous footage of a train racing towards them. Nowadays we have learned to distinguish between frighteningly sophisticated special effects and reality, and we do so every day.

Consumers 'are like roaches', says David Lubars of the advertising and media group Omnicom. 'You spray them and spray them and they get immune after a while.' And that is true of advertising, special effects and virtual reality. Human beings learn to deal with them. The main effect isn't a blurring between real and fake; instead we cling to what's real with more enthusiasm than before.

'Will we maintain enough power of additional awareness needed for both primary and secondary worlds – at the same time?' asks Professor Michael Heim, a critic of all things virtual. But we do in so many ways already. Politicians may prefer to *appear* active than actually to achieve anything; corporations may like to surround themselves with the *image* of business ethics and social responsibility. The truth is that it fools almost nobody. We are sophisticated enough to tell the difference and do so, sometimes, in a flash.

What holds all the different kinds of fake and virtual real together is that – at the very heart – there is some question about who is writing the script. In the computer-dating agency, the strings are actually being pulled by the computer and the staff who manage it. In the test-tube baby laboratory, it's by pipette. In *Big Brother*, it's the producers. In time banks, it's the time broker operating the software. Even organic chocolate has a mysterious process at its heart whereby the unsullied cocoa beans are turned into a highly processed product. Both virtual real and fake real are caused by invisible hands – which we choose to accept sometimes because the process gives a glimpse of an authentic experience, sometimes even a step into the authentic.

New Realists want depth to their reality. The difficulty is how authenticity can be delivered to the vast majority of people, and that's where the virtual real comes in. It is against that yardstick that we need to judge it. Does it provide us with enough of a real experience so that we can live a bit better? Is it a sustainably authentic experience? Time banks pass the test – though not as an alternative to old-fashioned neighbourliness – but organic chocolate and branded coffee bars do only to some extent.

Virtual reality that provides us with hands-on experience in training – like the equipment that helps us tackle glossophobia (fear of public speaking) – definitely passes. The kind of virtual reality that plunges us into a world of illusion and pretends somehow to be better than reality is seriously fake. While it may attract the experimentalist or occasional traveller, it isn't going to answer the new demand for what's real.

This is a distinction that one of the great modern manipulators of reality, the punk rock pioneer and Sex Pistols manager Malcolm McLaren, described using the metaphor of 'karaoke'. Now, to my mind, karaoke is definitely virtual real. It uses information technology and loudspeakers to draw the singer into an authentic experience of performance – which is often more fun for them than their listeners. But for McLaren, it sums up everything to do with the world of fake.

'Today our culture can be summed up by these two words – authentic and karaoke,' he said in 1998 . . .

> They can sit well together, but you have to be an artist to make it work. Today we live in a karaoke world. A world without any particular point of view – where high culture and low culture have had their edges blurred. This is life by proxy – liberated by hindsight, unencumbered by the messy process of creativity and free from any real responsibility beyond the actual performance. Tony Blair is the first karaoke Prime Minister. Television has made his 'Cool Britannia' a successful brand. However, there is a counterpoint to all this product placement and branding: the undeniable thirst and search for the authentic in our culture.

Karaoke and virtual real are also symptoms of that same search. The result has become a game, played between the marketeers, entrepreneurs and us – looking for new ways of providing a hint of the real. And behind that runs the Great Game between brands and authenticity, each side struggling to compromise the other. We may not always be able to tell them apart – we may not even *want* to be too authentic all the time – but above our heads, both sides are battling away hammer and tongs.

It didn't happen . . .

'Only ten or fifteen years hence, it could be possible for a housewife to walk into a new kind of commissary, look down a row of packets not unlike flower-seed packages, and pick her baby by label. Each packet would contain a frozen one-day-old embryo, and the label would tell the shopper what colour of hair and eyes to expect as well as the probable size and IQ of the child. It would

also offer assurance of freedom from genetic defects. After making the selection, the lady would take the packet to her doctor and have the embryo implanted in herself . . .'

Washington Post, 31 October 1966

4

Real Food

> **'The primary objective of texturization in protein food is the reproduction of the bite, chewiness, mouth feel and performance of a much-prized segment of the human food spectrum.'**
>
> A. D. Odell, General Mills Corporation, 1970

> **'You know you're truly Authentic when: you can keep an entire weekend's rations in your haversack and still have room for an extra pair of socks. You know you've gone too far when: your socks look better than the food . . .'**
>
> Internet joke, 2000

In the early hours of 21 July 1969, my mother woke me up to watch the flickering pictures of Neil Armstrong's first tentative steps on the moon. I was eleven years old; I remained obsessed by the moonshots for years afterwards.

For some reason, one of my main memories about Apollo 11 – and the tin can with the computing power of a Mini Metro that took them to the moon – was their food. There it was, that famous meal of beef and vegetables in a translucent plastic pack, which would turn to soft mush when a little hot water was added. This was the future of food, we were all told. All that fancy stuff we were eating then would soon be a thing of the past – if boiled cabbage and sausages could conceivably be described as fancy stuff. All meals would soon come in tubes or plastic bags, without fuss or effort.

It was also a labour-saving dream, and to that extent a feminist one. And with the arrival of serious fast food in the UK in the early 1970s, it seemed increasingly inevitable.

A year after Apollo 11, the presenters of the BBC programme *Tomorrow's World* – Raymond Baxter and James Burke, both familiar faces from moonshot commentating – published a vision of what Britain would be like in 2120. In some ways, it is surprisingly accurate thirty years on. We do have virtual reality, of a kind. We do now use cathedrals as concert halls, and we do have a minister responsible for leisure. We don't have mass tranquillization in the water supply – but with television, maybe we don't need it. This is how Baxter and Burke saw the future of food:

> Much of the food available will be based on protein substitutes and, as with a book club today, a family will contract with a company to supply it with part-cooked daily menus which will be delivered once a month in disposable vacuum packs. The most complicated dish will need only a few seconds under a microwave heater to make it ready for the table. As a result of this development, modern homes will no longer have kitchens for food preparation, and the resulting saving in space on a national scale will provide room for a million and a half extra full-sized living units.

But thirty years on, it hasn't happened like that. There is fake food in abundance – everything from Pot Noodle to Dunkin' Donuts. We do buy ready meals in their plastic-packaged millions, but it's pretty clear that the culture is also going another way entirely. We are not seeing the last gasp of authentic eating in a flurry of what was called 'analogue' food – the word 'artificial' was thought to frighten people. We're not embracing the brave new world of artificial smells, artificial tastes and artificial consistency.

Quite the reverse. There is an explosion of interest in organic food on both sides of the Atlantic. Cooking is the new rock 'n' roll: cookery TV programmes and books are some of the most popular. Farmers' markets, stuffed with fresh produce straight from the farm, are appearing in towns and cities all over the country. London has probably the most cosmopolitan restaurants in the world. The Campaign for Real Ale has transformed our drinking habits. It's not that the market for fast food has somehow disappeared – it clearly hasn't – but there is a growing demand for what is authentic, local and trustworthy.

Of course, you could explain it all away with the twin disasters of BSE and foot and mouth, but you can see a similar trend far beyond Britain, and even in the home of notoriously drab cuisine – England – eating out has become a major leisure activity.

I'm inclined to think that the British suddenly rediscovered the sensual experiences of eating and enjoying meals during the long hot summer of 1976, the year of my A levels. While rivers and ponds ran dry across the country, restaurant tables were finding their way outside onto London pavements for the first time. They've stayed there ever since, reappearing every spring with the cuckoo. Before 1976, Britain was stuck deep in a homely mix of puritanism and British reserve, with a strong sense that all these fripperies would fade away with the tubes and packets of the future. But ever since 1976, a dash of Mediterranean exuberance has stuck with us.

Before 1976, we laughed along with the futuristic robots on

the Smash advertisements for dried mashed potato, who fell around laughing at a previous generation's potato peelers. After 1976, somehow the whole idea of fake mashed potato has become almost impolite. The Smash robots no longer flit across our screens.

But if there's a heroine responsible for banishing the *Tomorrow's World* vision of fake meals, it was the pioneering cookery writer Elizabeth David. Her 1950 book *Mediterranean Food* fell like a hand grenade into the middle of British post-war austerity and rationing, with its boiled vegetables and rice pudding. The germ of the book had come from her trip from the south of France to Greece, just as war was breaking out. Back home after the war, trapped in a miserable hotel in an often flooded Ross-on-Wye, her lover suggested she cheer herself up by describing the Mediterranean she remembered: 'Even to write words like apricot, olives and butter, rice and lemons, oil and almonds produced assuagement,' she wrote. They had an inspirational effect on her readers too, just as fake protein meals were being dangled in front of them as the utilitarian dream of the future.

Like Terence Conran, who designed his shops to reflect the colourful piles of fruit and vegetables in the markets of the south of France, Elizabeth David began by injecting something of Provence back into British life in her regular columns for *Harper's Bazaar*.

It was her recipe for Turkish stuffing for a whole roast sheep – and its complete blindness to rationing – that persuaded John Lehmann to publish her first book. 'I grew up in a world devoid of olive oil, garlic and basil,' wrote cookery writer Nigel Slater. 'A world where no-one had ever heard of, let alone smelled fennel, Parmesan or coriander. A world that only drank wine at Christmas. I first read Elizabeth David's *A Book of Mediterranean Food* when I was twenty and already cooking for my living. Her words changed everything. It was as if a door had opened. A door to a different, more fragrant world.'

Half a century later we are besieged by celebrity chefs, the supermarkets are awash with some of the most sophisticated provincial tastes the world has to offer. We could hardly be further away from Apollo 11-style eating.

'After her death it seemed possible that the full extent and breadth of her influence might be forgotten,' said Elizabeth David's biographer Liza Chaney. 'This is not to say that she has gone out of favour, but precisely because her influence has been so pervasive (first in the home, then beyond it in the food shops, kitchen shops and restaurants) some of us, now and in the future, will be unaware of its source.'

Like some other pioneers of British authenticity, the poet and conservationist John Betjeman and the critic F. R. Leavis, there was more than a touch of snobbery about Elizabeth David – just as there is about some of modern foodies. What makes her such an exemplar of the new authenticity is that she graduated beyond a simplistic dismissal of everything stodgy and English, and the assumption that real food had to be elaborate, expensive and exclusive to be real.

By the end of her life, her main focus – much to the irritation of some of her original fans – was to rediscover the authentic lost traditions of English cooking. And, as so often in the authenticity story, that meant a determined search for roots. 'We need to go back to the recipes of a century ago and further, when an authentic and still strong English cooking tradition flourished,' she wrote. What had begun as her rejection of puritanism had grown into an equally powerful rejection of the kind of third-rate, fake food the technologists and food corporations were serving up for us all.

And nowhere more than in her defence of authentic bread in

her book *English Bread and Yeast Cookery* – which she finished writing just as the restaurant tables were coming out onto London pavements in that long hot summer. British bread by this time was the most chemically treated in Europe, and Elizabeth David turned her attention to defending small independent food producers, knowing that authentic food required diversity.

She wasn't alone. *Small is Beautiful* author E. F. Schumacher – another pioneer of authenticity – thoroughly embarrassed his dinner-party hostess by making the same point a few years before. He started buttering his perfectly white napkin, to make the point that it was indistinguishable from the perfectly white slice of fake bread on his side plate.

With Schumacher's help, bread has become a symbol of resistance to fake food. After all, just thirteen big bread manufacturers now control a £3 billion industry producing airy loaves with so few nutrients in them that they have to be injected with vitamins. Every environmentalist should learn to make their own bread, says Satish Kumar, editor of *Resurgence*: citing it as the same kind of act of defiance as Gandhi's learning to spin was in India.

Of course, most of us are not actually making bread. We may have tried to reject genetically-modified food in Europe, and dream of a future of authentic tastes and cuisine. But we are also cynical about all this.

How to be a Domestic Goddess was the title of the best-selling cookery book by Nigella Lawson. But the truth is most of us don't want to be domestic deities. We like watching *Ready Steady Cook*, but we don't always want to be so authentic as to actually cook for ourselves. Our kitchens may be the new centres of our homes, thanks to Elizabeth David – with gleaming new pots and stoves – but we don't always cook in them any more.

Even so, there is something about the spread of the giant

food corporations that scares people, and has driven the New Realists to bend the original 'analogue food' agenda. Now this looks like bringing them directly into conflict with the basic fakery behind big business food.

A friend of mine was horrified when her toddler came back from kindergarten, having been taught a multinational version of those children's chanting games we all learned at school – complete with gestures. It went 'McDonald's, McDonald's (*make arch signs here*), Kentucky Fried (*flap like a chicken*), Pizza Hut, Pizza Hut (*make sign like a hat*)'.

Although the toddlers loved it, there was something at once naïve and insidious about the game. Partly because McDonald's, Pizza Hut and KFC – together with Taco Bell, Burger King, Dunkin' Donuts and all the rest of them – are now to be found in nearly every main street in the Western world: they are a major force in the slow undermining of the reality of place. But also because children are in the front line of the battle for power by the increasingly powerful fake food sector.

Food companies have taken to using mobile phones and internet to reach children when their parents aren't around. At least 95 per cent of food and drink products advertised during children's TV viewing times are high in fat, sugar or salt. School textbooks are increasingly sponsored by food giants. School notebook are packed with smiling reminders of snack brands. One Scottish schools initiative called *The Balance: Get it Right*, promoting nutritious breakfasts and sponsored by Kelloggs, gave away a Coco-Pops-flavoured cereal and milk bar (16 per cent fat, 50 per cent sugar) to every child taking part. They targeted 400,000 primary school children.

In the USA, McDonald's and Burger King run more than 10,000 playgrounds between them. Their cross-promotions with TV channels, Hollywood studios and sports teams have spawned the most successful promotions to children in marketing history. McDonald's sold an average of four Happy Meals to every American child aged between three and nine in one ten-day period during their Teenie Beanie Baby promotion in 1997. Since 1996, they have signed a ten-year global marketing agreement with Disney. Dr Pepper, 7-Up and Pepsi even licence their logos to go on baby bottles. It is disturbing, through hardly surprising in these circumstances, that Americans spend more on fast food than they do on higher education.

And at the other end of the fast-food chain chickens are also in the front line. 'I have an idea,' McDonald's chairman Fred Turner told one of his suppliers in 1979. 'I want chicken finger-food without bones, about the size of your thumb. Can you do it?' The result was Chicken McNuggets, a whole industry in reconstituted chicken, a whole new breed of chicken with extra large breasts, and the transformation of US chicken farmers – according to Eric Schlosser in *Fast Food Nation* – into 'little more than serfs'.

Chicken has been a major element of American fast food since 1952, when former door-to-door salesman, amateur obstetrician, mule-tender and petrol-station manager Harland Saunders first dressed up as a Kentucky colonel to promote his Salt Lake City fried chicken emporium. But Chicken McNuggets made McDonald's the second biggest purchaser of chickens in the USA.

Fast chicken has become a centralized industry, where just eight chicken processors control two thirds of the US market; the once proud tradition of independent chicken farming has been transformed into a miserable franchise. It's a tough existence, where pathetically dependent growers earn just $12,000 on average after fifteen years of work, and where half of them sell up or lose everything after three years.

Fast Food Nation lifted the lid on the way the fast food industry has remade not just the food we eat, but also the places we live in, the farms we depend on and the way we employ people. Burger King, McDonald's and Tricon Global Restaurants – owners of KFC, Taco Bell and Pizza Hut – employ as many as 3.7 million people around the world in 60,000 restaurants, with new ones opening somewhere around the globe every two hours. Together it has a massive economic impact.

This provides a vision of a 'fake' future – of instant identikit food, virtually indistinguishable from TV and film tie-ins, of hopelessly dependent agriculture, of obedient, unimaginative, underpaid employees – poor, often illiterate, sometimes illegal – and monstrous industrial farming and meat megacorporations. The latest plants slaughter cows at the rate of 400 an hour. In Britain, health inspectors are expected to check chickens for health at the rate of well over 100 a minute.

'The basic thinking behind fast food has become the operating system of today's retail economy, wiping out small businesses, obliterating regional differences, and spreading identical stores throughout the country like a self-replicating code,' said Schlosser.

The problem goes far beyond snacks. The modern food industry is partly the product of urbanization. Big cities like London and New York lost most of their farms in the 1920s, as preservatives were increasingly used to keep the food edible while it was trucked or trained in from the countryside. It was standardized, marketed, branded, and it has been ever since – its original qualities removed by the industrial process, and reintroduced in the form of fats and secret chemicals.

The next generation of foods, following the highly successful Benecol margarine that actually reduces your cholesterol, are beginning a slow merging with pharmaceuticals. Cereals now contain folic acid because of a research link to healthy pregnancies. Food will soon be marked as suitable for specific conditions, even blood types – following the tried and tested American tradition that, if something's good for you, you might as well have too much of it.

Now the wider industry produces around 10,000 new processed food products every year, most packed with chemical additives and artificial flavours. The taste of ice cream, biscuits, sweets, burgers, toothpastes mostly comes from a series of little bottles on the shelves of International Flavors and Fragrances (IFF), in a big office just off the New Jersey Turnpike. The industry is immensely powerful, and it threatens a kind of global monoculture as supermarkets, big brands, big farms and convenient breeds drive out the rest. It's hardly surprising, for example, that Britain has lost 60 per cent of its apple orchards since 1970. Or that Wisconsin has lost more than 70 per cent of its cheese factories over the same period.

Behind all that there's a continuing push to limit food diversity, by forcing countries to accept genetically-modified food – like the USA's economic threats to Thailand in response to their requirement that genetically modified corn and soya be labelled. And whatever you might believe about the safety of GM farming, it does seem clear that it can affect the diversity of species in the countryside and of world food supplies. The real agenda of genetic modification is the patenting and control of crops.

But it was Schlosser's visit to IFF that was the most disturbing part of his book. 'Grainer's most remarkable creation took me by surprise,' he wrote. 'After closing my eyes, I suddenly smelled a grilled hamburger. It smelled like someone else in the room was flipping burgers on a hot grill. When I opened my eyes, there was just a narrow strip of white paper and a smiling flavorist.'

And behind this unreal world is a kind of mind control that forces it to be true and real, after all. Food conglomerates control enormous research budgets, locking academic departments in just as the pharmaceutical industry does – sometimes suppressing research findings that don't suit them. Some of the big brands sponsor teaching materials that are hazy, to say the least, about key issues like the health effects of sugar, or the implications of GM food.

This process of double-think has reached an extreme in thirteen American states, where they have enacted so-called 'veggie libel laws'. These make it illegal to criticize agricultural commodities in a way that's 'inconsistent with reasonable scientific evidence' – even Oprah Winfrey has fallen foul of these. In Colorado it is actually a criminal offence.

You only have to read the explanation on Ben & Jerry's ice cream tubs in the USA, almost apologizing for claiming to be GM-free – to realize how constrained freedom of speech has become. It's a strange unreal world we have entered, where the economy is built on exploitation and fakery, where our ideal of sturdy independent farming is rapidly disappearing, but the little boy is legally prevented from pointing out that the emperor is wearing no clothes.

But New Realists' strength of feeling has also been having an effect on the food conglomerates. That's why they are scrabbling to buy up local brands, like Campbell's soup, and snapping up salsa maker Pace Foods from San Antonio. And why they are launching their own regional brands, like the micro-breweries Mountain Red Lager and Elk Mountain amber ale, launched by the big American beer brands, both using exactly the same hops. That's why KFC sells tempura in Japan, gravy in Northern England, potato and onion croquettes in Holland, pastries in France and spicy chicken in China.

This was by no means the way giant global brands meant to develop. Even McDonald's has realized that Ray Kroc's simple 1950s formula isn't what people want any more. 'We thought we knew about service,' a McDonald's UK executive told the *Financial Times* in 1994. 'Get the order into the customer's hands in sixty seconds – that was service. Not according to our customers. They wanted warmth, helpfulness, time to think, friendliness and advice . . . what was revolutionary in the 70s was ghastly in the caring 90s.'

None of that makes real food exactly, but in the unequal fifty-year battle between authentic and fake eating, Goliath had blinked.

'Your mother was wrong. Television's a good thing,' said a recent advertisement for the modern doyenne of real living – and real food in particular – Martha Stewart. But although an advocate of authenticity, Martha is intricately enwrapped in the virtual world. Before her high-profile conviction for obstructing justice, she ran a $1 billion business mainly on-line. Her website got half a million hits a week. Her programme *Living Weekdays* was on CBS six days a week. Her radio programme series *AskMartha* was on 260 stations across the USA. She had a string of magazines, six personal fax numbers, fourteen personal phone numbers and seven car phone numbers.

'Her message is high touch; her medium is high tech,' said the futurist John Naisbitt. 'If the medium is the message, Martha is shifting to high tech.'

If your recipes end with phrases like 'Let it sit in a cool, dark place, sealed for about six months,' you might expect the medium to be a little more homespun – but that's unfair on the queen of Virtual Real. If the message needs to get out there, and there's a hunger for authenticity that needs satisfaction, then it needs to be delivered.

Martha Stewart is a phenomenon and a clear symptom of a world that's getting real, but – as a clear compromise between the real and the absurdly unreal – she's also an object lesson in the way the corporate world has moved to take advantage of the demand for authentic food.

Her official biography has Martha developing a passion for cooking, gardening and 'homekeeping' while being brought up in Nutley, New Jersey, in a family of six, and tracks her progress through stockbroking and catering to her first book, the immensely influential *Entertaining* in 1982. And from there in short steps how she became the ninth most powerful woman in American business, according to *Fortune* magazine.

The unofficial version is slightly different, but no less impressive. She was born Martha Kostyra, the daughter of Polish parents, and put herself through university by modelling. She then realized that people's hunger for the authentic actually came at a time when they had no time left to cook or bake. The resulting formula uses the guilt that seems to give people a greater appetite for ridiculously time-consuming recipes and handicrafts. Whether or not the 5.3 million viewers actually follow her instructions to make citrus grilled fish or their own haunted village (complete with gravestones) for Halloween – two of the offerings on the website when I last logged on – they love the idea of them. It reminds them of a time when people had that kind of leisure – rather as those best-selling 1970s self-sufficiency manuals bought by urban dwellers who wouldn't actually think of killing their own pig.

This is real in the sense that 'home-made' is real. It stands against mass production and impersonal identikit design. It flies in the face of a world where the preparation for the average meal is now fifteen minutes. But in another sense, Martha Stewart's world is hopelessly unreal: a straining towards impossible perfection rather than simplicity. It's expensive and, for the vast majority, absolutely unreachable.

Her Sunday morning TV show, according to the journalist Barbara Lippert, was 'a sort of alternative church service for those seeking aesthetic self-help'. When she flambéed bananas up Mount Kilimanjaro for a TV special, she packed thirty-six litres of bottled water and blusher and a number of changes of outdoor clothes in different autumnal shades. 'Tomorrow I think I'll wear russet,' she announced, pushing aside the cook to drum up a risotto at 15,000 feet – criticizing outdoor clothing for coming in 'such inappropriate shades'. This is authenticity as pornography.

Martha Stewart has yet to conquer Europe, but we are deep into the same phenomenon. The hunger for authentic food has led to a foodie explosion, now well into its second decade in the UK. The rise of fake food carries on apparently unchecked, but there is another side to people's personalities which simple convenience doesn't satisfy. And although they may not be Nigella-Lawson-style domestic goddesses – even enjoying the occasional visit to McDonald's McDonald's, Kentucky Fried, Pizza Hut Pizza Hut – they are having their effect on supermarkets and the food industry.

For, the growing demand for real food is beginning to divide the food industry. Supermarkets have been scouring the world for 'authentic' local tastes since the end of the 1970s, and responding to consumer demands for ethical food, free-range eggs, organic milk and GM-free soya. When McDonald's decided to ban genetically modified potatoes, following consumer pressure, it was a major setback for the biotech companies. Now big distributors like McCain Foods, Lamb Weston and Simplot are refusing to use GM varieties – and when New Leaf placed GM potatoes in the Canadian market, their sales slumped.

None of this helps the farmers much. American farmers now get just nine cents of every dollar spent on agricultural produce by consumers, with twenty-four cents going on seeds, energy, fertilizer and other inputs, and sixty-seven cents going to marketeers, middlemen, transport and supermarkets. Half a century ago, they got forty-one cents. Nor does it help the really desperate farmers in India, some of whom are even selling their own kidneys to get out of debt to the seed companies. But it is a chink in the armour protecting the inexorable expansion of fake food. Because it is clear that consumers – who have never been consulted about this massive shift – do have power, and enough of them are searching for authenticity to make a serious difference.

Consumer power is even having its effect in the heartland of fake food. By 1996, the *New York Times* could run the headline 'America's Quiet Rebellion Against McDonaldization' – a term coined by the sociologist George Ritzer. The article described a rediscovery of regional foods. According to the University of Chicago pollster Tom Smith, local brands and values were being passed on to kids before national brands could take hold. A decade ago, visitors to Dallas and Atlanta would have been taken out to eat French cuisine, said the *New York Times*. Now they're served *chile verde* and cheese grits.

All ten of the different descriptions of the new authenticity outlined in Chapter 1 are evident from any wander around most local supermarkets. Fair Trade coffee and Freedom Foods and other ethical foods are all there. The products occupying at least half of the shelf space are described on their packets as 'natural'.

Manufacturers have to be sincere about what's in their products by law, even if some of them tell less than the whole truth. The growth of 'organic' labels alone demonstrates the consumer's demand for what is simple, unspun and sustainable. The piles of coloured fruit and vegetables are intended to look thoroughly authentic, and if they don't quite meet continental standards of beauty – it's probably only a matter of time before they do.

The same trend is happening in the USA, according to the leading American food critic Ruth Reichl, who predicts that fresh local food will soon filter down to even the most impoverished inner-city dwellers.

The new trend towards raw food is another specifically American take on authenticity. It began, predictably, in California with the opening of Raw Experience, a San Francisco restaurant devoted to using only raw vegetables, herbs and spices. This was followed shortly afterwards by Organica in San Francisco and Quintessence in New York. 'It's a political act to eat raw foods, because major corporations are poisoning people with over-processed, denatured food,' says the founder of Quintessence, Dan Hoyt.

Back in the UK, one of the great authenticity success stories has been CAMRA, the immensely successful Campaign for Real Ale. No new breweries had been set up in the UK in the half century before CAMRA was founded in 1971, but the real ale revival has seen the arrival in the market of almost 300. CAMRA's biggest coup has been persuading the Monopolies and Mergers Commission that brewers shouldn't also own pubs.

A decade or so ago, the British beer market was dominated by giant breweries, producing nearly identical bitters and lagers. John Grant has revealed how his then client, the mega-brewery Courage, held a testing session for their staff at which only one person managed to identify their own lager. It was the same in the USA, where until recently Anheuser-Busch and Miller dominated American beer.

The first sign of a backlash was the unexpected rise of regional brands like John Smiths and Boddingtons, and the arrival of branded lagers from around the world. Their taste – even their design – made them seem more real: sometimes this was because the labels looked so Latin American that they had to be drunk with a slice of lime jammed into the neck, like Sol, or because their bottles were built to resemble a Germanic fortress, like Grolsch. Now successful beers reflect their specific roots, makes, and place of origin and are brewed by micro-breweries – there are now 1,600 in the USA alone.

CAMRA's successes have led to the big brewers introducing their own micro-brewery-style beers. And the leisure industry's stranglehold over the pubs – another focus of CAMRA's campaign – seems to get ever stronger. In Cheltenham, the confusion reached its height in 1996 when one city centre pub was renamed the Rat and Parrot while its neighbour was renamed the Rat and Carrot. Since British pub names sometimes stretch back over 1,000 years, these are important authenticity failures.

And then there's the inexorable rise of organic food, up 55 per cent in 2001 in the UK. Some outlets now only stock organic, like Iceland in the UK or the Danish chain Irma – which has given up non-organic milk entirely because there's no demand for it. The rise of organic products has been driven by supermarkets responding to consumer demand – it was supermarkets which also held back the tide of genetically modified ingredients. Marks & Spencer has even promised to prohibit seventy-nine pesticides, after being singled out for attention by Friends of the Earth.

Our modern take on organic farming goes back to the ideas of Sir Albert Howard, and his observations of the way that Indian peasant farms worked in *An Agricultural Testament*, published in the 1940s. His ideas have gathered incremental support the more entrenched processed and 'analogue' foods have become.

But there is a problem at the very heart of virtual real. The demand for organic food in the UK has long outstripped the ability of British organic farmers to supply it – and the UK government gives less support to farmers switching to organic than almost any other government in the European Union. As a result at least 70 per cent is imported, often from the other side of the world.

Yet consumers also want convenience organics. As a result, American agribusiness has fought a long, successful campaign to water down the definition of organic so that it can apply to factory farms or food processed with synthetic chemicals. European organic standards haven't been compromised to this extent, but on both sides of the Atlantic big manufacturers are now able to use 'permitted' organic additives which make organic TV dinners possible.

Organic farming has become big business in the USA, with farms like Cascadian – the biggest organic farm in Washington State – offering mass-market foods bearing the completely meaningless slogan 'taste you can believe in'. Five giant farms control half the organic market in California, shrinking price premiums, and as a result crushing the small organic farmers who need that premium to pay for the changeover.

At the same time, the mega food corporations have moved aggressively into the organic market. Rachel's Organic Dairy, the most successful organic farm in Wales, has been bought by the US giant Horizon. Mars spent £2 million marketing its new organic breakfast cereal in the summer of 2001. The Enjoy Organic company is actually owned by the giant Rank Hovis MacDougal.

And while the New Realists lap up these virtual real versions of vegetables and beer, the near monopolies of the food producers and retailers are also undermining the foundations of real places. It isn't just the species of butterflies disappearing on industrial farms. According to the Sussex Rural Community Council, a new supermarket will close every village shop within a seven mile radius.

When Sainsbury's arrived in my area in 1992, five small greengrocers, two butchers and many other independent businesses closed. When the planned Homebase outlet arrives next door, it will no doubt devastate all the local hardware shops too. Choice in food sometimes means less choice in other aspects of life.

So, this is the problem. The food might be real, but it isn't local. And the packages might have pictures of happy creatures gambolling about in rustic bliss on them, but many are actually produced in the equivalent of dark satanic mills for hens.

Most commentators believe that this is the natural outcome of consumers' demand for authenticity. The big corporations have moved to supply what people want at a lower cost. A colleague of mine was recently ridiculed by a Tesco executive at a conference on the future of food for suggesting that there was anywhere further for the revolution to go. I took part in a radio debate in 2001, at the height of the foot and mouth crisis, on which my opponent was a retail consultant working for one of the big four supermarkets; he was prepared to let British agriculture die out completely. It was an unnerving experience. What could I say, in the ten or so seconds available, that could do justice to the enormous waste involved, in skills and land – not to mention all that petrol wasted trucking in food from around the world instead? How could I sum up the extent of the economic devastation? Needless to say, I was frustrated by my performance.

But could people's demand for authenticity really lead them

to abandon that price advantage, or that convenience? Could we really get used to only having local fruit and vegetables available – and only when in season? Could we ever really organize food locally so that it is produced without chemicals, without exploitation and in a way that supports a thriving new generation of small farms?

Despite the fact that small shops are enjoying a revival in the UK, it seems unlikely. Even so, there is a growing backlash against agribusiness, partly because of irradiation, antibiotics, mad cow disease and foot and mouth, and partly because of a sense that they are leading somewhere even more unpleasant. The backlash is most apparent in France, where they have discovered a hero in a hippy-turned-sheep-farmer on the lower reaches of the Massif Central.

José Bové won that position when he burned down the new McDonald's restaurant in his home town of Millau, and was sentenced to three months in jail. His big bushy moustache inspires comparisons to Asterix – though his girth is nearer that of Obelix – and more than 40,000 people attended his trial, arriving in special trains. His wife Alice may have slightly dented the image when she accused him of running a macho organization and leaving her for another woman, but his campaign against *la malbouffe* – his word for fake food – has struck a real chord with the French.

His clash with McDonald's came as he rose up through the ranks of the radical small farmers outfit Confédération Paysanne, when Washington slapped a 100 per cent duty on Roquefort cheese in response to the continued European ban on the hormones in US beef. Bové makes Roquefort: 'The Americans took Roquefort hostage, so we had to act beyond the law to defend ourselves,' he said later. 'Hormones versus Roquefort. You couldn't get a better contrast between local quality and globalization.'

By February 2002 the revolt had spread. French restaurateurs took to the streets to protest against a tax on restaurants of 19.6 per cent, when fast-food takeaways only had to pay 5.5 per cent. Nearly three quarters of French restaurateurs took part in the one-day strike.

But then Bové, like Martha Stewart, has more than a hint of the virtual real about him. Since emerging as a modern French hero – much to the disgust of the French farmers' union – he has spent almost no time actually farming, but rushes across the world on speaking engagements and spreads the word through TV appearances.

'We have remained a culture where the time spent at the table is not just for consuming food,' says Bové. 'It's a social and family moment. There is a frightening statistic from America that the average time a family sits at the table is six minutes. That hasn't happened here yet.'

Consciously or not, Bové was echoing the words of an Italian journalist who has built up an enormous following around the world with his campaign to slow food down.

It was another run-in with McDonald's that was instrumental in launching Carlo Petrini's Slow Food campaign. It was in direct response to the arrival of hamburgers in Rome's Piazza di Spagna in 1986. But Petrini is no new Asterix, smashing the place up. He has a neat beard rather than a straggly moustache. His response has been a sophisticated campaign that now has 65,000 members across forty-two countries, an office in Brussels for lobbying Eurocrats and another in New York for organizing trade fairs.

Petrini and the poet Folco Portinari sat calmly down and

wrote the Slow Food Manifesto, declaring that 'a firm defence of quiet material pleasure [is] the only way to oppose the universal folly of Fast Life'. The organization developed out of Associazione Ricreativa Culturale Italiana, Petrini's network of social clubs linked to the Italian Communist Party.

Three years after the manifesto – choosing the snail as their official symbol – Petrini and 500 followers from fifteen countries met at the Opéra Comique in Paris to endorse the manifesto at a banquet. It was 1989, and the celebrations of the 200th anniversary of the French Revolution were in full swing. The choice of year was deliberate, because 1789 also marked the moment when the French court chefs suddenly found themselves out of a job and responded by opening the first restaurants.

From their headquarters in Bra in Piedmont, at the foot of the Alps – a region renowned for its truffles and red wine – Petrini and the Slow Food Movement have since taken up the cause of the long-tailed sheep of Laticauda, Sienese pigs, Vesuvian apricots and many other half-forgotten foods. They have a publishing house, a programme to protect endangered food, and about 500 local organizations known as *convivia*, where they basically meet to eat.

'We want to extend the kind of attention that environmentalism has dedicated to the panda and the tiger to domesticated plants and animals,' he says. 'A hundred years ago, people ate between 100 and 120 different species of food. Now our diet is made up of at most ten or twelve species.'

One of their success stories has been Renzo Sobrino, who bought an old mill outside Bra, and uses the old methods to grind traditional cereals and flours – including an ancient Egyptian grain called *kamut* that's good for people with wheat allergies. When he first tried to persuade local farmers to supply him with anything other than the high-yield American varieties, they dismissed him as mad, and he had to make ends meet by mixing concrete. A decade later, people are fascinated by the old dark grains, and he has all the orders he could need.

Another of their successes is the Pietmontese cow which was out of favour with the big commercial distributors because, although it produces very high quality beef and cheese, it grows slowly and produces less milk than modern dairy breeds. The Slow Food solution was to put together a consortium of sixteen farmers, using very strict organic rules of production. The strategy paid off even more quickly the moment BSE became evident in Europe.

But it isn't just industrial standardization that is inimical to slow food. A major threat comes from bureaucrats – often under pressure from lobbyists employed by the multinational food companies. In 1999, the EU passed rigid hygiene requirements for all food manufacturers based on rules originally developed for NASA. These are impossible requirements for small farmers, and Slow Food collected a petition with half a million signatures and won major exemptions for Italian artisan food-makers. The battle to protect unpasteurized milk in small-scale cheese-making continues on both sides of the Atlantic.

Even so, the mere existence of Slow Food thirty years after Apollo 11 – which also used NASA hygiene regulations – is a victory for the New Realists, and its popularity and imagination indicate that the authenticity revolution may have further to go than the current supermarket shelves.

In the short run, any kind of future for real food will depend on the survival of small farmers and artisan food-makers. Otherwise the diversity of food is going to carry on giving way to those that just grow fast and travel well – which is why the only kind of strawberry you find in supermarkets is the Elsanta, the so-called 'three bounce' variety, because it doesn't bruise.

The arrival of farmers' markets from across the Atlantic is one sign that they may survive after all. So is community-supported agriculture – a Japanese idea that has been taken up in the USA, whereby people support a local farm with a subscription and receive a guaranteed box of vegetables every week.

The first farmers' market I saw was in Ithaca in upstate New York. At the time it was one of the most beautiful things I'd ever seen, the piles of brightly coloured vegetables overflowing on the tables – and sold by the farmers that had grown them. The market was absolutely packed with customers looking for healthy, fresh and reliable food. In Ithaca, they even issue their own local currency – Ithaca *hours* – to make sure the money used at the farmers' markets stays circulating in the local economy. As many as 300 farmers' markets are now running regularly in the UK, occasionally even in supermarket car parks – and, as a by-product, encouraging people back into town centres. A range of websites run by small local food producers is helping to underpin food production by selling authentic food to a wider market. In the USA there are 2,800 farmers' markets, with a turnover of $12 million in the Seattle area alone.

A renewed interest in growing food commercially in cities is another sign. The first city farm in the UK opened next to a railway line in Kentish Town in 1971, with chickens, geese and goats collected by the American community theatre entrepreneur Ed Berman and a staircase borrowed from the stage props of the West End revival of *No, No Nanette*. But London was a little late – about 800 million city dwellers already grew their own food around the world.

There is a chain of twenty Washington restaurants, Clyde's of Georgetown, which are linked by computer to forty urban vegetable growers in the suburbs. The restaurants email their needs to the farms, send a van round to collect the produce, and are then honestly able to tell their customers that the vegetables have been freshly picked that day.

In Bogota, more than 100 women are employed growing food on rooftops, stairwells and patios in squatter areas, with the food picked up by local supermarkets three times a week. They've been so successful that they also now run a consulting service.

But the real issue is how small farmers can be sustained in country and city by providing local food for local needs. The global market in food may seem efficient in money terms – but by undermining tens of thousands of small producers who use the land effectively, it is inversely so in human terms or land terms. The re-emergence of local food is probably also the key to both the future of farming and a more authentic kind of small town. Which is why the organic farmer Sir Julian Rose – whose farm in Oxfordshire has been organic for over twenty-five years – is working with the local market town of Farringdon to make local agriculture central to their economic revival.

'The market town used to be the centre of rural commerce,' he says. 'And now it's a poor shell, with some trinket shops, a bank, maybe some travel agents and absolutely no sign of anything to do with the surrounding farmland and commercial activities associated with it. If you've got a town with 9,000 population surrounded by productive agricultural land, then essentially 9,000 acres around the town should be providing the majority of its food. That's almost unanswerable.'

Supermarkets can't play a role in that because their systems are so centralized, he says. 'If someone like me decides to provide products for a major supermarket in Reading, that product would have to go up to Manchester for packaging and distribution, and spend at least two days there. By the time it comes back, it's no longer fresh, it's lost much of its nutritional value and it's contributed to traffic jams and carbon dioxide emissions.'

Real food is going to have to emerge out of the wreckage of British agriculture – farms of 500 hectares making just 70p profit an hour – to fulfil the local needs not just of individuals, but also maybe of schools, hospitals, local businesses and authorities.

Sir Julian predicts a dual system emerging – one providing high-quality food for locals and the other, increasingly American-style, increasingly bland, mega-factory farms that really can compete without subsidy in the global economy. The local agriculture model still exists in Poland – even though this peasant-style farming, as they see it, is a source of embarrassment to the Polish government and a target of disapproval from the European Commission. 'But if these small farms can earn a living, which most of them do, with an average farm size of five hectares, and have a nice house, television, hot water, electricity and probably a car, without subsidies of any kind or the use of agrochemicals – because they can't afford them – there's probably something to be learned from these people.'

Rose has earned a reputation for himself as a representative of the International Coalition to Protect the Polish Countryside, and for wandering among the peasants of central Europe, urging them not to go down the high-production route for farming, and to use what they've got as the basis for improvement instead. The farmers are astonished that you can go bankrupt on a 500 hectare farm, even though Poland's entry into the EU looks set to send them the same way – and with it, destroying one of the most successful models of real, local food in the world.

Nobody can be completely confident that the authenticity revolution will go much further than filling the supermarket shelves with three-bounce strawberries – far from it. Authenticity is an ambiguous business. It always has been, but although the New Realists may not define it clearly, they know what they're looking for. It's just that, over the past few decades, it has been a moving target. Why should Elizabeth David's rediscovery of Mediterranean glamour be a search for authenticity in 1950, when Peter Mayle's *A Year in Provence* in 1989 just looks like an escape from reality? Why did packing supermarkets full of kiwi fruit and goat's cheese in 1980 look like authenticity, when now – with strawberries apparently in season all the year round – it somehow looks fake?

Of course the English search for colour, passion, real emotion and real food is much older than New Realism. But there is a progression here as well, the same authenticity progression that you can see in other areas of business; Elizabeth David's own life exemplified it. It's a progression that seems to be unfolding around us as we gradually become disillusioned with the corporate 'authenticity'. First she urged us to explore the experience of food, the foreign possibilities and sensuality of it. But by the end of her life, it wasn't enough to import authentic food from somewhere else – we had to rediscover our own.

The seemingly unassailable fake food industry is not where they said they would be three decades ago. Instead of limiting our diet to pills and tubes, they have found themselves struggling to provide some of the authenticity that consumers have demanded, through market pressure. And now that fascination for foreign tastes looks set to turn into a growing determination to rediscover our own traditions, and to protect the local economy and the reality – and the real taste – of seasonal foods, even perhaps to enjoy the seasonal inconvenience of that, as we enjoy complaining about the inconvenience of the changing weather. Because it's real.

* * *

‘Good cooking is honest, sincere and simple,’ wrote Elizabeth David. And it is – but, as she also pointed out, preparing it isn’t necessarily easy or quick. Authentic food, slow food, may – if we’re not careful – be a throwback to the pre-feminist, feudal days when women or servants cooked the food slowly and elaborately and the men or masters enjoyed it.

Maybe we can only rediscover slow food at the expense of other people’s lives. Yet, the new authenticity isn’t primarily about nostalgia. It’s fascinated by the past and determined to root modern life there, but it isn’t turning the clock back. This is how Paola Gho, the editor of Slow Food’s successful *Osterie d'Italia* for the past twelve years, answers the criticism:

> Here at Slow Food we have repeated ad nauseam: we are nostalgic for ‘grandma’s home cooking’, but we are also well aware that only blinkered reactionaries imagine they can hold on to customs and habits forever. This applies to cooking as well as music, language, clothing; what we appreciate is the renewal of traditions, which begins with a known and consolidated repertoire and skilfully updates it without distorting it: through different cooking methods, the addition or removal of an ingredient, or care over a new style of presentation. What frightens us is indiscriminate (and more or less conscious) kowtowing to fashions and trends. These may be the legendary destructured or crossover cuisine, the cult of enological and gastronomical status symbols, the multiplication of menus (for cigars, mineral water, coffees, oils, bread, liqueurs), the use of pretentious and absurd language, fashions, ephemeral phenomena by definition – they will never be reconciled with a model of cuisine that we would like to see: solid and in touch with its roots.

This clear description of a new kind of authenticity applies to much more than food. Even more so, when she follows it up sharply: 'Following fashion and trends is indicative of provincialism and a lack of education, short memory and scanty awareness of our own history; an inferiority complex that prevents us from recognizing the cultural value of our popular gastronomical heritage.'

The new drive towards authenticity has the same tension between old and new throughout, and tries to solve it in the same way – by rooting new traditions in local geography or local history. And – despite Paola Gho's comments – it recognizes how the mass media have undermined these roots, mainly by giving us an inferiority complex about what's local or ordinary 'or provincial'.

But it's hardly surprising that Slow Food has penetrated to the heart of the issue, because authentic food is an increasingly important issue. Local food may be the key to economic regeneration – as the geographer Sir Peter Hall says: 'The key to the heart of English regeneration is through its stomach.' Slow Food has now given birth to a parallel Slow Cities movement (Ludlow is Britain's first Slow City).

But it's even more fundamental than that. Petrini has constructed his own version of Ludwig Feuerbach's famous dictum that we are what we eat: 'If I wear a pair of Armani underpants, they do not become a part of Carlo Petrini. If I eat a slice of ham, it becomes a part of Carlo Petrini. That is why I worry more about ham than fashion.' That's what being real is all about.

It didn't happen . . .

'We shall escape the absurdity of growing a whole chicken in order to eat the breast or wing, by growing these parts separately, under a suitable medium.'

Winston Churchill, 'Fifty Years Hence',
Mechanics Illustrated, 1932

5

FAKE REAL #2: Out-Counter-Culturing

'Bliss was in that dawn to be alive,
But to be young was very heaven.'
William Wordsworth, *The Prelude*,
(on the French Revolution)

'How did we move from the optimistic, companionable, food-passing youngsters gathered on that field in Woodstock to the self-doubting, dark-hearted, tuned-in, death-praising, indifferent, wised-up, deconstructionist audience that now attends a grunge music concert?'
Robert Bly, *The Sibling Society*

Working as a campaigner for Christian Aid back in 1998, Andrew Simms managed to raise enough money to make a high-quality advertisement demanding action on Third World debt. You don't usually get that kind of advert on TV. Commercial breaks are usually packed with coffee and toilet cleaner adverts, rather than anything more challenging.

His film was tremendously effective: it showed a child in hospital and men in suits arriving to remove, one after the other, the intravenous drip and all the rest of the hospital's equipment. But then he faced the problem of raising enough money to get it shown on TV. When it occurred to him that the broadcasters might actually refuse to show it anyway, on the grounds that it was 'political' – rather as CBC refused to show Kalle Lasn's television slot attacking the forestry giants – it inspired his public relations ruse to get the advert seen and thought and talked about without pouring money into the television advertising department's coffers.

For when, sure enough, the television authorities ruled that Third World debt was too political for their audiences, suddenly Andrew found that his advert – shoved in a cardboard box before the ban – had developed an instant underground cachet. Soon, radio stations around the country were polishing their radical credentials by playing the soundtrack and Andrew was being repeatedly interviewed about the implications of the 'ban'. Leaflets with pictures from the ad were snapped up, and best of all – during that year's G8 summit in Birmingham – one of the city centre cinemas showed the advert repeatedly.

It was a highly successful example of how public relations can go far beyond simple advertising. Coinciding with the extraordinary Jubilee 2000 event where a chain of 70,000 people linked hands around the world leaders – the G8 summit resulted in a major new initiative on Third World debt – and Andrew's advert helped create the mood that led to it. Adbusters' *Uncommercial*, advertising TV Turn-off Week in 2000, followed a similar trajectory. Banned by the Advertising Regulation Bureau in France, it became a TV news story in its own right. Both these demonstrate the amazing currency of the underground and anti-establishment, not just to specific individuals who want to promote themselves as mildly dangerous, but to mainstream business as well.

I first realized this while researching a book about money in New York City, when Dennis Rodman – the 6′ 6″ star basketball player for the Chicago Bulls, famous for wearing a leather skirt and sequined top – had just head-butted the referee. And he turned himself into a considerably hotter property than ever before. By the end of the week, he was swamped with endorsement offers. Nike and McDonald's both joined the queue of his prospective sponsors and he looked set to earn an extra $1 million. A ghostwriter was rapidly signed up to write his autobiography, entitled *Bad As I Wanna Be*.

Thanks to the head-butt, Rodman was no longer a simple cross-dressing basketball genius, he was now 'bad'. 'Bad' had, of course, been the title of a Michael Jackson album, using the word in its reversed 'street' sense. It was a very modern boiling down of the old phrase 'naughty but nice' into something with a more threatening nuance. Because in the modern world of marketing, with its desperate focus on youth, the key to giving an impression of authenticity is rebellion.

High-pressure marketing to young people – probably *the* critical audience – now tends to mean developing a rebellious atmosphere around your product. That means sports players who break the rules, former terrorists, reformed criminals and mild Mafiosi are in demand. It means that discomfiture and a hint of polite violence have now become an accepted method of sales communication, and the power of marketing money is sometimes being shifted to encourage the louts – which is going to cost even more money to deal with later. It's a phenomenon that is surprisingly little commented on, partly I suppose because it's such an obvious facet of modern life. But brands want to capture some of the sense of real that their younger consumers are searching for, and that means being a little bit 'bad' – because bad means in your face, uncompromising, romantic and authentic. Bad has the ring of truth about it, or it seems to.

That is one of the reasons the small upstart local brands, succeeding by making a virtue out of their challenging independence, are being snapped up by the big players. And it's why the big names are also trying to wrap themselves up with a hint of that independent, anti-establishment verve. And if they can't have or be the real thing – an independent brand – they launch their own lookalike independent 'indie' label, which is why we are now awash with fake micro-brewery beer. It's cheeky and unofficial. That's why it sells.

Coca-Cola recently declared itself the 'unofficial state drink' for Wisconsin – after all, who wants to read an *official* biography these days, when all the controversy is bound to be in the unofficial one. Old Navy, an arm of Gap, set up a pirate radio station in Chicago to promote its clothing brand. If a product manages to gather a hint of the underground, it seems more real. After the Seattle anti-globalization clashes, Gap used graffiti to decorate their shop fronts all over the world. And the advertising agencies have been rapidly assimilating the symbolism of black street culture – or any other kind of protest culture – to suffuse their products with that same anti-establishment glow. Even for the middle-aged market, they have been rediscovering Jack Kerouac and Jimi Hendrix. Pepsi paid $5 million to be the only soft drink logo at the thoroughly commercialized Woodstock II.

Add a little heroin chic, and a strong whiff of decadence, and in the battle for the minds of younger consumers, your product looks considerably more authentic. And the more anti-establishment you are as a performer, the more you direct your rage at the commercial mainstream – as bands like Pearl Jam or Nirvana did – the more you become grist to the marketing mill.

French Connection's fcuk campaign – with its aggressive anagrammatic hint of Anglo-Saxon – transformed a trailing brand name into an anti-fashion market leader. Fcuk T-shirts sold as many as 100,000. Club 18-30 Holidays, notorious for their 'sun, sea and sex' ethos, noticed that their bookings shot up after just one disapproving article. If you can make customers think that by using your product they are somehow striking a blow against the kill-joys, the bureaucrats, the mean-minded and the censors, you have won considerably more than half the battle. No matter that these caricatures belong to a different generation, like the anal retentive with a small moustache who lives next door and refuses to give your ball back – they don't exist any more, but we still want to hit back.

One of the earliest exponents of this kind of advertising was the British agency Howell Henry Chaldecott Lury. They made their names by injecting a revolutionary moral core into products like Fuji film and Tango fizzy orangeade. The highly-successful Tango campaign, which involved people slapping each other about the ears, became a youthful craze around Britain – until a case of burst eardrums meant the advert was banned. 'It went from Ronald McDonald to Sid Vicious in a matter of months,' said John Grant of rival agency St Luke's.

HHCL even managed to produce a hoax broadcast claiming that 'Still Tango' was a bootleg product, and nothing to do with the brand, urging people to report it to the authorities. It was a wonderful example of persuading people they were selling the real thing by making it seem 'bad'.

Nor is this just about being cheeky to your elders – like Richard Branson's campaign against British Airways' 'dirty tricks' and his unexpected accusation of bribery against a rival National Lottery bidder, both of which helped the Virgin brand to look anti-establishment. It helps to wrap up your brand in radical opinions as well. MTV discovered this fighting back against genuinely local broadcasters who had been drawing off some of their viewers. Their solution was to fill in the spaces between videos with campaigns against AIDS, racism and environmental degradation. This worked like a charm; twinned with the launch of their highly successful *Unplugged* series featuring famous stars performing acoustically, without any of their usual razzmatazz and amplification. This seemed authentic just because it was raw: it also implied an attack on the record industry for their artificial arts of recording music.

The adverts for Fuji film created in the early 1990s by HHCL used the radical idea that photos taken with their film might allow us to see the world differently – and, in this case, disabled people in particular. It implied a mild revolution. And in their own way, so do Benetton's controversial advertisements: one showing a man with AIDS on the verge of death, surrounded by his distraught family; another more recently, the mug-shots of prisoners on death row.

The Body Shop has led the radical field by embracing campaigns against global warming, Shell's behaviour in Nigeria, the cosmetics industry and much else besides. But they are in a slightly different category, because Body Shop founder Anita Roddick genuinely believed in the campaigns – often rather more than she may have believed in the retailing that lay behind it. There was at least one attempt to oust her within the Body Shop because of fears that her public radicalism was damaging the company.

So what is going on? Why has the corporate world embraced adolescent revolt?

This is a phenomenon that goes back to the 'invention' of teenagers in the 1950s, when the need first to differentiate themselves from their parents and then from each other led – paradoxically – to a teenage culture where most dressed exactly the same. Youth culture has always demanded what is 'real', what is somehow 'on the street', yet for half a century or so they have been manipulated about what that is by the big fashion houses and record companies.

Once every generation or so, a genuine new wave manages to break the stranglehold, as punk did in the 1970s. But now the pressure is more intense, on both the kids and the marketeers. Advertising to children increased by 50 per cent between 1993 and 1996. At the same time, black street culture was hijacked by the music industry in what seemed like a blatant attempt to heighten the already present undercurrents of violence and frustration. 'Hip-hop' began when an early New York rapper called Lovebug Starski, used the phrase 'chap hippity hop don't stop keep on body rock'. By the mid-1990s, as many as 97 per cent of African American teenagers between twelve and twenty were listening to rap, a fifth of them buying five or more albums a month. One rap song 'Assassin', from the Ghetto Boys, included a line that rhymed spaghetti with 'slicing up somebody's guts with a machete.'

Rap and hip-hop are extreme examples. Marketing's use of the range from adolescent rebellion to outright violence reflects their need to shock us out of our increasing immunity to advertising. This requires larger and larger doses of shocking cultural antibiotics. Once again, it means endless adverts and posters showing prudish old people, pompous officials and authority figures being humiliated by fun-loving youngsters – and all pushing a product that has to seem much cooler and desirable than ever before.

The phenomenon was first tracked by the French sociologist Jean-Marie Dru in his 1996 book *Disruption*. Dru argued that the key challenge for modern marketing was to align products with liberation. Modern sales are achieved by identifying a social convention, some idea that maintains the status quo, he said, and smashing it visibly. That clashing of atoms together creates a sense of authenticity – or appears to. It's a process that seems to take the idea of the generation gap just a little too seriously, but it still means Nike lining up to declare itself a 'bearer of revolution',

Benetton to commit to fighting racism, Reebok to back non-conformity and Apple to struggle publicly with technocracy.

It doesn't matter that people don't entirely buy the link – they still believe in the underlying battle. 'This belief in the significance of the war between hip and square is accepted as holy writ not only by avatars of academic cultural studies but by our entertainment and marketing industries as well,' says the cultural critic Thomas Frank:

> The billion-dollar megaphone of advertising goes on telling us that the problem with society is conformity and that the answer is carnival, as long as there remains a discretionary dollar in the last teenager's allowance. If our famously fragmented society has anything approaching a master narrative it's more of a constant struggle, not with the communists, but with the puritanical, spirit-crushing fakeness-pushing power of consumer society itself. We resist by going to eat in 'ethnic' chain restaurants or watching Madonna videos or consorting with more authentic people in our four-wheel drives. Or simply by celebrating the consumers who do these things.

There is a major authenticity game going on here. It is being played out on the front line of marketing by people whose job it is to infiltrate youth culture and create demand for a new product. The terrible irony about out-counter-culturing your commercial opponents is that actually this isn't really a battle that belongs to young people at all. It isn't real in that sense. They are the objects of the game, the pawns moved across the chessboard. And when some of the more sophisticated consumers wake up to it, they find themselves at a whole new level in the game – caught between the fake rebellion encouraged by the marketeers and the 'real' rebellion against brand marketing encouraged by the anti-globalization movement.

'This is where liberation management comes in,' writes Thomas Frank. 'It imagines consumers, with the help of the brand, breaking free from the old enforcers of order, tearing loose from the shackles with which industrial order has bound us, escaping the routine of bureaucracy and hierarchy, getting in touch with our true selves. And finally finding authenticity, that holiest of consumer grails.'

Well, maybe. But I suspect that while the brands are out-counter-culturing each other, we're more likely to find our true selves elsewhere – and probably not by handing over our credit cards. This is because consumer power has to some extent left people with more foreshortened lives. Frank – whose underground magazines have done so much to puncture modern branding rhetoric – conjures up a picture of consumers driving down the road from their homes, mortgaged and heavily indebted, driving a sponsored car covered with corporate logos. That may be many things, but it isn't rebellious, authentic living.

Many conventions certainly do need to be flouted. It's just that the search for authenticity isn't really about packaged revolt. It only *seems* to be.

It may sound hopelessly pompous to blame the wave of consumerism we have all grown up with on Byron, but be patient with me for a moment because I think it's at least worth considering. And not just Byron either, but all those other overwrought fathers of Romantic poetry, Wordsworth running off to the French revolution, Keats on his sickbed, Shelley reciting Greek to babies on Oxford's Magdalen Bridge.

Imagine a series of sulky adolescents, in the second half of the eighteenth century, waking up one morning revolted by their parents' habits – those wigs, those sensible, reasonable, reasoned opinions, that pretentious wit. Where was the sense of mystery, of fate, of glory? And most of all, where were their wild animal instincts, and their primary duty to themselves and their passion? Their favourite philosopher was Jean-Jacques Rousseau and his rediscovery of the 'noble savage', who was in touch with its natural instincts, blissfully ignorant of the old basis of philosophy, coined by Rousseau's countryman René Descartes 'I think therefore I am'. For Rousseau – the Romantics, it was the other way round: 'I felt before I thought.'

Byron was a hopeless spendthrift, a riotous exponent of the idea that he could be, think and sleep with whoever he liked. He wouldn't have known the awkward word 'self-actualization' but he certainly lived it.

To claim that we have inherited the demand for instant gratification from the Romantics wouldn't be fair to the tradition that gave us Coleridge, Wordsworth and Tom Paine. But we have inherited their insistence that life has to be lived – for at least part of it – on the very edge. That doesn't mean that we have to die in a garret like Chatterton or go mad drinking absinthe like Toulouse-Lautrec, but by recognizing the rules and living outside them like Oscar Wilde and Aubrey Beardsley. It means buying into the great dream of bohemian living – we have to become what we best could and should be, and as young as possible.

It was the group of writers and painters born a century ago that repopularized bohemia. 'You are the lost generation,' said Gertrude Stein to Ernest Hemingway, and he wore it like a badge of pride – as almost every generation has done since. 'There were two schools among us: those who painted the floors black (they were the last of the Aesthetes) and those who did not paint the floors,' wrote the American critic Malcolm Cowley, who described his contemporaries's journey from Paris garrets to Greenwich Village garrets and their reaction against the new mass markets and mass producers.

Every generation since has dressed differently from the last – even if they didn't dress differently from each other. They believed in self-actualization, and struggled against becoming subsumed in the nine-to-five workaday world. But it is an ironic paradox that gets sharper with every new generation: they are increasingly lured by marketing into the consumer world in order to afford to buy themselves the badges and outfits of revolt – but the further they get drawn in, and the more they spend, the more they find themselves part of the very world they were trying to break free from.

The fashions that allowed them to stand out and shock their parents were there to buy – and labelled for that purpose – and buying them seemed a blow to that miserable work ethic that threatened to engulf them at any moment. 'Since the 1920s, consumerism has given voice to an order in revolt against older production-orientated values,' says Thomas Frank. 'It emphasizes pleasure and gratification against the restraint and repression of the puritan tradition.'

It's a schizophrenia, embedded in the mixed messages that society gives us all as we grow up and start spending. Enjoy yourself, we're told – consume and live life to the full, because thrift is bad for the economy. 'Our enormously productive economy,' wrote the post-war retail analyst Victor Lebow, 'demands that we make consumption our way of life, that we convert the buying and the use of goods into rituals, that we seek our spiritual satisfaction, our ego satisfaction, in consumption . . . We need things consumed, burned up, worn out, replaced and discarded at an ever increasing rate.'

But we are also told the exact opposite at the same time, that we must also knuckle down, forget enjoyment, work hard and do what we're told. We must be spendthrifts and workaholics at the same time. Big Brother wants us to do everything harder, whether it's working or spending.

It is partly in reaction to this impossible set of demands that so many of us start by despising the workaholic world. Either way, we are all bohemians now.

'We guarantee to give each person a look which is unique to them,' said one shop I went into recently in New York's SoHo. As modern bohemians we receive our marketing information and keep the economy afloat by our endless ability to buy the extreme, the bizarre and the shocking. We still live in garrets, although they are now fitted out very differently from Chatterton's. We still believe that the rules of society don't apply to us.

What holds both ideas together – and allows us to be spendthrifts as well as bohemians – is the concept of 'cool'. We buy what's cool and feel we are remaining true to our bohemian principles. And so suddenly cool becomes important to the economy. When Levi's blue jeans suddenly ceased to seem cool, they had to close half their plants in the USA and lay off 6,000 workers. These things matter.

Executives' current obsession with whether their products are cool or not dates back to 1992, the first time the number of teenagers had increased since the days of the baby-boomers. Teenagers also buy 35 per cent of all groceries – partly the kind of food they eat, and partly the stuff they've been sent out to buy by their parents – so cool food is regarded as important. Cool is, or seems to be, the real thing.

Since then, learning has been promoted as 'cool', Britannia is promoted as 'cool' and – according to the authors Dick Pountain and David Robins, authors of *Cool Rules* – loft living was 'cool' until recently, and for a peculiar reason. The abstract expressionists of the 1950s and 1960s moved into lofts to get in the way of modernist development plans in New York and created a whole trend of their own. But by the late 1980s, Docklands loft apartments were among the most expensive properties you could buy. The artists' stand against authority was crucial to the recipe of Cool, which is why Tony Blair's concept of 'Cool Britannia' could have never worked. It was too bloodless; it lacked the sense of revolt and defiance that makes Cool what it is. You can't have official Cool.

Cool also has a less acceptable face, as we saw when Rodman head-butted the basketball referee. Because, like 'bad', there's an undercurrent of violence – this time, self-violence and an obsession with the effects of 'cool' drugs like heroin and cocaine, or romantic tales of self-immolation. *Nevermind*, the title of the first album by Nirvana, was originally called 'I Hate Myself and I Want to Die'. This idea reached its epitome in April 1999, when two youths – both dressed as 'goths' – gunned down twenty-five of their classmates at Columbine High School in Denver, convinced that they were cooler than all the rest, having gorged themselves on drugs and satanic websites.

And this brings us back to the Romantic poets, for if our consumer bohemianism could be seen as Byron's legacy, then the strange brooding on death – particularly shared by youthful followers of Kurt Cobain – is the legacy of the author of 'Ode to a Nightingale'.

'They're already here, but we can't see them,' says a disembodied voice, addressing eight 8–13 year-old boys in a darkened office belonging to the toy-maker Hasbro in the South Side of Chicago. The voice informs them that extraterrestrial aliens called 'Pox' –

a disturbing name in these days of anthrax spores in letters – have escaped from a laboratory. 'Mankind's only hope is to enlist a secret army of the world's most skilled hand-held-game players,' says the voice as the boys swivel nervously in their chairs. 'We chose you because you are the coolest, funniest guys in your school. Raise your hand if you're cool.'

The slightly sinister scene, featured in a notorious PBS documentary in the USA called *The Marketing of Cool*, reveals the latest stage in an innovative campaign by Hasbro to take the 'cool' message to ever younger generations. Their sales reps concentrated on Chicago, and asked teachers, school children – anyone they met connected with education – to name the most popular boys in their school. It was always boys, too, because girls are not known for their interest in computer games.

These 'alpha pups', as they were then called, were paid $30 to learn Hasbro's new electronic game Pox, basically game plus radio transmitter. They were also given ten game units to distribute to whoever they wanted, as a way of enhancing their 'cool' status among their peers. Having 'bought' these boys, Hasbro needed to make sure they were cool enough to deliver. In small groups, they were also taken for the treatment with the video in a darkened room – with Hasbro's marketing men watching them behind a hidden mirror.

The alpha pups were predictably thrilled by the game, and the idea that they could play with anyone less than thirty feet away. 'Get the name of the kid who said it's the best game ever,' said the publicist behind the mirror. The children went off happily with their $30 and their ten game units – their status somewhere in the stratosphere.

The South Side of Chicago is famous as Al Capone's old stamping ground. These days it's a Latino neighbourhood, but also a strongly religious one. Some parents had banned their children from using computer games. Some schools had banned them too – and officially of course Hasbro said these weren't for using in school, just for talking about there, but the kids knew better. Yet all these factors pale into insignificance beside the deep unease at intervening in this way in the strange status battles of the children's playground.

The issue here is the extraordinary lengths companies will go to make viral marketing work, and to do so with younger and younger consumers – by deliberately playing up the idea of 'cool'. One result has been a rash of new cool consultancies, who keep their ear to the ground and find out the way the cool wind is supposed to be blowing, and setting up regular positions in marketing departments for people who are 'professionally cool' – experts in youth culture. Cool seems real and engaged in a way that other products are not. It seems aggressively contemporary. It means turning your back on the past, and in that sense it's desperately fake.

But it's fake in another sense too. In practice, the boundary between listening to the authentic offerings of youth culture and actually injecting your fashion ideas, games or products is now completely blurred. It isn't as if 'cool' comes somehow authentically from the streets to be discovered by manufacturers: it is normally put there by the manufacturers in the first place. In the US, big record labels hire street teams of urban black youths to take hip-hop albums into communities. They organize guerrilla bands of bill stickers. Nike even has a word for this borrowing of black street culture – 'bro-ing'.

This is how Nike's designer Aaron Cooper described a bro-ing operation in Harlem: 'We go to the playground and we dump the shoes out. It's unbelievable. The kids go nuts. That's when you realize the importance of Nike. Having kids tell you Nike is the number one thing in their life – number two is their girlfriend.'

In practice, the cool consultants are listening to each other's rumours of cool filtered through each other's bro-ing whispers. You have to question, in the end, whether any of it is genuine in any sense at all. And when you look at a brand like Sprite, with its deliberate slogan of authentic cool – 'Image is nothing' – then it just seems empty. 'The raw authentic is hunted down by cool hunters, snatched up, stripped clean, and mass marketed,' writes John Naisbitt. 'It's no wonder we question what is genuine.'

Of course, youth culture occasionally breaks free and throws up something of its own that takes a while before it is swallowed up. But in practice they are increasingly bound in by the competing forces of the twenty-first-century Great Game – into acting out the battle between different interpretations of cool until there isn't anything authentic left. There is, in short, very little remaining of youth culture. It's injected marketing, pulling the strings of the benighted consumers online and in their clubs and playgrounds about what is specified as cool.

A dangerous by-product of the battle is the increasing worship of cool – from the schoolkids transformed from overactive pre-adolescent boys into demigods by Hasbro, right through into adulthood. The result: the band of accepted youthful behaviour and fashion gets narrower and narrower – and increasingly expensive – forced into shape by the desperate search for trendsetters and the deliberate whispers of the cool consultants.

And behind all that, there is the myth that somehow youth culture is moving faster and faster – which in a way it is. But in another way, this cool rebellion has been deliberately speeded up by the marketeers. The hope for the future is just that occasionally this gets recognized by young people themselves. This is what one of them said in *The Marketing of Cool*:

> They were talking about the rebelliousness – but it's not rebelling at all. They're capitalising on the fact that people want to be rebellious, and they're talking about how teachers are nerds and authority figures are laughable. I mean, they're basically saying, 'Everybody sucks except for us' . . . They're basically telling us what to like and what we should like. They're trying to make money, obviously, and it's not about trying to make anybody happy. It's not a business in that it's trying to help people; it's a business in that it's making money.

If the brands can co-opt the whole of youthful rebellion, they can also – if they're clever – co-opt the anti-globalization movement lock, stock and barrel.

Negativland, the band that coined the phrase 'culture jamming', were asked by one advertising agency to make the soundtrack for the new Miller Genuine Draft. The fashion chain Gap now paints its own slogans across its windows. 'Criticism of capitalism has become, in a very strange way, capitalism's lifeblood,' writes Thomas Frank, and this is a phenomenon that Naomi Klein tracked in *No Logo*:

> When the youth culture feeding frenzy began in the early nineties, many of us who were young at the time saw ourselves as victims of a predatory marketing machine that co-opted our identities, our styles and our ideas and turned them into brand food. Nothing was immune: not punk, not hip-hop, not fetish, not techno – not even . . . campus feminism and multiculturalism. Few of us asked, at least not right away, why it was that these scenes and ideas were proving so packageable, so unthreatening – and so profitable. Many of us had been certain we were doing something subversive and rebellious but . . . what was it again?

It's no wonder then that young people embrace a tone of Byronic world-weariness, but then even that comes from the marketeers. Because if marketing comes with an increasingly ironic tone, it can wrongfoot the critics of mass advertising, and that little voice in our head that shouts 'Shut up!' at the TV screen. After all, what's the point?

It's just another part of the out-counter-culturing mind game. The poet Robert Bly describes us all as a 'sibling society', both suspicious of any messages from above and endlessly accepting of them, displaying both a nonchalant rejection of rules in general, and a fierce need to accept the rules of cool.

These were always the paradoxes of adolescence, but thanks to the battle for brand authenticity they are now everyone's paradoxes. And perhaps that's not surprising, says Bly – because the marketeers want us to stay young and unable to control our buying urges. 'The advertising industry is utterly opposed to ending infantilism,' he writes in *The Sibling Society*. 'The ad companies want the boy's infantile desirousness to continue – he should keep his desire for fast food, for M&Ms, for CDs, for refrigerators.'

Counter-culturing means that we are constantly urged to turn our back on anything traditional, to reject roots of any kind, and to desire anything new. We have been told so many times that we have become convinced that new technology blows away the old ways of doing things – even though e-commerce has just allowed us to rediscover the joys of having our purchases delivered in a van, which was actually the way our grandparents did their shopping.

In reaction to this, and to the discovery that we are now the slavish, indebted devotees of each latest fad of marketing cool, is an increasing demand for something genuinely real. We want authenticity – something which isn't cool or constructed –

because we resent the way our minds are being manipulated. The counter-culture wars, in fact, are spawning resistance to that kind of marketing.

I'm in my forties, so perhaps I haven't got the right any more to comment on what young people do. I'm at the age when inner-city bars suddenly seem too loud for conversation, after all. But equally, I'm nostalgic for a time when young people could control their own culture and construct their own rebellion. Perhaps they never could, but it certainly seemed so at the time.

'Our counter culture was a complete rethink of Western Civilization (still on the drawing-board, that one),' wrote the pioneer hippy and former editor of *Oz* magazine, Richard Neville, in a wonderful diatribe against the next generation. 'Your counter culture is the shopping counter – Prada, Tommy Hilfiger, Stussy, Moschino, Calvin Klein. Born free, you are everywhere in chain stores.'

It never happened . . .

'Waking to cool, 1970-style music from the tiny phonograph built into her pillow, the housewife yawned, flicked a bedside switch to turn on the electronic recipe maker, then rose and stepped into her ultrasound shower. While sound waves cleaned and vigorously massaged her, breakfast got itself ready in the kitchen. The recipe maker, taking its cue from a menu coded on a punch card, perked the coffee, dropped six eggs from an egg compartment into a bowl, mixed them with a dash of milk and scrambled them.'

The 60s, *Newsweek*, 14 December 1959

6

Real Culture

> **'Once we're wired for a virtual world, the present world goes dim.'**
>
> Richard Degrandpre, *Adbusters* magazine, March/April 2001

> **'To retreat behind the notion that the audience simply wants to dump its troubles at the door and escape reality is a cowardly abandonment of the artist's responsibility. Story isn't a flight from reality but a vehicle that carries us on our search for reality, our best effort to make sense out of the reality of existence.'**
>
> Robert McKee, *Story*

There's a disturbing moment in Willy Russell's play *Educating Rita*, when the heroine describes why she is determined to carry on with her Open University literature course, despite the pressure from her husband and family. In the pub for a family evening out, her mother suddenly stopped singing along to the fatuous song being played on the juke box with the rest of them and was crying.

'Everyone just said she was pissed an' we should get her home. So we did, an' on the way I asked her why. I said, "Why are y' cryin', Mother?" She said: "Because – because we could sing better songs than those."'

In the film, we get to see the scene as well – Julie Walters' Rita is shown next to her mother while, over and over again, the rest of her family all drones through the same old fake jaunty jingle. 'You think we're all surviving with our spirit intact,' Rita shouts at her university tutor in the form of Michael Caine: 'There must be better songs to sing than this.' Rita's mother represents a community without culture, without ritual to fall back on and without much meaning, except – as Kipling put it – 'the will that says to them, hold on'.

But we're in dangerous territory here. Willy Russell can get away with writing this kind of scene, where whatever is left of popular culture is portrayed as grindingly pointless repetition of some stupid sub-television tune, stripped of all meaning, squeezed dry of any emotional content – because nobody can accuse Willy Russell, with his impeccable Merseyside credentials, of being a snob. But you don't have to be urging a return to some kind of long-lost 'genuine' folk-song tradition – a cross between Bob Cratchit and Rambling Sid Rumpole – to believe that there's something missing these days.

Once again, it's all too easy to be boxed into sounding snobbish or nostalgic or both when talking about our renewed demand for what's authentic. But once again, the phenomenon I'm talking about is neither snobbish nor nostalgic, though it occasionally bears some of those elements. *Educating Rita* puts the case for me: Rita isn't looking for nostalgia when she wants to learn about literature, and she spends most of the play battling with snobs. What she wants is a sense of the life she's afraid she's been missing – a sense of the emotional fulfilment she fears she'll lose completely once she stops secretly taking the pill every night.

In the two decades since *Educating Rita* was first shown in London's West End, the situation has got much worse. We have a packaged culture, geared to our common ability to jump from TV channel to channel every three seconds. Our attention span has shortened to such an extent that the average time we spend in front of a painting in an art gallery has gone down from ten seconds to the same three seconds since 1987. From the age of seven, the average child sees about 20,000 adverts every year – and that's just on television. We have a concentration of media ownership so that most of what we read in the news, watch in the cinema, buy in the shape of toys in a toyshop, is mediated through a dwindling number of corporate giants. Our lives proceed with a constant soundtrack wallpaper from CDs or radios on for such a large proportion of our waking moments that some of us sink into depression.

Even the emotional reality of watching the same programmes as everyone else has now disappeared – when I was a child, everyone you knew would have watched *Morecambe and Wise* or *Monty Python's Flying Circus* the night before and be talking about it; now we have over 100 channels to choose from.

I'm not being puritanical about this – we enjoy a lot of it, after all. But there's also a growing sense that we want something more authentic too. It's a demand that proves to me that human beings are well able to protect themselves – both from the well-paid people who say the virtual world will sweep the old one away completely, and from the doomsters who believe it will destroy us.

There are, after all, critics on both sides of the Atlantic, predicting the end of human-scale culture altogether. The MIT internet guru Nicholas Negroponte predicts a future television with an 'audience of one', where the whole resources of broadcasting can be tailored for us to watch exactly what we want, when we want it. It's a scenario that threatens to undermine TV completely by removing its last vestiges of being an 'event'. It's also a disturbing image because, although music is often about dulling the silence of being alone, television and cinema can be a social as well as a solitary activity. Negroponte's vision is of a lonely world.

It's also a world without surprises. The cyber-critic Paulina Borsook describes interviewing Microsoft co-founder Paul Allen, while he waxed lyrical about custom-made newspapers delivered to you virtually, just containing the news you are interested in. She talked about serendipity, but 'he was puzzled, poor dear, and didn't know what I was talking about'.

On the other side of the fence, critics like Jerry Mander, president of the International Forum on Globalization, sees television as the force that homogenizes the world, to 'remake human beings themselves – our minds, our ideas, our values, our behaviors, our desires; to create a monoculture of humans that is compatible with the redesigned eternal landscape'. What results, he says, is 'a homogenized mental landscape that nicely matches the franchises, freeway suburbs, high-rise buildings, clearcut and speeded-up physical life of the external universe'. And Mander isn't the only cultural critic to make a connection between fake culture and fake places.

He wrote *Four Arguments for the Elimination of Television* (1973), after discovering there had been 10,000 books written in the USA since 1945 about television, but not one that questioned its existence. Mander even predicted a political leader for the television age with a simple message, absolutely no history and an assertive style with absolutely no content – over seven years before the election of Ronald Reagan as US President.

Television does remake the world. Watched for an average of four hours a day by children from the age of eight to thirteen, becoming for many the main thing they do in life, it must create an unreal mental world. It must have an effect. Toddlers spend between twenty-five and thirty-two hours a week in front of the TV. When the anthropologist Margaret Mead predicted that TV would become a second parent, she was clearly right.

The *New York Times* dismissed television in 1939 because 'people must sit and keep their eyes glued to the screen; the average American family hasn't time for it'. Six decades later, we know that the issue is whether they have time for anything else. But whatever else we might think about it, we have to take our exposure to TV seriously – the glittering, unreal world it promotes, and the illusion of intimacy. The French philosopher Jacques Ellul says that TV satisfies the need for intimacy without the hassles of a real friendship or relationship. TV saturation must have an effect – but people are increasingly choosing things that can combat it.

It is true that modern culture has a world-weary quality. It has to be 'cool'. It also comes along with a metropolitan sophistication that sneers at anything home-made, local or traditional. If we live in Europe or the USA, we learn to be ashamed of our current clothes, or family, or car, or trainers – and rush out to the shops to spend over the odds getting something that allows us to break 'free'. If we live in developing countries, we learn to reject the rural, agricultural life – and to rush to the nearest burgeoning, over-stretched city, to seek our fortune.

It is true, also, that modern culture is about instant hits – instant emotion and instant solutions. The poet Don Paterson was once phoned by the BBC's *Newsnight* programme explaining that they were doing an item on how poetry had been trivialized by the media, and if they sent a taxi to pick him up at 5.30, could he think about putting some of his thoughts into verse? It was then 4.30.

Yet maybe because of all this, or maybe in spite of it, there does seem to be a demand for authentic culture of a different kind. There is the completely unpredictable renaissance of poetry, which had been pronounced dead almost everywhere except for the in-trays of obscure professors of semiotics. There's the rise of reading circles: over 50,000 people are now regular members in Britain alone. There's the rise of art galleries – Britain's new Tate Modern, in an old power station on the Thames, was packed, receiving over five million visitors in its first year, while the hopelessly middle-brow Millennium Dome struggled to achieve half its target audience. The new Lowry Gallery in Manchester has been very popular while the National Museum of Pop in Sheffield has stayed empty. Galleries and concert halls here successfully led the regeneration of imperished cities like Gateshead, Salford and Walsall. 'People want high culture to stay high,' wrote the *Daily Telegraph* editor Charles Moore. 'The millions of us who do not know as much about art as we would like do not want it dumbed down: we want to be lifted up.'

As well as the revival of museums, the ubiquitous hype of virtual life – with the internet gurus claiming that we can transcend our bodies – has left artists with an absolute fascination with real bodies and body fluids. Now Damien Hirst, originally famous for his dead sheep and his dead shark, is one of the best-known artists in the world – his 1994 piece 'Couple Fucking Dead (Twice)' was banned by the New York authorities before he had even finished it.

Conceptual art is one of those difficult areas where you can argue about authenticity forever. A great deal owes more to hype and the arts establishment embracing 'cool' counter-culture than anything real. It is hardly surprising that one of the leading figures in advertising over the past generation, Charles Saatchi, should have been so involved in its creation as a phenomenon. Damien Hirst himself managed the hype brilliantly from the first, organizing his own *Freeze* show in an abandoned warehouse in the London Docklands in 1988, when still an art student. Other conceptual art bears most of the hallmarks of the counter-culture wars. It is 'cool', nihilistic, ironic, world-weary and carries more than a hint of violence.

On the other hand, leaving aside the business of light bulbs going on and off, Damien Hirst's work is very much concerned with authenticity. It's about the real cow, or shark. It's about the stark fact of death, just as Tracey Emin's unmade bed was about her own real life. Their success bears testament to our fascination with the immediate and the tangible – even if the gallery staff won't let us touch the works.

Over 60 per cent of the population of Mannheim in Germany queued to see artist and anatomy professor Gunther von Hagen's 200 human cadavers in plastic in 1998, and 2,000 people have donated their bodies for his future work. Somehow, the shock of the real thing draws in a horrified crowd. An estimated eight million have seen the show around the world, including a successful British tour ending in Glasgow in 2002 – where exhibits had to be moved away from the entrance to the Registry Office in case they were seen by bereaved relatives. 'Authenticity is key,' says artist Mark Dion. 'One of the reasons why museums are incredibly important now, and people seem to be flocking to them like never before, is that, despite the popularity of new technologies, people are still incredible hung up on the actual thing, the object, the specimen – as a means of communication.'

As if to confirm that, a recent poster for the Royal Academy in London with a picture by a famous modern artist urged people to 'just once see his work in a gallery, not on a tube of hair gel'.

The revival of traditional music and folk is more unambiguously about authenticity. There's even an attempt to claw television back for the 'authentic' camp, mainly by using technology differently. Michael Lewis predicted in the *New York Times* that machines like ReplayTV and TiVo – which don't record the ads when recording television programmes – spell the end of the mass market. Even top television personalities have been bailing out: Clive James set up his own internet TV channel, run from his front room.

Television executives seem only to be helping this process along. When Britain's commercial television's share of the audience fell below 50 per cent in 2001 – down from 67.5 per cent only five years before – they added another two and a half minutes of advertising every hour at prime time. The much-praised British TV looks set to threaten the record length of advertising break, currently held by NBC, of five minutes, twenty seconds.

There is cynicism about television: its obsession with viewing figures, timidity about new ideas, the stern belief that young people aren't interested in news, and especially not news about anywhere 'abroad' – and, in fact, can't bear to hear about anything they don't immediately understand. But despite all this, Britain's most detailed, sophisticated and longest television news programme – Channel 4 News – attracts the highest proportion of young viewers. Although we enjoy all the happy pap, the smiling faces, the distant hope of being a millionaire, people want something authentic. We don't necessarily want it *instead*. We don't want to give up television or pop culture, but we also want something real.

But cultural debate is a hall of mirrors: even just claiming this about culture is a confusing business – because 'real' is used in so many very specific senses. The Impressionists claimed to be capturing images of real, modern life, and were ridiculed for it – contemporary critics accused them of shocking women into premature labour. The abstract artist Kasimir Malevich claimed to have discovered what he called 'symbolic reality' in 1913, painting an isolated black square on a white background. Poets like Sylvia Plath dedicated themselves to recording the fierceness they perceived at the heart of the real world. Artists have often claimed to be the real thing, and we have to see through all that.

Three decades ago, it was widely predicted that reality would be so awful that the population would embrace the idea of mass tranquillization – echoed in the BBC's *Tomorrow's World* in 1970, which also predicted the demise of 'real food' and real kitchens. The following year, the author Stanislaw Lem published a short novel, *The Futurological Congress*, in which he imagined most of society taking what he called 'psycho-chemical' drugs as routine, because they preferred realistic hallucinations or waking dreams to reality. Instead of just watching television, they lived out the fantasies of television as if it was happening to them. 'We keep this civilization narcotized, for otherwise it would not endure itself. That is why its sleep must not be disturbed,' the hero is told by the pharmacological dictator who rules the new deluded world.

In some ways, these predictions have come true. We are stuck with the neo-brutalist housing blocks, most of which are still not paid for. Chunks of civilized society spend much of the time trying to escape into alcoholic or drug-induced unreality. And we do live out our lives in a kind of 'hyper-reality' constructed with the help of Disney, which does in fact come to pass because that's the way so many people believe the world to be.

This is another paradox about the modern world. Some kinds of escape into oblivion are unlawful; some are positively encouraged. It's a bit like the issue of consumerism: in some ways we are encouraged to consume and spend like Beau Brummel; in others we are urged to work hard and save.

But what the 1970s predictions failed to see was that this

escape into fantasy isn't the whole story. People also want to escape from a manufactured universe where feature films are made to sell us toys, or subtly place products in our heads; where advertisements carry layer upon layer of reference points to films, TV programmes and other ads; where the whole world is constructed by cinema executives; and where even the latest pop stars – like Japan's computer-animated Date Kyoto – don't actually exist. Virtual stars Gorillaz picked up two awards at the MTV Europe trophies in 2001, just as the Soggy Bottom Boys – who were an invention of the Coen brothers' film *O Brother, Where Art Thou?* – won a top award at the 2001 Country and Western Awards.

But we need something else. We need to see things happening to real people. We need to take part emotionally in real spectacles. We need to be at the heart of the carnival, rather than just on the sidelines looking in like couch potatoes. And according to the artist and musician Brian Eno, carnival is the key to 'real culture'. When spectators become part of the proceedings themselves, then the event takes on an authenticity it didn't previously have. 'Carnival is good when it leaves people with the feeling that life in all its bizarre manifestations is unbeatably lovely and touching and funny and worthwhile,' he writes.

As a vision of real culture, it is a real antidote to Negroponte's audience of one.

You wouldn't think that a TV documentary where the plot surrounds a pan of uncooked potatoes would make for prime-time television success – but you'd be wrong. That was exactly the issue between the chef and the head waiter at the Adelphi Hotel in Liverpool that turned the BBC's fly-on-the-wall documentary

Hotel from a mad idea by an in-house producer into a blockbuster.

'It was in episode two, and it was hardly the stuff of great drama or the basis for a novel or anything,' says *Hotel*'s executive producer – and one of the people behind TV's shift into the 'authentic' – Jeremy Mills. 'But it was a catalyst through which we could examine the relationships between the key players.'

The chef and head waiter became famous, and were constantly being recognized in the street, as millions tuned in every week to watch the latest episode of their inner lives. The point was that television documentaries had temporarily turned away from covering the inside story of great events, or even ordinary people going through extraordinary or disastrous events. *Hotel* was showing ordinary people doing ordinary things, and that somehow seemed a shift towards reality. These were instant TV stars: they hadn't been coached – they weren't even wearing make-up. They were authentic.

Hotel wasn't the first fly-on-the-wall documentary to examine ordinary life. That was probably the famous series *The Family* made by documentary-maker Paul Watson, where an unsuspecting family was dissected for the watching public and finally destroyed. The BBC made a name for itself in the 1970s with its naval series *Sailor*, which observed life aboard the aircraft carrier *Ark Royal*. But *Hotel*, more than a decade later, was the real watershed.

'I had spent a lot of time doing "big subjects" – life-changing stories,' says Jeremy Mills. 'What we discovered during the making of *Airport* was that the most engaging bits were very ordinary – like lost baggage or missed planes. We found ourselves making a series about how ordinary people coped with ordinary life.'

Hotel was followed by *Paddington Green*, an in-depth study of various inhabitants of a strange, transient neighbourhood. Since then, Mills has been pushing the idea of authentic TV further, into what he calls 'constructed situations' – where ordinary people are put into strange scenarios which force them to work together with people in new ways. *Trading Places* swapped people doing similar jobs in very different environments to see how they coped. *Turning the Tables* swapped public officials – headmasters or doctors – from top-performing schools with their opposite numbers from the bottom of the league tables.

And from there, it was just a small step to the BBC's £2.4 million *Castaway 2000* – with Mills as executive producer – where thirty-six ordinary people were left on a small Hebridean island, to fend for themselves. But by this time documentary soaps – 'docu-soaps' was a term coined to make the point to one recalcitrant BBC controller that these programmes had the virtues of both – had become too frequent and their popularity was waning. The stage was set for the arrival of 'reality TV'.

Reality TV claims to meet the needs of people for authentic television – and watching real people interact in real situations is more authentic than the scripted nature of so much else on television. But it is authenticity that is still mediated via the virtual world. It's virtual real.

It began with an MTV series, *The Real World*, in 1992, which showed seven young people who lived together for twenty weeks. It came at a time when 'transformation' had become the buzzword for commissioning editors. The success of a programme like *Changing Rooms*, which transforms people's homes with a small budget and lots of camp imagination before their very eyes, convinced executives that this kind of authenticity was what the viewers wanted. The result was a positive deluge of reality programmes: *Ready Steady Cook*, *Charlie's Garden Army*, *The Trench*, *The 1900s House* and many more.

By the millennium, *The Real World* had been reborn as *Big*

Brother – this specific model adapted from the Dutch original – where viewers spy on the daily goings-on of a group of people penned inside a poky house, and vote out one participant a week. In each series, the participants became briefly the most famous people in the country. The sub-text of *Big Brother*, and *I'm a Celebrity – Get Me Out of Here*, is always sex, even if it only happens after the cameras have gone.

Other countries had already gone much further. The Portuguese *Big Brother* included mixed showers. The French version, *Loft Story*, included a double bed in both bedrooms and a jacuzzi built for two – and two of the contestants had sex in a swimming pool. There was even an official website run by the producers allowing viewers to vote on the likelihood of which participants were likely to sleep with each other that week. *Loft Story* was complicated when several hundred viewers took the authenticity of the proceedings so seriously that they stormed the studios to liberate the participants trapped in the loft.

The American *Temptation Island* took the idea to its most ludicrous extremes by separating unmarried couples, taking them to an island where they are surrounded by attractive members of the opposite sex who try to seduce them. Then there was the BBC's bizarre First World War version of *Big Brother – The Trench* – where twenty-five young men are put into an environment vaguely like the Western Front, complete with the smell of rotting corpses, poor rations, mud instead of sleep, and every so often one would be whisked away. Maybe there were some genuinely experimental aspects but then the twenty-five were not blown to pieces, and even BBC executives stopped short of actual bombardments and mustard gas.

In other words, this kind of reality TV is about as authentic as a package tour. The people are real, the clashes between them are real, but the whole situation is contrived – and the strings are also being pulled regularly by the producers. The American 'reality' programme *Manhunt* set on a Hawaiian island – credited with turning round the fortunes of CBS – proved the point when it became clear that some scenes had been filmed in a Los Angeles park with body doubles and then cut into the original footage. 'I absolutely couldn't care less,' said the British-born former paratrooper Mark Burnett, who directed the show. 'I'm making great television.'

The defence of the television executives, similar to that of the marketeers about advertising, is that nothing is real anyway and that all judgements are subjective. 'I resent the idea that this programme is high quality and this one is not,' said Peter Bazalgette, the man responsible for *Big Brother*.

So are viewers who want more authentic television being conned by reality TV? The audience certainly responds to *Big Brother* because they sense that it is more authentic, even though the manipulation of the poor unfortunates is blatant and ever increasing. The ratings for *I'm a Celebrity* increase as the series continues and the inhabitants become less conscious of the surrounding cameras and their real feelings start coming out.

Jeremy Mills sees a clear difference between the 'reality TV' that emerged from the entertainment and game-show departments – like *Big Brother* and *Survivor* – and those that emerged from documentary departments like *The Trench*. *Castaway* aimed to be a genuine 'experiment'. '*Big Brother* owes more to *Blind Date* and *Opportunity Knocks*,' he said. 'In *Castaway*, we found how reliant the participants had become on other people, and the producers were largely hated by them for it. But if we fell out and if we provided support, we tried to include the truth about it in the programmes.'

And they did fall out. The *Castaway* thirty-six focused all their discontent on the producers, enraged at their failure to note that their plough horse was pregnant and wouldn't plough, furious for not securing them against meningitis when it hit a neighbouring island, sometimes venting their rage via previously cunningly hidden mobile phones to the newspapers. The one thing they weren't was castaways – but this TV experiment had to be authentic, and that meant being honest about the dishonesty.

The world of television production has never been known for its commitment to authenticity. Anyone who's been involved in television news – and I have – will know how often the subjects of news stories are asked to pop outside and repeat what they have just done for the cameras. *Big Brother* and similar so-called reality TV is more fake real than virtual real, more choreographed than authentic. Yet there is still a growing demand for authenticity on TV, which is being satisfied not only by the growing popularity of television history – from Simon Schama to David Starkey – but also at the docu-soap end of reality television.

'It's about the skills of the producer,' said one docu-soap producer. 'It's about looking at the person you are filming, spending time with them off camera, so when they behave in a way that isn't true to themselves, then you can change the way you're working. The point is that you're always trying to reveal the real person.'

So does that mean that what you're actually getting is the producers' view of reality? Well, yes, it does – but the key division here is between those who think that reality is no more than a muddle of different perceptions – and those who don't. You may not be able to reach that reality – but at least some TV is attempting to find it. That's nothing new in television, but its continuing success in the current climate of exhausted formulaic searches for audience share is proof of the appeal of authenticity.

Behind people's demand for authenticity may be a fear that the reductionists are right – that there's no 'real' anyway, so none of this matters, that we are deluded victims of the spin of those who want our money or commitment. In that sense, *Big Brother* tells the story of all our lives. We are all living with the constant but indefinable sense that we are being controlled and directed. We are living out the virtual real.

Even the places we live in are increasingly constructed according to the way the producers of our lives say the world is. The prevailing culture in the 1970s said that reality was so awful we would all have to be lobotomized just to face it. The prevailing culture in the 1990s saw the world as a vast shopping mall, and so it seemed hardly surprising that – wherever we lived – we saw the vast shopping mall appearing in concrete reality. And through this shopping experience, the real Big Brother is watching us through security cameras, and storing data about our purchases and choices electronically. Privacy is dead.

When the prevailing culture was convinced that there was no such thing as reality, we got an environment that matched that idea. In the USA, it was 'Edge City', a phrase coined by the *Washington Post* journalist Joel Garreau. These were the burgeoning suburban cities – 'technoburbs' or 'pepperoni-pizza cities' – shooting up around motorway interchanges, out-of-control shopping malls, each covering at least five million square feet of office space, but without any civic government. The example Garreau used in his 1991 book was Tyson's Corner, just outside Washington, DC, which in a decade or so had grown from a small village into the biggest retail area on the American east coast south of New York, with over 100,000 jobs – yet featured on no map and had no elected government.

Non-places, gates against the poor and the dispossessed, outside the normal democratic structures and served by identikit highways – if that's the culture we have, that's the places we get. Strangely enough, Jerry Mander's original title for *Four Arguments for the Elimination of Television* had been *The Freewayification of the Mind*.

We have our own Edge Cities in the UK. The once delightful Hertfordshire town of Bishop's Stortford is now joined to its surrounding towns by mile upon mile of identikit modern homes, in thousands of indistinguishable cul-de-sacs, the roads between them designed by highway engineers so you can accelerate to 30 mph and yet have enough warning if children are playing outside.

Just as in the USA, these virtual places echo those featured on television. So if you've ever wondered why so many modern housing developments look like *Trumpton* or *Camberwick Green*, this could be the answer. Bishop's Stortford, Basingstoke, Swindon and Ashford – and all those other towns designated for expansion over the past decade – are virtual real. And our reaction has been, once again, a growing demand for authentic places and authenticity in culture.

The main demand is for café culture and people places, thanks partly to architects like Richard Rogers. Unfortunately, this process is a much slower one. Instead we dream that future British towns will be more like Barcelona, with colourful markets, bustling squares and an al fresco life lived out of coffee shops and tapas bars. That isn't real either – or rather, it may be real for Barcelona, but it isn't necessarily going to create authentic places that are somehow *of* the country we live in. For one thing the British haven't traditionally regarded flat-living as authentic and have emphasized the importance of their gardens, and who's to say they're wrong?

* * *

When new volumes of short stories are published, they don't normally get much attention. So what was it about the publication of *All Hail the New Puritans* that led to major features in all the broadsheet newspapers and colour supplements – making it probably the best-publicized book of its kind in publishing history?

The young editors of the book, crime writer Nicholas Blincoe and rave-scene novelist Matt Thorne, had hit on the idea of a 'literary manifesto'. It was published alongside the collection of stories it inspired, and although most of the stories won't be remembered for long, the manifesto might. 'It was exciting,' said Matt Thorne. 'Every major cultural critic had a comment on it. It was nice to see people speaking honestly about writing. By putting a manifesto together in this way, we forced people to define what writing should be.'

Their main tenet was that writers should concentrate on writing the truth. 'We went to talk to the other people, and they immediately agreed with what we said,' said Thorne. 'It was about simplicity and directness, no flashbacks, no foreshadowing. That was the idea. If music production is unvarnished then it seems more authentic. You can't do that with writing – but you can concentrate on the narrative.'

The oldest of the New Puritans was Alex Garland, author of *The Beach*, and the youngest contributor was just twenty. Their self-confessed intention in the introduction was to 'blow the dinosaurs out of the water'. New Puritanism was, of course, also all about getting one over the literary élite – Salman Rushdie, Ian McEwan or Martin Amis. But it was also clear that the editors were serious about their manifesto, about stripping writing down to its truthful basics, promising to 'shun poetry and poetic licence in all its forms'. The other nine points of the manifesto urged writers to accept a 'recognizable ethical reality' and to 'avoid the cult of personality'.

There was no sign of Rushdie quaking in his boots, but the media loved it. It was very successful in the USA and France, and, rather unexpectedly, in Croatia, where the local literary establishment saw it as a call for more personal and thus less state-sponsored writing. The commentators junked some of the manifesto – especially the renunciation of flashbacks. But they took the purity and simplicity and their commitment to story-telling seriously. 'For all the ink that's been spilled about post-modern fiction and its indifference to distinctions between "high" and "low", plot is still tainted by an association with the baser genres, with action movies and soap operas,' wrote one American critic. 'It's nice to see somebody speak up for it.'

The title *All Hail the New Puritans* came from a song by the punk band The Fall, but the idea of the manifesto emerged from an earlier one calling for similar ideas, this time in film. Dogme 95 was organized by the Danish directors Lars von Trier and Thomas Vinterberg with a similar 'ethical reality' behind it – no artificial lighting, no camera tripods, no trickery.

In some ways the Dogme film-makers went even further. 'The *auteur* concept is bourgeois romanticism from the start and thereby false,' they wrote, dumping the central idea of post-modernism, that we can understand a film by the language, the grammar of editing, the context, layers of historical background and the social background of the director. 'To Dogme 95, cinema is not individual.'

'The supreme task of the decadent film-makers is to fool the audience. Is that what we're so proud of? Is that what the 100 years [of cinema] have brought us? . . . By using technology, anyone at any time can wash the last grains of truth away in the deadly embrace of sensation.' The alternative was what Dogme called the 'Vow of Chastity', which included hand-held cameras, no props and sets, no extra lights, optical work or filters, no flashbacks or foreshadowing – the film had to take place here and now: 'My supreme goal is to force the truth out of my characters and settings,' boasts their vow. 'I swear to do so by all the means available and at the cost of any good taste and any aesthetic considerations.'

The promise not to sign your name on the end of a film as director has possibly deterred some ambitious young directors from taking up the cause – but some Dogme films have been made and there's no doubt that Dogme 95 has made an impact. How and whether it will be remembered is another matter. Both manifestos are fascinating because they clearly display the first twitching of the global phenomenon this book is about – the determined rejection of spin or manipulation and the demand for something real.

Dogme 95 shares the New Puritans' emphasis on unspun authenticity – the determination that there is a 'truth' that can be revealed. Despite Hollywood's idea that somehow 'spectacle' comes before anything, and almost anything comes before the story, both share a commitment to clear, unvarnished narrative. Both reject all those layers of reference, all that subliminal selling of products and ideas, all those literary flashes of sound and fury or cinematic special effects to confuse us. What's important is simple story-telling.

Both manifestos look towards a more authentic future. But there's no doubt that the main symptoms of the search for authentic culture is evidenced in nostalgia – whether in the emergence of over 100 different group across the UK re-enacting battles from every era from Boadicea to Waterloo, or the website jollygoodshow.org, which allows us to stage an authentic World War II dance. You can see it in people's longing for TV programmes and music from past decades, as if they were somehow more real then. The biggest-selling band in 2001 was the Eagles, whose previous major hit had been *Hotel California* in 1976.

'My generation will go down the pub on a Friday night and, instead of talking about politics, or philosophy – or the future – we'll remember the theme-tune to *The Singing Ringing Tree*, or discuss some public information film from the 70s,' said the poet Simon Armitage. In *Fever Pitch*, novelist Nick Hornby managed to give a nostalgic edge to football, transforming a game beset by hooliganism and violence into 'the beautiful game'. Coke sales leapt by a quarter after they recreated their traditional curvy bottle in 1994.

Then there's the growing demand for accuracy. One of the first signs of this was the bizarre announcement in 1990 by the American music industry that the year's Best New Artist award had been taken back for 'misrepresenting their contributions to their own music'. Milli Vanilli – two rather camp performers called Rob Pilatus and Fan Morvan – had just mimed to a track.

But this was hardly a new phenomenon. You could almost say that pop culture has been built on the ability to mime. So the idea of bringing a class action suit against them – so that anyone who had bought a copy of 'Girl, You Know It's True' could eventually send for their portion of fraud damages – was a little extreme. Unable to escape from the universal disapproval, Pilatus tried to kill himself the following year by jumping from the balcony of his hotel suite in Beverly Hills. What was new was the way the industry suddenly felt they had to prove themselves more authentic by sacrificing a successful band.

Something similar seems to be happening in cinema. Everyone knows that Hollywood has built itself on the broadest possible interpretation of historical truth, but suddenly – when the £120 million film *Pearl Harbor* emerged in 2001 – it was widely accused of getting the history wrong. Long lists of mistakes appeared around the world in the newspapers. There were the wrong number of stars on the US flag; the film showed blanks fired from an anti-aircraft cannon; naval officers shouted from the sinking battleship *Arizona* that they didn't know how to swim – when all officers in the US Navy had to demonstrate that they could.

A website called moviemistakes.com was set up as long ago as 1996, and has so far listed almost 9,000 errors. There are more serious mistakes one might mention – the film *U-571* was based on the idea that the American navy managed to capture a German Enigma machine, and so allowed code-breakers to crack the Nazi code, whereas it was actually the British navy. British soldiers rioted in protest when Errol Flynn was shown fighting in the jungles of Burma during the war, but previously, nobody has really expected Hollywood to be historically accurate, or even internally accurate. They do now.

Perhaps it isn't so surprising, in those circumstances, that the audience had some doubt over the most successful film of 1999 – *The Blair Witch Project* – about whether what they were seeing was real or not. The actors were, after all, using their real names, and much of the footage came from their genuine reactions of extreme fright. The eventual film was consequently terrifying and, in that sense at least, authentic. And a film reputedly made for $25,000 took $150 million at the box office.

The Blair Witch Project relates to authenticity rather as Damien Hirst's animals do. They're virtual real – using the language of authenticity, but relying on innovative marketing and modern internet whisper campaigns. The filming famously took just eight days, in the small village of Burkittsville in Maryland. The three hapless actors were left on their own in the woods, with directions but no script, with food, batteries and acting notes dropped at key locations every day – with dwindling supplies of food. The final reels included a number of impromptu outbursts and genuine screaming.

That was authentic. But the virtual real hidden hand was at work too. The film website, including notes from a diary, photos, witness interviews and a history of the Blair Witch over the past 200 years, was an amazing success. The site recorded over 50 million hits before the film had even been released in 1999. A documentary on the Sci-Fi channel deliberately confused viewers about what was true and what was fiction. The answerphone at the Burkittsville town hall was forced to carry a recorded message that said: 'If you're phoning about *The Blair Witch Project*, it is FICTION!' The Maryland police were overwhelmed with calls asking whether it was safe to camp in the area.

The simplest explanation for the film's amazing success was that it tapped into people's demand for something genuine. This same demand for unvarnished narrative has also given rise to the unexpected rebirth of storytelling. Like 'real food', the demise of storytelling has been predicted over and over again for the past generation or so in the face of radio, television and film video games industries. Why listen to bedtime stories, after all, when the best special effects that $100 million can buy will be available to you at the touch of a button? And yet here it is back again – in fact it was the widespread return of the bedtime story that has been credited with turning Harry Potter into a publishing phenomenon.

Why do people like storytelling? Maybe it's the authentic feel of live performance. Maybe it's the way that the division between performance and audience begins to blur – rather as Brian Eno described carnivals. Maybe it's the sheer buzz of the professional storytelling at the Crick Crack Club in London, or its Edinburgh equivalent, the Guid Crack Club. Maybe there's also something real about a simple narrative, which is why history and autobiographies are now suddenly publishing blockbusters.

There is something about stories that allows people to solve problems in ways they couldn't do with just the facts. That's the idea behind 'narrative-based medicine', the school of doctors who argue that there's more to diagnosis than just feeding facts into a computer. It's also the idea behind the corporate consultants who want to dump the ubiquitous Microsoft PowerPoint, which seems all too often to stop people from understanding the emotions behind situations or from thinking about them afresh. Storytelling is increasingly used, not just in service industries, but in business too. There are even communications consultancies pioneering the idea of storytelling as a tool in corporate change, and a former World Bank director and senior IBM executive teamed up to run the first Organizational Storytelling conference in New York City in 2001.

There is something authentic about stories that TV, cinema and all the rest seem to leave out, and it's the human touch. It's the presence of the storyteller: 'More powerful and more holy than all writing is the presence of a man who is simply and immediately present,' the theologian Martin Buber wrote in 1914.

We don't need to know the storyteller's name – as the Dogme 95 authors said. We don't need to be cajoled by special effects or new technology. We don't need to be staggered by flashes of bizarre imagination or their literary equivalent. But we do need authenticity in the shape of the human and emotional truth that the storyteller offers.

Aldwych underground station no longer exists. Its platforms are used occasionally by film companies wanting to create the authentic atmosphere of the Second World War. Almost its last role was as the venue on a freezing cold morning in January 1986 for the launch of what seemed a slightly crazy project called Poems on the Underground.

The idea was that, over a few experimental months, the Arts Council and two poetry publishers would support some posters with poems on to be read by commuters and exhausted shoppers, alongside adverts for car insurance or holidays in Tenerife. The commentators were pretty vitriolic. 'Far-fetched if not preposterous . . . the exposure of an obscure and esoteric passion,' wrote one. But the public loved it. Surprised London Transport officials started receiving wild letters of enthusiasm saying 'Thank you, whoever you are' – not something they were used to, to say the least.

Poems on the Underground have grown a little every year, and now spread to cities like Stuttgart, Melbourne and Dublin. 'Such poetry should not be an occasional delight, displayed as now for just two months,' wrote Simon Jenkins, a former editor of *The Times*. 'It should be compulsory in each of London Underground's 4,000 carriages, like a smoke alarm or a mind-the-step announcement. The absence of a poem should be a signal passed at danger.'

Poems on the Underground are probably a symptom rather than the cause of a much bigger change in the position of poetry over the past decade. What started the 1990s as an obscure craft, passed between academics in ivory towers and hammered out in short-lived poetry magazines, has become something – if not exactly universally popular – at least talked about. Nationwide polls for people's favourite poem touched an enormous chord, as did the one the following year for the nation's favourite modern poem – people chose Jenny Josephs' 'When I am old I shall wear purple'. Armies of poets were sent out by the Poetry Society to be 'poet in residence' in schools, factories, prisons or Marks & Spencers. The so-called New Generation poets carved out a niche for themselves in the national consciousness, and when one of them – Simon Armitage – described writing poetry as like talking down the toilet, he made headlines.

The virtual world hit back by asking the Poetry Society director Christina Patterson to comment on a poem by a computer program called the Cybernetic Poet, which used mathematical models to string words together. 'Whatever else a computer might be able to achieve,' said Patterson, 'I think we can safely bet that the fundamental ingredient of poetry – that electrical spark that brings it alive – can only be produced by living, breathing human beings.'

Why should poetry have resurfaced when its demise has been predicted for so long? Perhaps it's because poetry is an antidote to a world where almost all public language is trying to sell you something, or manipulate you in some way. Marketing and spin compromises the vast majority of what we see, hear and read. The news is compromised by a combination of spin-doctors and media ownership. Even soap operas try to catch us with cliff-hanging events so that we watch the following night. But poetry is so carefully crafted to seek out such personal truths that it really isn't like that at all. The poets we run across are the real thing.

There may be layer upon layer of meaning and reference in a poem, but you know it's there for its own sake – and in search of truth – not because it is manipulating us to buy or vote or spend time. If marketing and television are closing down our understanding of language, then poetry is refocusing and rebuilding it. 'The essence of poetry with us in this age of stark and unlovely actualities is a stark directness, without a shadow of a lie, or a shadow of a deflection whatever,' said D. H. Lawrence in the 1920s, and it still is.

Accountants don't examine poetry for costs and benefits. Auditors don't measure its effectiveness. It's a haven of authenticity in our virtual, relative world. Focused on what feels real and true, it makes it possible to reclaim our imaginations. Most people don't necessarily give poetry a thought from day to day, but they are somehow also glad that poets are active somewhere, doing their bit.

And at times of crisis or high national emotion we turn to poets and novelists as if their search for truth has made them wiser than the rest of us. In the days following the terrorist attacks of 9/11, the *Guardian* commissioned articles from novelists such as Martin Amis and Ian McEwan. And two weeks later, they were on the stage of the Queen's Theatre in London, just talking: it was a sell-out success. A generation ago, we turned to the space scientists and microbiologists. Now we turn to storytellers and poets.

So am I suggesting that the new popularity of poetry and a literature manifesto that urges writers to 'shun poetry and poetic licence' are both somehow symptoms of the same thing? Am I also suggesting that a commitment to real life and real emotion on TV is a symptom of authenticity, yet so is sitting down and telling stories?

Well, yes I am. I'm not saying that there's a coherent 'reality movement', or that everyone defines it in the same way. There's a growing sense that people want things they feel are real – and that usually means direct human emotions. Poems, simple narratives, real lives and storytellers are all, in different ways, authentic in a way that virtual books, special effects, television advertising and advanced music mixing are not. Does the culture we imbibe add to our sense of the possibilities and depths of life, or does it get in the way? Does it make us feel more human, or does it leave us with the feeling of having stayed indoors in the same room a bit too long, rather as Rita's mother felt singing the jingle over and over again?

Once again, there's a progression going on here. Just as we have searched for a hint of something authentic in foreign tastes and elaborate cooking, but then progressed to local food production and farmers' markets, something similar seems to be happening with culture. The demand that started with docusoaps can't be satisfied any more with *Big Brother*, and people look for something more – even if the something more seems a contradiction. The search for authenticity is as addictive as smoking: after a while, a couple of puffs on low-tar authenticity just isn't enough.

And that makes the search for real stories rather less of a contradiction in terms. It also explains the success of efforts of people such as Hollywood story-consultant Robert McKee to persuade modern movie-makers to turn their backs on spectacle, using all the tricks of the film-makers' every technological gizmo that the cinema can invent, and to embrace something real. He doesn't mean hand-held cameras, like Dogme 95. He means a return to stories that are based on 'eternal, universal forms, not formulas'.

McKee and those like him are followers of the great mythologist Joseph Campbell, whose influence you can see strongly in George Lucas's plots for his *Star Wars* films. It also might explain why many recent films which appear to be little more than vehicles for special effects – *Godzilla* springs to mind – should have disappointed at the box office and taken such a pounding from the critics. *Godzilla* took $136 million in the USA, when over $200 million had been spent just on making it.

'When a society repeatedly experiences glossy, hollowed out, pseudo-stories, it degenerates,' writes McKee in his book *Story*. 'We need true satires and tragedies, dramas and comedies that shine a clean light into the dingy corners of human psyche and society.'

So much that comes out of Hollywood, or on television, ignores the deep sources of where stories come from – the structures of human reality. Thanks to structuralists and post-modern theorists, all too often, they're either about special effects or about language codes or context or stereotypes that have no relation to real human life. The result – according to McKee (and Aristotle) – is decadence.

It also goes some way to explaining why the backlash against this – the increasing expectations on storytelling, the demand for something real – is part of this same search for authenticity. Not everybody shares it, of course. Many people loved *Godzilla*. But a significant section of the population want something more – and a significantly large number, when they want something, will get it.

It's also an answer to those who say that our need for fantasy and fairy stories is an escape from reality, not a demand for authenticity. That's too puritanical for me: Robert McKee says that real stories are about making sense of reality, and I think he's right. That might make dour kitchen-sink dramas potentially fake, while the obvious success of *Harry Potter* and *Lord of the Rings* a glorious return to authenticity. That would make fairy stories, if not quite real, then at least true to the basic structures of human life.

The truth is that stories may be very ordinary or they may be full of fantastical creatures, but some of them have a resonance that haunts us because it seems to touch basic human realities. We need real stories to make sense of the complexities of our lives. But when all we get is TV soaps or when the school syllabus tests children about their comprehension of short passages, ignoring the book – as they increasingly do – then we lose these authentic stories. And when we lose real stories, something inside us begins to shrivel.

It was an issue that concerned J. R. R. Tolkien, author of *Lord of the Rings*, who spent his last years railing against the modern world. He never watched television and only rarely listened to the radio. But he also attacked the narrow view of reality that the modern world was foisting upon him – as if the increase in traffic around his home town of Oxford was somehow more real than the monsters that he was writing about. This is what he wrote in his 1964 essay 'Tree and Leaf':

> The notion that motor-cars are more 'alive' than, say, centaurs or dragons is curious; that they are more 'real' than, say, horses is pathetically absurd. How real, how startlingly alive is a factory chimney compared with an elm tree: poor obsolete thing, insubstantial drama of an escapist! For my part, I cannot convince myself that the roof of Bletchley Station is more 'real' than the clouds. And as an artefact I find it less inspiring than the legendary dome of heaven.

That brings us back to the way that real culture relates to real places. Tolkien felt that the places he loved were, in some ways, becoming less real as they became more similar. And if you wade down the long-dead high streets of London – Lambeth High Street, St Giles High Street, for example – and look at the street-level façades of blank brick and concrete, and the occasional ventilator, you can see what he meant. As Gertrude Stein put it when she left Paris and went home to California: 'There's no there there.'

'The bigger things get, the smaller and duller or flatter the globe gets,' wrote Tolkien to his son during the war. 'It is getting to be all one blasted little provincial suburb.' I'm rather keen on provincial suburbs myself, but to be 'real' they do need a sense of place. The idea that a sense of place is possible, even desirable, is another symptom of the rise of authenticity.

The critic Roz Kaveney, writing in the *New Statesman* in 1991, described Tolkien's work as 'a broadside attack on modernism and even realism'. I'm sure she's right, but his was an attack on realism in its narrowest sense – he wanted to defend the real world as it should be, in the face of its dwindling meaning, mystery and moral sense. The appearance of *The Lord of the Rings* on the world's cinema screen's in 2001 offers evidence that he was actually ahead of the trend.

It never happened . . .

'The whole urban complex may be constructed on artificial land as one of the several floating cities tethered to the coasts of Britain. In areas where weather control has been instituted, he will still be able to see the stars at night. But if he lives anywhere else – and most people will – the chances are that his area will be enclosed in a municipal dome half a mile high and approximately five miles across. Set into the upper part of the semi-opaque protective canopy will be sources of artificial infra-red and ultra-violet light for use during the day and simulated moonlight for night. During some phases of the year, a 24-hour day cycle will be adjusted to 18 hours or so to allow visiting foreign dignitaries to arrive at hours convenient to them.'

Raymond Baxter and James Burke, BBC *Tomorrow's World 1*, 1970: predictions for the year 2120

7

FAKE REAL #3: Living Real

> **'Industrialism renders most forms of work utterly uninteresting and meaningless . . . nothing but a more or less unpleasant necessity, and the less there is of it the better . . . This work utilizes only the smallest part of human potential capabilities.'**
>
> E. F. Schumacher, *Small is Beautiful*

> **'Why are you unhappy?**
> **Because 99.9% of what you think,**
> **And everything you do**
> **Is for your self.**
> **And there isn't one.'**
>
> Wu Wei Wu, contemporary Taoist thinker

Of all the unreal ways of living your life, those who consider a country called Norrath as the place they live probably take the biscuit. Norrath is a virtual place, part of Sony's internet game *EverQuest*, a virtual Tolkien-esque world, and the brainchild of computer game creator Brad McQuaid – he's called Aradune in Norrath. EverQuest is so popular around the world that over 100,000 people are playing online at any one time.

It probably isn't surprising that 84 per cent of those are male – Norrath is not a good place for boy-meets-girl. What is strange is that up to 20 per cent of them claim that Norrath is their main 'place of residence'.

But, surely, that's just pretend, isn't it? I mean, you can't earn money to live there, can you? Well, actually, it isn't as simple as that. Players can create their own characters in Norrath. They can buy horses to get across Norrath more quickly, and can earn what they need to buy them by working there for the Norrath currency 'platinum pieces'. And then they can sell or exchange all these things in the 'real' world.

The economist Edward Castronova studied thousands of *EverQuest* transactions through the auction website eBay to work out Norrath's real-world economic value. He found that Norrath's GNP per capita is $2,266. If Norrath was a country, it would be the 77th most wealthy in the world, just behind Russia. In fact, *EverQuest* players earn an average of $3.42 for every hour spent playing the game.

Nobody is claiming that Norrath is somehow real. But it does make internal sense. It is both logical, and you can make your own decisions there. It is genuine in the sense of being internally consistent – just as some modern 'real world' leisure pursuits also have an authentic element.

But before we look at the strange authenticity games people play when it comes to living real, it's worth looking at the extremes they are reacting against – the whole virtual world of computer games. This is quite explicitly presented as an alternative to real life. As Sony's games website puts it: 'Pause life – Play games.'

I have to confess that I'm fascinated by computer games. I always cared far too much about winning when I was playing Monopoly, so I try to avoid actually playing myself but there is something thrilling about the attempt to create a new world.

They may have disturbing links to the military. They almost

certainly do inoculate a small minority dangerously against the usual human horror of violence. But the mixture of skills required to make a computer game – screenwriter, artist, programmer – has the potential to open a whole new vista of human creativity. There is something powerful about the way you can move a man running with a gun – for example – across a thrillingly realistic cartoon landscape, as I did at the recent exhibition of computer games at the Barbican in London. But my attempts to get the man to jump overboard just didn't work. The programmers hadn't envisaged suicidal behaviour, and whatever we may believe, this is their world not ours.

But for every *Grand Theft Auto III*, there are games that point the other way: some are beautiful, like the search game *Myst*; some quaint, like the Japanese ones that let you take a dog for a walk or drive a bus; some ethical, like *Black and White*, where your moral decisions affect the world you're building.

What makes them relevant to the rise of New Realism is the way the games are merging, not just with cinema, but with sports too. You can already play the top tennis games or manage football teams in games. Japanese game designers are now looking at how we can interact more directly with the 'real' games. Anything we imagine can be a game.

There are also some people, like those who think they live in Norrath, who live dual lives in both worlds. South Korea's game *Lineage* is played by 2.5 million people. That's one in eight households.

These are fake worlds, of course. But the best of them attempt to satisfy our needs for authentic stories. Researchers find that many involved in multi-player games like *EverQuest* spend longer in the chat-rooms discussing the games they have just played – the stories they created – than playing the games in the first place. Even so, the hands of the programmers are everywhere, because these are constructed worlds full of rules that make them different from the real one.

Even games like *The Sims* – where people build up whole soap operas of characters – are constructed universes. It may soon not be possible to tell the difference between computer-generated 3-D images and real news footage – though that may cause people to cling more closely to real news – but the games will still differ from reality in the narrowness of what can be done there.

So it's not that games are getting more like real life. The issue here is that life is getting more like computer games, constrained by complex rules and requiring advanced juggling skills to play at all. Managing a career, mortgage, family and bank balance requires gaming skills. We are plunged into a strange world with staggeringly complicated financial regulations, bizarre codes and bureaucratic procedures at work that we submit ourselves to, exhausting child-rearing structures. Modern life is a little like being locked inside a computer game where there clearly are rules, but many remain secret – to most of us at least. Life in the Disney town of Celebration, for example, is packed full of rules and unspoken constraints. Modern life is often the same.

We suffer from longer working hours, increasingly complicated lives, enormous pressures to succeed – these days from our arrival at junior school – all given an added twist by the cycle of debt. And the debt spiral is made all the sharper by the way we are repeatedly persuaded to invest in things we don't need – often using the lure of authenticity to persuade us. Like the success of the Fun 'n' Fresh deodorant for 7–12 year olds, giving children the chance to feel like authentic adults – when perspiration odours don't usually become a problem until after puberty.

Debt is actually a critical cog in the way modern economies work. Most money in circulation is created by debt, and exists because people are prepared to go into debt. Since the 1990s, the average British family has paid more on debt repayments than it has on food, but the real killer has been mortgages: a massive £400 billion is now outstanding in the UK, representing about 60 per cent of the money in circulation. In the USA it doubled between 1987 and 1997, with about half the population carrying gigantic debts of approximately half the value of their over-valued homes. Back in the 1930s, mortgages were normally for less than ten years and took about 8 per cent of average income. Now they crucify us – and all the more so in Japan with the advent of 'grandparent mortgages' that will eventually be paid off by the generation after next.

Now 3.3 million British people work more than fifty hours a week, nearly a quarter of those taking no paid holiday at all. So, it is hardly surprising that a quarter of British men and a third of British women are depressed or anxious at any one time. Or that 48 per cent of American executives say their lives are empty and meaningless.

We lead lives of indebted slavery, interspersed with brief holidays to distant, more authentic places and alcoholic or narcotic oblivion – real at neither extreme – unable to find much pleasure in the pursuit of either, unable to see what's in front of our faces. The constant cacophony of media and music surrounding us cuts us off from reality and – if only because of the enormous choice of channels – allows us to censor any uncomfortable emotion. Todd Gitlin, the radical culture professor and author of *Media Unlimited*, describes it thus:

> The most important thing about the communications we live among is not that they deceive (which they do); or that they broadcast a limiting ideology (which they do); or emphasize sex and violence (which they do); or convey diminished images of the good, the true, and the normal

> (which they do); or corrode the quality of art (which they also do); or reduce language (which they surely do) – but that with all their lies, skews, and shallow pleasures, they saturate our way of life with a promise of feeling, even if we may not know exactly how we feel about one or another batch of images except that they are there.

Perhaps it isn't surprising that there's such demand for some kind of balance, whether by slowing down, or simplifying, or re-emphasizing what's really important about life. At any rate, for living it as intended – whatever that might be. And in that fuzziness lies some of the difficulty: where do you go to find out? Religion? The New Age? A smallholding? Do you read a self-help book to give you some insight into what the rules of the *Life* computer game are supposed to be? Or do you just take a holiday to experience somewhere real?

The most enthusiastic propagandists of virtual living don't see it that way. For them, the idea that life is somehow 'supposed' to be anything is meaningless. The head of BT's laboratories Peter Cochrane says virtual reality will be able to deliver such realism that travel will become an anathema. 'Stroll with your love along a virtual Champs-Elysées,' urges Ray Kurzweil in *The Age of Spiritual Machines*. 'Mingle with the animals in a simulated Mozambique game reserve.'

For people who want to retain some authenticity in their lives, this promise hasn't been enough. But the world of marketing has responded to the demand with an authenticity 'game' that has confused the whole business. They have been trying to persuade us, with some success, that real life is only liveable when we're on holiday.

* * *

Head spinning with the success of the new American industrial revolution – Coke bottles and Fords rolling down the production lines, and with the memory of the British General Strike at the forefront of his mind – the eminent scientist Julian Huxley addressed the Young Men's Hebrew Association in New York in 1926. There's a limit to how much of the products of this automation humanity can consume, he told them: a two-day working week and a five-day weekend was inevitable.

Huxley probably wasn't the first to make this – one of the most famous wrong predictions of a century packed with wrong predictions – but he was followed by a regiment of futurists who agreed with him. 'When we reach the point when the world produces all the goods that it needs in two days, as it inevitably will,' wrote John Maynard Keynes in 1932, 'we must turn our attention to the great problem of what to do with our leisure.'

That same year, a book called *The Challenge of Leisure* by Arthur Pack predicted the same thing – one of its heroes was a man in Maine who had spent his leisure time building a three-mile model railway – urging us to take up painting, stamp collecting or public service. It was one of those almost 'official' predictions – like food from tubes and calming drugs in the water supply – which almost everyone seemed to subscribe to. Work was running dry and the world where people worked forty-eight hours a week, forty-eight weeks a year for forty-eight years of their life, and died obediently within eighteen months of retirement, was on its way out.

'People will start to go to work at about age twenty-five,' a spokesperson for General Motors promised in a 1966 BBC documentary. 'Six-month vacations would not be out of the question.' That holds an element of truth: so did the prediction in *Vogue* magazine, by the author of *2001: A Space Odyssey*. Arthur C. Clarke said that 'our descendants' in 2001 might be 'faced with a future of utter boredom, where the main problem in life is deciding which of the several hundred TV channels to select.' But the basic idea underlying it hasn't happened. Quite the reverse.

How could someone who correctly predicted satellites get it so wrong? That dream of unreal idleness, wandering from the labour-saving machines in the kitchen to the golf course and back, simply hasn't come to pass. For one thing, you only have to walk through any of our inner cities to see how much work now just isn't being done. Looking after parks, visiting older people, watching over railway station lavatories – nobody does it any more, and not because the work has been automated or computerized, but because society has decided it can't afford it. The work hasn't disappeared; it's just that because it isn't *paid* work, we forget it exists. Because these aren't marketable tasks, they just don't get noticed any more.

For another thing, those of us in employment in the Western world have actually been working harder than ever. Modern executives increasingly have to squeeze their sleeping time into less than six hours a night. As many as 37 per cent of British people work on Sundays. Even children as young as eight have an hour's homework every night and formal tests in each area of school work every week – and where they have such busy schedules filled with CV-building after-school activities that 'windows' for play are often a week or so apart. It all goes together to create what the Harvard economist Juliet Schor, author of *The Overworked American*, called 'a profound structural crisis in time'.

It's true that those who are rejected by the increasingly competitive economy, or those who have retired from it, face vistas of empty time stretching for years ahead of them – though that wasn't what Huxley, Keynes and Clarke really meant. The rest of us mix up work and leisure, taking mobile phones to sports games, listening to books to teach ourselves French in the commute to work, and sending emails to friends when we get there.

Schor has her critics who say that, actually, we just underestimate the time we have available now – but, even so, the sheer complexity of life makes us very much busier. New technology like mobile phones means that we can be on call twenty-four hours a day, and that those decisions that simply had to be left to the local offices or junior staff can now be taken by the big boss.

The peculiar thing is that both the myth of the leisure society and its opposite – the reality of our complex, overworked lives – has led to the all-pervasive belief that somehow we are only living authentically when we're not working. Maybe this is because of the failure of the leisure society to emerge, maybe despite it, or maybe leisure needs to be scarce to be marketed in the way it is. Either way, we are now encouraged to believe that the only real life is leisure. Tourism is reality.

It's a strange reversal. What started as the idea that we should escape from the drudgery of our 'real' lives has now been reversed. Reality is when we are resting or travelling. Or when we're drunk, or high, or canoeing, or halfway up a mountain in a blizzard. Or so we are encouraged to believe by the powerful industries that have grown up to serve our leisure needs.

In the 1970s it was widely believed that real life was so awful that it was better to have valium in the water supply – to permanently escape to some other mental place. Now we seem to believe the opposite: that we are at our most real when we are acting our some kind of fantasy from *Deliverance*, involving canyons, shooting rapids and Mountain Men.

The most potent part of this 'authenticity game' is the way adventure holidays, unpackaged vacations and other paid-for ordeals are offered as 'real living'. There are now so many backpackers in the world that there are even PhDs written on the phenomenon. In 1998, one Chicago family (including children under ten) held their family reunion on top of Mount Kilimanjaro. As American adventure clothing company North Face puts it: 'I am not alive in an office, I am not alive in a taxi cab, I am not alive on a sidewalk.'

They are not wrong, of course. People increasingly crave the 'authentic experience' of leaving their family comfort zones, getting lost, connecting with others they never usually speak to – all of which are ways of paradoxically finding yourself. In this sense, all travel is part pilgrimage, part mythic journey as written by Joseph Campbell. And 'real travel' – about doing it yourself on an unpackaged holiday – is clearly catering to people's need for an authentic experience.

But the leisure myth doesn't quite satisfy the New Realists. For one thing, it has been pushed to such an extreme that people find themselves swapping their hard work for equally hard play. The latest electronic gizmos are marketed as adult 'toys'. Night club attendance in the UK doubled during the 1990s. Thus we can be young again – and whole business empires have been founded on the proposition. Although the industry is still mercifully dominated by small businesses – selling anything from B&B to walking boots, from holiday cottages to guidebooks – the big leisure brands are beginning to emerge. Richard Branson's Virgin is involved in insurance, airlines, leisure drinks, railway travel, and – with the recent launch of Virgin Galactic Airways – space trips by 2010. It's a massive creation to service the myth of leisure.

For another thing, we seem to need increasing levels of adrenalin to kick-start our reality starter motor each time. Perhaps this is why the Dangerous Sports Club became so popular in the 1980s. Or why 'reality tours' with holidaymakers going off on tours of war zones, and meeting land-mine victims, became so successful in the USA. For them, authenticity has to be about climbing mountains without oxygen, or jumping off the Empire State Building without the automatic safety systems that open your parachutes.

The leisure myth leads us to giggle at the wealthy New Yorker Sandy Pittman, who took both TV and VCR on an Antarctic holiday in the 1990s because she couldn't bear to leave them behind. This is suggested as an example of how we can't let go of the technological props of our existence: we're supposed to laugh at the poor woman for her failure to embrace 'reality'. I'm not so sure. What if it was connection with the real world that Ms Pittman couldn't quite bear to let go, in an otherwise fantastical journey into empty whiteness?

There's nothing wrong with people having leisure time, of course – and nothing unreal about it. People do work too hard. But there's a lie at the heart of this idea, as 'pioneers' find out crawling up Mount Everest through all the abandoned detritus from previous pioneers all around them. If modern life is now so hopelessly compromised that authenticity or natural living is impossible, then that's just as true on holiday as it is at home.

The leisure myth gets in the way of the truth – which is that we are an increasingly divided society. We are divided between an exhausted mainstream, ground down by mortgage payments and the necessary work to achieve them, and the unwillingly idle old, unemployed and unemployable, with the dwindling self-esteem and purpose that involves. We are also increasingly divided internally, between our complex ordinary lives and the escapism of our leisure time.

Over the last few decades we've seen people test out a range of new directions towards the same ideal – anything from downshifting to new kinds of personnel management at work.

The only thing that is absolutely clear after this time is that, while authentic living may be a wonderful ideal – and probably well worth the attempt – it is still Never Never Land. However hard you try, you never quite reach it.

When Tom and Barbara Good, the characters in the popular BBC sitcom *The Good Life*, hit British TV screens in the 1970s, the word 'downshifting' wasn't in common use. But the idea of living more simply, or going back to the land, was very much in people's minds.

These were the days of the Energy Crisis, of the IRA and the Symbionese Liberation Army – kidnappers of Patty Hearst – and there was a widespread 1970s sense that society was about to collapse. A military cousin of mine stocked his loft with £200 worth of flour, sugar and grain, just in case. People bought books on how to kill your own pig and run your own smallholding. Most had no intention of actually doing so, but the books gave them the sense that there was an emergency exit from complexity if they wanted one.

Downshifting by the 1990s was about being less busy, taking more time, and trying to get off the treadmill to live a bit more authentically – which by then usually meant making relationships more central in our lives. The simple definition of downshifting – deliberately earning slightly less – would mean that anything up to a quarter of the British and US population are downshifters in one sense or another.

As many as 77 per cent of Americans say they want to take steps to 'simplify their lives'. Of course, this doesn't necessarily mean downshifting at all. The latest technological gizmos are often marketed as ways to simplify living – to avoid domestic chores or to keep in touch – and it takes decades sometimes to realize how technology actually makes things more complex. Even the mobile phone – with all its benefits – means we can almost never feel the relaxation of being completely out of reach.

It isn't as if downshifting is an entirely modern phenomenon. Henry David Thoreau was definitely downshifting when he went to live on Walden Pond – even though his friends came and dragged him off every so often for a slap-up meal. St Simon Stylites was probably downshifting when he went to live on a high pillar. He was certainly simplifying his life.

In fact, Thoreau, St Simon and the Goods are representative samples of the various different strands that have gone to make up the phenomenon of downshifting, tracked in Britain by Polly Ghazi and Judy Jones in *Getting a Life*. There's a religious strand represented by the Life Style Movement in the UK, of which more later. There's the self-sufficiency strand represented by the Goods, and there is the Waldenesque idea that somehow more simplicity can give us life more abundantly. Duane Elgin, the American author of the influential book *Voluntary Simplicity*, defined it as 'the deliberate choice to live with less in the belief that more of life will be returned to us in the process'.

Downshifting is, in other words, a search for authenticity – and a stark contrast to the idea that we are somehow only alive during rigorous leisure time stolen from 'dead' time at work. All these other movements, voluntary simplicity and downshifting, are about bringing these divisions of life back into harmony – work and leisure, work and family.

Go into any bookstore in a city of downshifters like Boulder, Colorado, and you will find the divisions of this particular authenticity game mapped out on the different shelves of the magazine rack – there's a shelf on ski-ing, dangerous sports and body-building. There's another shelf on the environment, nature and sustainability, and a third shelf on meditation, Buddhism and spirituality. These strands aren't necessarily at war – though if you listen carefully you can hear the spiritual types referring to the body-builders as 'body fascists'. These are different interpretations of what authentic living might be like.

Downshifting takes Thoreau's dictum that the 'mass of men lead lives of quiet desperation' as its premise. We have become so infused with the Whig view of history – a process of endless social and constitutional improvement – that we imagine this isn't true any more, however much it might have applied in Thoreau's day, when most big cities were hideous, damp, bug-infested corners of depravity. But there is a sense in which modern life, wealthy in terms of money, remains quietly desperate because it's cut off from human contact and nature.

This view was encouraged by Mother Theresa, who commented on a visit to Britain that she had seen poverty far worse than anything in the slums of Calcutta. She was referring mainly to loneliness but also to unmet spiritual needs – which might not have been recognized by the very people she was referring to.

Gerald Celente – who also correctly predicted the 1987 Crash – estimates that, by the mid-1990s, 15 per cent of Americans were already living a simpler life, three times the number five years before. 'Western societies right now are very miserable places,' he wrote. 'People are very empty and they are looking for much deeper passions in life than those provided through material accumulation or through vicarious association with status symbols and people who represent them.'

Of course it isn't all about materialism. Downshifting is also about escaping the cacophony of modern life. I know I feel distinctly gloomy after a day where every moment has been filled with the radio, TV news and background music. That may be another explanation as to why a quarter of clubbers in the UK suffer mental health problems, rather than the conventional connection with taking Ecstasy. One village downshifted *en masse* by choosing to be the first community in the USA to reject cable TV. The tiny village of Waterford in the Blue Ridge Mountains of Virginia said they were proud of their bad TV reception, because 'people here have time to talk to each other'.

'When there's no silence, there's no room for thought,' wrote the futurist John Naisbitt in *High-Tech/High-Touch*. 'We've become so accustomed to the noise, we no longer hear it. In a beeping, ringing, flashing world it is no wonder 77 million baby boomers are searching for meaning.'

Downshifting is also about spiritual change. Sales of religious books rose 150 per cent in the USA between 1991 and 1997, compared to only 35 per cent for all books. Going back to reading is another sign that the New Realists are flexing their muscles. 'Today we see millions desperately searching for their own shadows,' wrote Alvin Toffler, 'devouring movies, plays, novels, and self-help books, no matter how obscure, that promise to help them locate their missing identities.'

There are downshifters motivated primarily by health, such as public relations entrepreneur Lynne Franks, said to be the inspiration for the BBC sitcom *Absolutely Fabulous*, who changed her life in 1992 after two friends died from stress-induced illnesses. She sold her company for £6 million, went to live in California to start an organization called Sustainable Enterprise and Empowerment Dynamics – and lights a candle every day on her home 'altar of dreams'.

There are also downshifters motivated primarily by morality. The idea of 'voluntary simplicity' goes back to Gandhi, a phrase coined by one of his disciples in 1936, but popularized in the 1990s by Duane Elgin. The British equivalent was specifically

Christian, emerging as the Life Style Movement, named after a parable of sharing by the Dean of Bristol, Horace Dammers, in 1972, and uniting around the phrase – which has since become a cliché – that we should 'live more simply that others may simply live'.

And there are downshifters who just want to spend less, such as Amy Dacyczyn. She and her husband Jim had both been working for twenty years – she as a graphic designer, he in the navy – but had amassed savings of just $1,500, so they set about the task of not spending money with enormous enthusiasm. After seven years, they had saved $49,000 and bought a farmhouse in Maine. Amy then put her discoveries into a newsletter called *The Tightwad Gazette*, so that everybody else could benefit from her ideas, which include avoiding make-up when nobody is coming to visit, and eking out cheap sneakers over a three-year cycle to make them last longer.

Vicki Rubin and Joe Dominguez of the New Road Map Foundation made the US bestseller lists with their book *Your Money or Your Life*, which took tightwadding to a new, practical level. The book even appeared as a forlorn symbol of its opposite – the hopeless middle-class spending and debt spiral – in the detritus of the family car in *American Beauty*.

But there is also an idealism in the downshifting idea that can be adapted to rescue a range of other aspects of life – from agriculture to urban design and community development. The Philadelphia publisher Robert Rodale coined the term 'regeneration' to cover all these things, creating a campaign out of his fascination with small-scale agriculture. Inspired by the way the land regenerates itself once the farmers leave it alone, he believed that this must be a natural process, something we must be able to work with rather than against – but which also probably applies to everything else too.

His *Regeneration* newsletter spent the 1980s tracking ideas about regenerating lives, jobs, communities or environment. This meant anything from learning craft skills to the traditional songs of your region. It reached a high point with the decision of the mayor of North Bergen, New Jersey, to give away free broccoli, cauliflower and cabbage plants to his constituents, to help prevent cancer. Up to 40,000 plants were given away, and appeared on fire escapes, balconies and front doorsteps all over the town.

Rodale was carrying on an interest of his father, who had known Sir Albert Howard, the organic farming pioneer I wrote about earlier. But he didn't live long enough to see the regeneration idea really flower. Rodale was killed in a car crash outside Moscow in 1990 and his newsletter barely outlived him – though the publishing company he started has.

Living with less is confusing. Many of the advertisements we see every day seem to imply simplicity. If only we had a Toyota, nothing else would matter. Microsoft software means we have to throw away every bit of paper we have ever owned. It's a dilemma summed up by the futurist Faith Popcorn. 'We don't want more anything any more,' she wrote. 'What we want now is less. More and more less.'

It's an idea that is embarrassingly easy to ridicule. You only have to think of the advocates of simplicity howling at the moon or drumming in the woods. The only way to avoid this is to have a sense of humour about it. In 1988, Rodale's newsletter reprinted a Ziegler cartoon in the *New Yorker* with an enthusiastic-looking family in the garden 'enjoying the calm night breezes while claiming to be inside enjoying a re-run of *Falcon Crest*'.

But there's a much bigger problem than that. It just isn't possible to withdraw from the world to live a lonely but authentic life. Not all of us can save like Amy Dacyczyn. How about the difficulties of being a woman trying to succeed in a man's world, or an Asian in a white world? There may be structural problems to society that prevent us living 'authentically'. History is littered with examples of utopian communities crushed by the failure of society to understand what they meant. And even for those of us who happen to fit in with the world as it is, there may be other factors that keep us from authenticity. Maybe the dioxins in the air crept into our mother's milk. Maybe war has engulfed our lives. We are not actually in control – and maybe being in control isn't very authentic either, since it clearly isn't truly human.

The engine behind New Realism is partly people's anger that their life choices are being closed to them – by pollution or health problems or racism or sexism – and getting between them and their chances of some kind of imagined authenticity. You can't get there, and even *trying* to live authentically needs a great deal of effort. Nor is it something we can do completely on our own. And the main problem for most of us – however many gears we downshift – is that we need to earn at least some money. We have to work: it's part of the human condition. Authenticity without work may not be very authentic at all.

The poster boy of the New Realists has to be Truman Burbank, the hero of Peter Weir's film *The Truman Show*, in which the hapless Burbank finds he is actually just part of a hideous 'virtual real' TV soap, controlled by an all-powerful producer in the sky called simply Christoff. Burbank is, incidentally, also the name of the town where the Disney Corporation has its headquarters – and Truman's virtual world smacks more than a little of Celebration.

The film can be seen partly as a side-swipe at television, and the way it re-creates the world we exist in. But it also says something rather frightening about human existence and God. For probably the closest to Truman Burbank's experience most of us come is at work. The poet David Whyte – author of a book subtitled 'Poetry and the Preservation of the Soul in Corporate America' – says he felt this when the Berlin wall came down. The closest we get to living behind the Iron Curtain, he said, is when we go through the office doors every morning. Inside, we find ourselves subject to the whims and instructions – sometimes by video, sometimes just by target and statistic – of people who may reorganize our lives right out of the building, giving no reason. They are people who can remake reality, airbrush people out of the annual report – and often do. Most of us have our Christoffs – like Truman Burbank – on the floor upstairs.

'Rather than breathing life and vitality into work from the greater perspective which is our birthright, we allow our dreams and desires to be constructed and replaced by those of the organization, and then wonder why it has such a stranglehold over our lives,' said Whyte.

Whyte is among a growing band of business consultants trying to bring creativity into the workplace. Not just the kind of creativity that can come up with patentable ideas for the company, but something that builds the souls of the people who work there too. Since the success of the film *Shakespeare in Love*, that often seems to mean Shakespeare. By 2001, the Cranfield School of Management had one course called 'Stepping into leadership with *Henry V*' ('Once more unto the breach, dear friends'?). There's also Shakespeare Inc., an American repertory theatre that takes the ideas into business, and a book by Tina Packer – who runs it – and the dean of Harvard Business School John Whitney, called *Shakespeare's Lessons in Leadership and*

Management ('How can you avoid Macbeth's mistakes?'). At the same time, Laurence Olivier's son Richard has been teaching his own business courses at Shakespeare's Globe in London. Some corporations flew their employees in from all over the world for his course called 'Hamlet: Managing the Edge of Chaos'.

The best companies know that fulfilment is absolutely crucial to creativity, and that unless all their employees are creative – and thus finding some aspects of authenticity at work – modern businesses are never going to stay profitable. The idea that 'the creativity of artists and the practicality of business people may once again become allies' – as Whitney and Packer put it – seems sensible. The recognition by business that we need to lead authentic lives at work is in stark contrast to the 'mind control' tendency in business training – reducing processes to numbers, reducing creativity to formulae and best practice. Or worse still 'internal branding'. This was excitedly described by the magazine *Business 2.0* as a method for turning employees into 'walking, talking brand representatives'. To get there, the benighted participants are expected to stand up, confess their weaknesses and describe their biggest failure in the past twenty-four hours – and confess what it cost the company. Helping people be authentic can turn into brain-washing extremely fast.

What is exciting about taking creativity and poetry into corporations is that it is also about setting people free – and once you've set them free to be themselves at work, they may decide to leave. It's a risk for the company. But if they stay, being able to use those creative parts of the self that usually get banned from corporate life, they might turn that to the company's benefit, whilst leading more authentic, less divided lives.

Until recently, the only people who could afford to be 'real' at the office were either the boss or they were supremely confident – sometimes both. Two in this category felt safe enough to use the word 'love' a lot: Herb Kelleher, who managed to develop Southwest Airlines with the slogan 'the airline that love built', and the fearsome Jack Welch of GE, who told his successor Jeff Immelt after a bad year: 'I love you, and I know you can do better.'

You could dismiss this as corporate flannel, but the truth is that most managers wouldn't dare use words like that. Yet unless love and passion are involved somewhere in our working lives – whether because the company we work for has real ideas, or because we can be ourselves there – we're going to lead pretty unbalanced lives. That has been the fate of working people for generations, leading half lives – alive like vampires, only after the long commute home.

The rhetoric of 'real work' is increasingly common these days, as a new breed of corporate consultants emerges – like David Whyte – who are certainly inner-directed, some on the verge of New Age, talking about life as 'as mystery to be lived rather than a problem to be solved'. Former Apple executive John Sculley puts it like this: 'The new corporate contract is that we'll offer you an opportunity to express yourself and grow, if you promise to leash yourself to our dream, at least for a while.' This is true, but it won't work unless you share at least some of those corporate dreams: a fantastic bottom line isn't enough.

But if you *can* share them – and they can maybe enable some of your dreams in return, beyond the simple exchange of contracts and pay-cheques – then the search for authentic living could become a much bigger phenomenon than just downshifting. We don't have to work less to be authentic then. Even the heads of corporations can lead authentic lives, as long as they manage to be themselves at work. But we do have to break out of the computer-game worlds that trap us, including the consumer-orientated one of built-in, restless dissatisfaction.

That makes authenticity not something you do – like downshifting – but something you are, striking a balance between your working life and your other lives, between your inner and outer worlds. It's about knowing what you think and feel and being able to live that, rather than being buffeted by employers, marketeers or demanding friends and partners. In this sense, what Freud, Marx and many of the others meant by authenticity begins to come together. It means being true to yourself. Sometimes that means resigning your job and living on much less money, but it might not always and it might not for everyone. And it certainly requires more than that.

It hardly needs saying that this is difficult and full of delusions and pitfalls. Employers like that are rare. We are so constrained by all the intractable aspects of modern life that life and work seem to have been designed to exclude many of us. Not even the New Realists can hope to get very close to genuinely authentic living. It isn't easy, yet the process is clearly more important than the probably impossible end-point. Even in *The Truman Show*, we have no idea where Truman Burbank gets to in the end, and whether he achieves some reality. But we see him have the courage and imagination to break out of his fake world, and start the process.

Truman's journey is also a metaphorical one, because – difficult as it is – authentic living is also terribly ordinary. It's about simplifying our lives enough to look around us and, as T. S. Eliot put it, 'know the place for the first time'. In short, we have an authentic self already somewhere. Hovering like a platonic ideal, it may be impossible to find, but the search and the journey itself – the setbacks and the failures too – are what authentic living is all about. Or as Henry Moore put it: 'The secret of life is to have a task, something you devote your entire life to, something you bring everything to every minute of the day for the rest of your life. And the most important thing is, it must be something you cannot possibly do.'

It never happened . . .

'1991: Hybrid soft fruit perfected that ripens in the open during the European winter months.
1998: World's first international city completed in the South Pole ice cap (population of half a million).
1999: Creation of intelligent artificial life achieved.
2000: Semi-voluntary enthanasia at the age of 60 encouraged by the Department of Health.'

Predictions in Raymond Baxter and James Burke, BBC *Tomorrow's World 1*, 1970

8

Real Relationships

'Technology is not the basis of our society. Compassion is the basis of society.'

The Dalai Lama

'I want a real person. I want a real member of the opposite sex with me, not some goddam virtual . . . and I don't want to communicate with somebody on the other side of the world, I want my neighbors to come over and play bridge, and I want to touch 'em and look at 'em and knock 'em on the back.'

Ted Turner on online chat rooms, *Fortune*, 16 April 2001

The futuristic agenda of the Institute of Contemporary Arts in London has always been obsessed with the debate between real and unreal. Fifteen years ago, long before the conceptual art of Damien Hirst, I ran across a notice in an upper room there which read simply: 'The exhibit entitled "Carcass" has been removed because of complaints about the smell.' It sounded, at the time, like 'real' art.

So it wasn't surprising that the ICA should be a venue for a high-profile debate in November 2001 about a virtual future, complete with an experimental robot and 'intelligent' cat produced for the occasion by Sony, and a panel that included the originator of virtual reality – the dreadlocked musician Jaron Lanier, whom we first met in Chapter 3.

But then, Lanier is no predictable nethead. He finds the idea of technology being used to replace the real, living world very disturbing. The organizers produced the robot cat halfway through and encouraged the speakers to stroke it. Instead of running his hand along its back, Lanier picked it up by its head – and Sony executives horrifiedly watched its legs come off and the whole thing fall apart in his hands. There was a shocked silence, which Lanier filled by denouncing any confusion between real and unreal life.

'If we allow our self-congratulatory adoration of technology to distract us from our own contact with each other, then somehow the original agenda has been lost,' he told a journalist from the *Guardian* afterwards, as meeting organizers muttered about legal action.

The encounter between the virtual reality pioneer and a pile of circuits and software pretending to be a cat may not be remembered for long in the annals of artificial intelligence – but it was a symbolic moment in the argument between those who believe the internet revolution has ushered in an age where we will relate to each other in completely new ways, and those who don't.

The advocates of unreal business, fast food or fake culture may have done very well financially, but you rarely find impassioned advocates – who don't happen to be in their pay – who argue that the future is going to be all theirs. Maybe they are now rich enough not to need to, but the predictions of a primarily technological future by the millennium have clearly lost the argument.

But when we get onto real relationships, the argument is still in full torrent. Conversations, newspapers and films are full of predictions that the future will overtake old-fashioned face-to-face relationships with new online communities, virtual doctors, teachers and therapists, telephone bankers, even electronic lovers. We argue whether online relationships or face-to-face relationships between people are better, worse or just different.

There is a widely accepted idea that people are withdrawing from society into their own homes, and that inside their homes they are withdrawing into themselves in front of a screen – which in turn provides a gateway to a whole range of other connections. In 1988, I reviewed a creation sponsored by British Gas at the Ideal Home Exhibition in London, claiming to be a house from 2020. It was a home turned inside out, with no privacy at all inside – a house designed for divorce – but defended by elaborate security systems and high walls from the outside world. What's more, the main window in the front room could give you a computerized picture of the Rocky Mountains or New England in the fall, depending on your mood. The unhappy family who lived there would have had no privacy from each other, because all the rooms opened wide into a tree in the centre of the house, and they would interact with the frightening world outside through their computerized finance unit, their holographic encyclopaedia and the machine that automatically tested them for AIDS every morning. A future like that just wouldn't be sustainable.

This chapter is primarily concerned, not with intense loving relationships – though the demand for authenticity applies very strongly there too – but with the everyday relationships we have with other people. The arrival of e-commerce and the crisis in public services are both feeding into new ways of interacting with people – and not just with shopkeepers. Websites and phone lines like NHS Direct are increasingly being offered as an alternative to seeing a live flesh-and-blood doctor. There are said to be as many as 350 online therapists in the USA alone, with sites like cyberanalysis.com prepared to carry out therapeutic support without relying on facial expression, body language or intuition. Teaching is increasingly being carried out by computer, especially for adults.

At the same time, professionals are using programs to assist them in their jobs, rather than relying on the mixture of knowledge and common sense they used to use. Psychiatrists are increasingly using computerized checklists to diagnose patients: Matsushita have even developed a 'smart toilet' that measures our various body fluids and sends the data automatically to our doctor. And there – one day – perhaps we can relax in the knowledge that the powerful computers at the surgery will scan us automatically for abnormalities over the phone line.

We are also told that geographical communities are being replaced by a new age of virtual communities, that physical friendships are making way for friendships mediated – without regard to the usual boundaries of space or time – by the internet. We are told that not only will we buy the bulk of our purchases online, but our dealings with professionals will be carried out in the same way.

There is nothing wrong with this process. It gives people choices. There are 120,000 people in the UK waiting for mental health treatment, and at least a third of them don't want to go through their GP. But if their *only* choice is virtual, they are all going to be considerably worse off. And it's only too inevitable that these impoverished relationships with doctors, teachers or bank managers are likely to be *all* the poor are offered in the future (virtual dentists are more difficult, of course). Real meetings with officials and professionals will be reserved for the wealthy; the rest will find themselves slipping into a virtual world where the only problems that exist have to be on a computerized checklist.

This process is already happening in customer relations. Face-to-face meetings are reserved for wealthy clients. The rest of us have to make do with getting answers through the internet or being put on hold at a customer service centre. There's no reason to believe this process won't extent to public services as well.

But there is resistance to this kind of future. Some of it surfaces in hopelessness: 'The real world is perhaps in terminal decline,' wrote Julian Stallabrass in the *New Left Review*. But there is something feistier in the air too – the human reaction against the inevitability of virtual relationships, demanding the choice at least of authenticity. Now it is threatened, people are realizing they want to cling onto the last vestiges of human contact. Like the 'conversation cafés' springing up around Seattle. Or like *Guardian* columnist Simon Hoggart who couldn't bear to upgrade his filofax because of all the detail, memories and crossed out meaning that can't be transferred: 'If I junked my filofax for a palmtop, it would be like heaving my life into a skip.'

Or even like the extraordinary rediscovery of geographical communities, just when we thought the whole idea had been banished by modern life. 'The more our lives are steeped in technology, the more people want to be with other people (at movies, museums, book clubs, kids' soccer games),' wrote the futurist John Naisbitt. 'The more high-tech medicine becomes, the greater the interest in alternative healing practices; the more we toil on computers using our brains not our bodies, the more high-touch and sensual our leisure activities become (gardening, cooking, carpentry, bird watching).'

New Realism doesn't mean turning our backs on modern life. If we want to escape from suffocating families or prying communities, we can do so. If we want new challenges we can find new jobs online. We can leave the country. We don't determine the whole of our lives by decisions taken after a careers interview at school. You can't over-emphasize the importance of the personal freedom we have won over the past century or so. But – like Americans who go home once a year for Thanksgiving, shedding a sentimental tear for the old home town – we don't want to lose the possibility of belonging either. We want to keep the authentic option open.

And for all their benefits, virtual communities can be intolerant. If a member of it violates the rules, or even gets slightly boring, you don't have to listen or talk to them – you can just switch them off. Virtual communities are self-selecting affairs, with shared ideals and shared ideas but without any responsibility. Geographical communities, on the other hand, may be inconvenient collections of families, but their very inconvenience contains the possibility of socializing, educating and caring for people.

Geographical communities that ignore problems unravel very fast, as the Harvard School of Public Health found in a major 1997 study of crime rates in Chicago. They found the 'real' communities – where people were prepared to intervene when they saw children behaving badly, for instance – had lower crime, regardless of their socio-economic problems. That's inconvenient too, but it's about the only means of preventing disorder that we've got. The isolated alternative doesn't bear thinking about.

So, yes, communities may sometimes be restricting and claustrophobic, but they are also the only guarantor that society can function securely and peacefully enough to support virtual communities in the first place. 'If it takes a village to raise a child, as Gandhi said, what does it take to raise a village?' asked Edgar Cahn, the civil rights lawyer and most interesting of the communitarian writers. It's a key question, and virtual communities – for all their benefits – can't answer it.

The communitarians were enormously influential on the so-called 'Third Way' that Tony Blair used to characterize his political philosophy – though if you look in his pamphlet of the same title you find there's a considerable gap where communitarian solutions might perhaps have been expected. The original communitarian, Amitai Etzioni, hasn't got much in the way of solutions to offer either. Neither does Robert Putnam, though he believes society will regenerate itself. Cahn is the exception. The communitarians do, however, all share a sense that our modern disconnected lives, alienated from geography, seasons, nature, time and each other, is somehow unreal. Real life at least acknowledges responsibilities to people around you – and acknowledges that you need things from them too. A real life is one that is embedded and rooted.

The classic description of unreal life is Etzioni's description of a lorry driver called Rod Grimm, for whom – thanks to economic pressures and the new possibilities of mobile phones – has disappeared into a virtual half-life:

> Rod Grimm (his real name) is an American truck driver who delivers loads from coast to coast, specifically from Los Angeles to Maine. He is part of the "just in time" system. If his load of frozen shrimps is not delivered on schedule, restaurants will be forced to shut down. He is on the road 340 days a year, so his wife moved in with him and they now practically live in the cabin of the truck. Meals are taken at truck stops, or eaten while driving. Friendships are reduced largely to casual encounters with other truckers at gas pumps. Rod's only child has been left with a succession of babysitters since she was six years old; birthdays are marked by calls on Grimm's cellphone.

The Grimm life gives a whole new precision to the depressing description of the modern world by French philosopher Henri

Lefebvre: 'We are surrounded by emptiness, but it is an emptiness filled with signs.' Etzioni compares the story to that of Phineas Fogg in *Around the World in 80 Days*, where the engine runs out of coal on the last stretch, and Fogg uses the furnishing and the carriages as fuel instead. We are doing the same to society with our obsession with economic competitiveness. Yet there's nothing about Rod Grimm's life that should seriously upset those who predict our new virtual lives, plugged into computers attached to the lenses of our eyeballs, connected to mobile phones in our brains, powered by the energy we generate from our heads – and always on the move.

I don't agree with their contention that there's no qualitative difference between real and virtual relationships. In fact, I read about the eponymous Rod Grimm with a shiver of recognition. There are aspects of my life – immersed in my word processor, too busy for relationships – that I recognize in his. Etzioni uses him as a *memento mori* to make us realize what this kind of alienation does to the next generation: that they need at least some human contact – from parents and others – if they are not going to inflict similar insanities on their own children. It is the vision of Rod Grimm, and aspects of him all around us – not just the descent into virtual isolation – that has reawakened our determination that at least some of our relationships should be real.

The most recent vision of the future written by Microsoft's enigmatic founder, Bill Gates, *Business @ the Speed of Thought*, includes a strange nostalgic piece about dating a woman who lived somewhere else. It's ever so slightly reminiscent of Rod Grimm, though from the entirely different end of the great economic divide.

Gates describes how they spent time together on email, because they were too busy actually to meet. 'We figured out a way we could sort of go to the movies together,' he writes. 'We would find a film that was playing about the same time in both our cities. We would drive to our respective theatres, chatting on our cellular phones. We would watch the movies and on the way home we would use our cellular phones again to discuss the show.'

He goes on to promise that this kind of 'virtual dating' will be even better when combined with video-conferencing. Gates shows no signs that he understands that virtual dating is a pretty miserable business compared to the real thing. As Howard Rheingold of the WELL network says, 'You can't kiss anybody' in virtual communities – however wonderful the virtual kiss might be.

This blindness is shared by many of the cheerleaders of the virtual revolution, with the notable exception of Jaron Lanier who believes the new technologies must help people engage more closely, rather than escape from each other – and, to prove the point, he doesn't 'disengage' by using drugs, alcohol or chocolate. But few virtual writers accept that there's a qualitative difference, for example, between real and virtual teachers.

We hear that providing more computers in schools is imperative – which is why education systems are cutting back on arts and music to provide them, especially in the USA, after the Clinton administration's determination to make computers 'as much part of the classroom as blackboards'. We have even heard about virtual examiners. The New Jersey-based Educational Testing Service now uses 'e-raters' to mark G-MAT test essays for entry to graduate management courses. The best way forward for education, says the philosopher Theodore Roszak, is to 'find out what Bill Gates wants schools to do and don't do it'.

Of course there should be computers in schools. Children

need to be technologically proficient, and computers can help them study and find out information for themselves. But they can't ever be a substitute for the kind of real education in the meeting of minds between pupil and teacher. That may not happen often enough – and it's a difficult alchemy to create – but that isn't the point. Computer education by itself is push-button, relationship-less education, and infinitely poorer because it is less human.

Real knowledge, real education can be a passionate business at its best, but it's also inconvenient. Computer programs that lead you through science experiments to perfect answers tend to leave out those inconvenient facts or findings that don't fit, and might encourage pupils to think a little more. 'Because it offers a manageable little "reality" of its own, it may tempt its users attention away from the messy, frustrating angularities of imperfect daily life,' says Roszak about computers in education.

Most educationalists balk at the idea of teaching with computers alone – just as doctors argue in those endless articles on the subject 'Will computers make doctors redundant?' But, in a world of squeezing budgets for hospitals and schools, it is very tempting for the accountants to start the replacement process going, because it allows human teachers and doctors to spread their efforts further.

It's the same argument about sex. It's closeness with another fallible, imperfect human being that makes real sex exciting – but the enthusiasts for a virtual world don't seem to realize that. Virtual artist Myron Krueger – inventor of an artistic concept called 'artificial reality' – describes a computer program that can administer electronic sex as 'a sequence of ministrations ordinarily requiring two hands'. Well yes, but . . .

Even the author of the highly influential *Age of Spiritual Machines*, Ray Kurzweil seems to have a narrow view of what sex could be. His excitement at the idea of virtual sex where we can change the appearance of our partners without their knowledge – realizing, of course, that they may be doing the same to us – seems to cut out half the passion of a real, fallible lover. 'Even when proximate, virtual sex will be better in some ways and certainly safer,' he writes, 'virtual sex will provide sensations that are more intense and pleasurable than conventional sex, as well as physical experiences that currently do not exist.'

Our demand for authenticity is partly in response to very well-funded, very powerful people who want us to believe that online affairs – talking far into the night to someone with an assumed name we'll never meet – are no different to real ones. Maybe it's a sign of how impoverished the world has become that highly intelligent people don't seem to be able to tell the difference between virtual teaching or virtual sex and the real thing.

But it isn't just the virtual world that's threatening to drag us somewhere unreal. It's the demands of market forces – as we saw in the sad story of Rod Grimm – transforming billions like him into the modern equivalent of pit-ponies. And it's the descent into drug-induced virtuality. I don't mean alcohol or recreational drugs, which have always been with us. I mean the way we increasingly resort to drugs to treat problems which might, in previous generations, have been seen as perfectly normal aspects of growing up.

Like the discovery of Attention Deficit Disorder in 1980 and the increasing prescription of Ritalin for difficult children, especially in North America, where at least four million schoolchildren take it regularly. A recent *New York Times* article described the exhaustion of the school nurse, going from classroom to classroom, doling out Ritalin to outstretched hands –

often on the advice of teachers who would prefer them to be 'less argumentative'.

'How has it come to pass,' asks the Washington writer Mary Eberstadt, 'that in *fin de siècle* America, where every child from pre-school onwards can recite the anti-drug catechism by heart, millions of middle and upper-middle class children are being legally drugged with a substance so similar to cocaine that, as one journalist accurately summarized the science, it takes a chemist to know the difference?'

That isn't to say that some children don't have a serious medical problem. But there is something rather horrible – and certainly fake – in the way we increasingly drug our children to make them submissive, open vessels in the classroom waiting to be pumped full of knowledge. Or, outside the classroom, as they wait to be pumped full of CV-building activities that will make them stand out. The truth is that children and adults both need time to assimilate or dream or imagine. This is real, in a way that drug-induced states of open-mindedness simply aren't.

Then there's the emergence of Prozac as a 'designer' drug for anything from spots to bulimia and shyness. It is taken now by 40 million people around the world, including one in ten Americans. As Mariella Frostrup explained after she took it to lose weight – it may not have helped her slim, but it stopped her minding about it when she didn't.

Eli Lilly's invention was launched in Belgium in 1986 and has become one of those wonder drugs that might not cure you or your basic problems, but whose solution is far more spectacular. It's a bit like Lily the Pink's medicinal compound ('Ebenezer/thought he was Julius Caesar/so they put him in a home/where they gave him medicinal compound/Now he's emperor of Rome').

There are more than thirty books on the website depressionbookstore.com with 'Prozac' in the title. You can even buy Prozac ear-rings – there is none of the stigma of other anti-depressants. We know it can be a lifeline for people with depression, but we also know that it makes about 10 per cent of those who take it restless, and a small proportion of those it makes angry, fearful and suicidal.

Prozac has never been marketed for children – though there were rumours that orange and peppermint flavours were being planned. But it does seem to go rather well with the culture of Nirvana and grunge. 'Every so often,' wrote Elizabeth Wurtzel in *Prozac Nation*, 'I find myself with the urge to make sure people know that I'm not just on Prozac but on Lithium too, that I am a real sicko, a depressive of a much higher order than all those happy-pill poppers with their low-level sorrow. Or else I feel compelled to remind people that I've been on Prozac since the FDA first approved it, that I've been taking it longer than anyone else on earth, save for a few laboratory rats in cages, trapped but happy.'

Some of us clearly need Prozac or Ritalin to make 'real relationships' at all. On the other hand, their widespread use as 'lifestyle drugs' must also get in the way of this, by insulating us from real living. A friend of mine was prescribed Prozac before she moved house, as her doctor put it, 'just in case'. The demand for real relationships starts, I think, from asserting people's right to tell the difference between drugs that tackle conditions that prevent us relating in proportion to reality, and those that iron out all the wrinkles of life so that this is impossible.

Because if we don't make that distinction, we fall foul of the emerging link between unreal relationships and depression. Maybe it's the effects of living in a hyper-real world, surrounded by perfect models in magazines with airbrushed blemish-free skin, courtesy of the cosmetics industry. Maybe it's the heavy marketing of toys to children whose parents can't afford them, or trainers or clothes or cars – or anything else we are urged to desire so hopelessly day after day. Maybe it's a matter of suppressing the consequences of living like Rod Grimm, cut-off, indebted and exhausted, or of being forced into a state of constant Ritalin-induced over-stimulation. Who knows?

But it may also be, to some extent, a result of living in a world of virtual relationships. When we buy by computer, we don't have to deal with shopkeepers – even with check-out staff. When we wander down the street listening to a Walkman, we don't have to be aware of the street around us. When we learn by computer we don't have to face the relationships with our teacher or our fellow pupils. When we are kept indoors as we grow up – because of a morbid fear of psychopaths or motor cars – we may have a sense that our lives and experiences are being moulded for us.

People who watch TV chronically are known to have low involvement in their communities – perhaps that's just obvious – but also to be more loutish, less sociable. But even more to the point, spending time on the internet may lead directly to depression and loneliness, according to a 1998 research project by Carnegie Mellon University – sponsored, much to their horror I expect, by Apple, AT&T, Intel, Hewlett Packard and Netscape. 'Sad, Lonely World Discovered in Cyberspace', said the *New York Times* headline.

I'm sure that's accurate for some, but most of us are still able to adapt to the modern world, by taking something real as a balance. That might explain the contradictory findings of the Institute for Social and Economic Research in the UK, which found that people go out to cinemas and restaurants more when they use the internet.

None of this matters to the ideologues of virtuality because it can all be tackled with the sort of fine-tuned drugs that iron out all the other awkward edges of real living, in what Peter Kramer called 'cosmetic psycho-pharmacology' in his book *Listening to Prozac*. Kramer believes it heralds an age when humans can be 'better than well'.

Maybe the average Briton over thirty always had just one close friend – as they do now. But the virtual world isolates us further, and makes us long for something that we can't quite put our finger on. Of course we can turn in on ourselves, take the precise combination of drugs and find the right combination of online acquaintanceships. We can iron out abnormalities, peculiarities, uncomfortable truths. But somehow when we do that we find ourselves plunging into a background depression that threatens to engulf us whenever we dare to emerge from our cosmetic state of 'better than well'. Real life has awkward edges, as we know, and we learn from them. That's why people are increasingly clinging to it, together with all those face-to-face relationships we used to have, not because we should but because – in the end – they are life-enhancing. Let's face it: real people are fun.

One of the many ramifications of 11 September 2001 was for the intelligence services, which hadn't been able to predict or prevent the catastrophe. 'At one point in time, we thought that electronic intelligence was going to replace human intelligence,' said Richard DiSabatino, director of the US company Intelligence Support Group. 'I think we're seeing right now that you can never replace human intelligence. Electronic intelligence will only augment it.'

Even the first President George Bush – a former director of the CIA – agreed after the disaster that human intelligence had been sidelined through an over-reliance on high-tech listening and translating equipment. This seemed to have been confirmed a few days later with the news that one of the key Pentagon advisers on Iraq could speak none of the local languages.

Of course electronic intelligence gathering is crucial, a vital new dimension that no generation has had at its disposal before. But after 9/11, it was increasingly understood that electronic eavesdropping missed vital information unless it was supplemented by that crucial human factor.

It's the same story with intelligence as with everything else. But technocrats seem to wake up to it over and over again, without the lesson ever sinking in. It is now two decades since the French government report *The Intelligence Revolution* concluded that Japanese commercial success wasn't – as thought at the time – anything to do with robots in factories, but with good training, good ideas, and an industry prepared to act on imagination. It was the human factor. Remember that, Jack Welch.

I mention the legendary GE chief executive because the same is true of marketing – despite Welch's famous pronouncement that 'human relationships are declining in the selling game'. He was only partly right: simply because it is now possible to sell something as valuable as a £50,000 scanner over the internet, human relationships with customers and potential customers are one of the few remaining things that can differentiate your products from anybody else's. And when *Fortune* columnist Geoffrey Colvin asked the chiefs of the top dot.com survivors, Amazon, AOL/Time Warner and Yahoo, what the source of their competitive advantage was, none of them mentioned technology.

It's the same with the elusive concept of customer loyalty. The virtual tailoring that 'personalizes' Amazon's service is nothing like a real relationship. The source of their success, their new-found profitability and the affection that many of us have for them have been because of their overwhelming efficiency. That's enough to endear a company to you, but don't think for a moment that it's a relationship in anything more than a metaphorical sense.

Just as the corporate world tells us there's no difference between virtual shopping and real shopping, virtual bank managers and real ones – so they also tell themselves there's no difference between virtual and real customer loyalty. The industry has deluded itself that if customers use their services online, then that is loyalty. Or if they use a customer loyalty card, and interact through an internet-enabled customer call centre, then they are somehow 'loyal'.

Actually, there's all the difference in the world – as AOL found in 1996 when a busy signal led to swathes of their 'loyal' locked-in customers flooding immediately off to other internet providers. Research shows that as many as 70 per cent of British shoppers will pick up and use a loyalty card if they're offered one. As the chairman of one UK hardware company put it, after a survey found that most shoppers didn't actually know which branded DIY chain store they were in at the time: 'If you want loyalty, buy a dog.' For real loyalty you need to meet your customers face to face.

People use e-commerce because it's convenient: they don't necessarily want to join in the pretence that it means they never need to leave the house. And so it is that British high-street banks have been forced to end their branch closures after public outcry; and governments on both sides of the Atlantic face powerful calls for more police on the streets. We are fascinated by imaginary communities like *EastEnders* or the fifty-year-old radio soap *The Archers*, and this belies all the talk about the end of geographical proximity. Everyone from Prince Charles to Tony Blair has embraced the idea of 'real communities'.

Yet this seems to be accompanied by extraordinary official ignorance – or official blinkers at least – about how communities work. Governments are flailing as they search for any levers they can pull to recover them, and to do so without the intolerance against outsiders that is so often the by-product when a neighbourhood pulls itself together to unite against a common enemy. And as they struggle to hold back the atomizing of social capital, the virtual world has its effect. Online shopping means we don't have to interact with anyone, but it also sucks money out of real shopping centres and removes those choices. Next time we want real shops, they might not be there.

Politicians tend to fall back on virtual real solutions. There must be some simple method – a mixture of rules and money – that can remould local relationships, or so they imagine. This same search for an instruction manual to authenticity also seems to have fuelled a whole new industry of self-help books which purport to guide people into 'real' relationships, with titles like *Dare to Connect* or *Men Are from Mars, Women Are from Venus*.

One of the most interesting has been *The Rules* – the bestseller by Ellen Fein and Sherrie Schneider – subtitled 'Time-tested secrets for capturing the heart of Mr Right'. These include 'don't call him', only return his calls rarely, and don't accept a date for Saturday night after Wednesday. Follow these injuctions, says *The Rules*, and you'll soon be swanning up the aisle – after which, presumably, you can be nice.

I've always wondered about why a prescription for a real relationship after the wedding has to be so different from a prescription for a real relationship before it. If it's all about deferred gratification, it might turn out to be bizarrely unreal after all. Or is marriage by *The Rules* a kind of dignified but permanently separate living – something that isn't real either?

No, the 'time-tested' tag is a clue. This appeal to the past, as if we have lost what John Grant calls 'the instructions to life', as if we used to know the secret but have forgotten it, is a time-tested appeal to authenticity. It isn't real, of course – How could a formula for authentic relationships be real? – but it *is* virtual real.

We shouldn't be too hard on virtual real. Online relationships can open up whole new worlds for people, especially isolated ones. The internet can set people free from too much reliance on geography. Writing an internet essay in 1997 about the death of her online friend whom she'd never met, Rose Vines wrote: 'If you compare offline relationships to online, you can't say one type is real and the other not. It's simply not true. They each have their advantages and their disadvantages. It's just that online relationships are a whole new area of human interaction, one that we're still sorting out.'

Online communities can be an important part of people's lives, especially as an estimated 10 million people are online, taking part in virtual relationships, around the world at any one time. And I'm sure many would subscribe to Rose Vines's view that there's no qualitative difference between them. Virtual relationships can challenge you, after all. They can cheer you up. I'm not saying that humanity should forgo these pleasures – just that there is also a growing reaction against spending our entire lives in a virtual cocoon.

Sony's robot cat certainly wasn't the first. It followed in the path of their AIBO robot dog, retailing at about £1,000, which hit the stores in 1999. This could recognize its name, and two years on it can retrieve email messages and read them out. AIBO made no attempt to look like a 'real' dog. It gloried in its shiny resemblance to a robot, and was snapped up by Japanese shoppers – for whom real and virtual are sharper and more extreme distinctions than they are for most of us.

There are now many kinds of robotic pets in Japan, from a robot human with 'real emotions' to a robot jellyfish. So it was only a matter of time before American rivals hit back with a far cheaper version, and in 2001 Tiger Electronics launched the £130 i-Cybie robot dog, which respond to clapping and voice commands, learns tricks and barks. In February 2002 a Honda robot called Asimo (Advanced Steps in Innovative Mobility) rang the opening bell for the New York Stock Exchange.

These are highly sophisticated toys. The animals may be marketed as robot pets – they can 'learn' after all – but people aren't really going to have relationships with robots as they might with their pets. 'There's a major upside to i-Cybie's low price,' said *Fortune* magazine, giving the game away. 'You won't feel so bad when you tire of it and drop-kick it across the yard.'

The same was true of those Tamagochi toys that had to be nurtured by pressing buttons, or they would die. Japanese restaurants even opened crèches to look after the Tamagochis belonging to their executive customers during their meal; schools provided bereavement counselling to former owners. But then the schoolgirls – who were supposed to be learning nurturing skills from these machines – soon changed the rules of the game to compete over how quickly and ingeniously they could kill them.

But this version of consumer tough love doesn't put off the prophets of a virtual future who believe that many of our closest relationships will be with machines. 'Once your house can talk to you, you may never feel lonely again,' said *The Futurist* magazine. I'm not so sure. Nor am I convinced by *Machines That Think* author Pamela McCorduck about the geriatric-minder robot that looks after geriatrics by saying 'Tell me again' to their stories – 'and means it'.

Those aren't real relationships; they are the kind of relationship we might have with our cars or televisions. However 'intelligent' the computer is, you are actually having a relationship – and at least one remove – with the person who originally programmed it. For those who believe otherwise – that there is really no distinction between artificial and real intelligence – the idea of authenticity is meaningless.

Most authorities date the birth of AI back to the famous conference at Dartmouth College in 1956, where Marvin Minsky and other AI pioneers started the long battle against the indifference of the scientific establishment. Until 1985, IBM even had a rule forbidding employees to describe computers as 'smart' – to calm people's fears about taking home a desktop that wrested control of their house. Minsky now looks forward to 'artificial scientists, artists, composers, and personal companions'.

Another beginning was the so-called Turing Test, invented by the brilliant mathematician and code-breaker Alan Turing. Turing was the man who cracked the Nazi naval code as part of his wartime work at the top secret British code centre at Bletchley Park – where he used to padlock his coffee mug to the nearest radiator. The Turing Test dates back to 1950. The idea was that if a human being and a computer are both trying to convince you they're the same and you can't tell the difference, then they *are* the same.

Turing himself was rather a tragic figure, a homosexual who died at the age of only forty-one – apparently by suicide – after developing breasts due to hormone treatment intended to reverse his homosexuality. Jaron Lanier's view is that he was 'running away from sexuality and mortality by becoming a computer'. But whether that's true or not, the Test isn't very objective. For we might be mistaken. We might discover later that we were wrong about this 'intelligent machine'. The trouble with the Turing Test is that it assumes the very issue being debated – that there is no difference between real and imaginary.

It's Turing's doctrine, brilliantly brought to life in Ray Kurzweil's *The Age of Spiritual Machines*, that Lanier calls 'cybernetic totalism' – the idea that life will eventually be reduced to computer software and that people are no more than cybernetic patterns. Kurzweil argues that computers will massively overtake human intelligence within decades, but behind this prediction is the idea that real and virtual, real and imaginary have collapsed together in a new manufactured world.

The Turing Test has been extremely influential nonetheless. During the dot.com boom, the whole world seemed to be in its grip. The future was virtual: we no longer needed nations or governments or communities – and soon we wouldn't need bodies either. But it's also a belief system, as vulnerable as any other belief – despite the billions pumped into it by an increasingly powerful computer industry. British Telecom's SoulCatcher project even calculated that it could capture and save every sense experience in a human life of eighty years, and put it on the equivalent of 7,142,857,142,860,000 floppy disks. Jim Gray of Microsoft Research has predicted that, within twenty years, we will be able to store a complete video record of our lives digitally.

Lanier denies this is a possible future, because the more sophisticated our software becomes, the more glitches there are. But there's a more fundamental reason why Kurzweil and Minsky and BT and Microsoft have got it wrong – they are muddling two very different kinds of thinking.

Computers are extremely sophisticated databases. They have the capacity to store, sort and retrieve information far beyond anything humans can manage. But information is not the same as knowledge – still less wisdom, as T. S. Eliot pointed out. Computers don't have ideas. It isn't a matter of the *level* of intelligence computers might be able to have, it's about the *kind* of intelligence they have. Computers will always be better, quicker and more accurate data processors.

When IBM's Big Blue beat Gary Kasparov, it did so by swiftly researching all the possible chess moves it could make. But Kasparov and other humans don't do it like that. They use their intuition about the next move or the next and edge towards it. That's why poets often talk about hearing the poem first in the back of their minds – like Coleridge dreaming the words to *Kubla Khan* and rushing to write them down before being interrupted by a 'person from Porlock' — and completely losing the rest of the poem; Michelangelo carving the statue that he could already sense from the shape and textures of the stone; John Maynard Keynes' ideas appearing in his head like 'great woolly monsters' as he struggled to express them. Computers may be able to write poems and carve sculptures, but they do it by searching for possible random combinations, not through flashes of inspiration. They deduce, they don't intuit. They can't explain the meaning of their work.

So those who believe we can have a 'relationship' with computers, as teachers, companions or lovers are really talking about a relationship with a highly sophisticated data processor – and that involves taking a very narrow view indeed of what human warmth is all about.

If you've ever been phoned by a computerized pollster, for example, it's a disturbing experience. Of course, the whole business is also pretty crude, but the fact that the machine is responding to what we say isn't in the least bit reassuring – because we know it's a machine, and is searching its databanks in order to respond.

I heard of one computer used to do so-called push-polling in a US state primary race between two Democrats, phoning up voters at home and grilling them on their voting intentions. 'Why are you voting for him?' the computer was programmed to reply if you gave the wrong answer: 'He's a jerk.' Somehow it's even more disturbing to hear a computer doing that. It gives you a shudder of disgust at this pretence at intelligence. The closer the robot gets to being human, in other words, the less you want to have a relationship with it.

The truth is that only if you define humanity as a simple matter of data processing can you ever believe that human beings and machines are alike. It's a classic circular argument: humans are just machines so we can recreate them using machines.

Still, this is another prediction in its way, and 'never' is a tough call. If one day a computer could think and feel like a human being, and was indistinguishable from human company because it wanted to be with you, not because it responded to a program – and because it had common sense and intuition, then maybe that would construe an authentic relationship. But we're nowhere near that yet. It is possible, after all, that human consciousness is somehow the product of our sheer complexity, that our awareness of the world somehow achieves freedom by balancing the twin extremes of chaos and determinism. In those circumstances, a sufficiently complex computer might achieve something similar.

It seems to me that the opposite is far more likely – that we will take on computer functions ourselves, so that we become so interconnected with our machines that we become a little robotic.

This is hardly so strange: at least 10 per cent of us carry artificial implants of one kind or another. When the aeronaut and writer Antoine de Saint-Exupéry wrote more than half a century ago how he had become part of his plane, he little realized that he was predicting the future. Fighter pilots and military robots are increasingly alike, with the distinction between pilot and computer increasingly hard to define. Military hardware is now so complicated that, as we have discovered all too often, it's sometimes too complex to actually work.

The so-called 'post-human' debate in cultural studies takes this even further, believing that human beings and intelligent machines are being merged – so that all power divisions between male and female are no longer relevant. 'Post-human' sounds even more of a challenge to authenticity than straight AI – but in some ways it is also humanizing it, asserting the humanity of these human/machines against all those virtual enthusiasts who would like to define out those illogical, awkward human characteristics that make for real relationships.

A string of influential 'post-human' exhibitions travelled around Europe in the 1990s, and the most prominent post-human is probably the feminist and anti-Vietnam War protester, Donna Haraway – now Professor of the History of Consciousness at the University of California at Santa Cruz. It was Haraway who took the academic feminist world by storm with her 1985 essay 'Manifesto for Cyborgs'.

For Donna Haraway, we are already on the verge of being part-human, part-machine, and it's something to celebrate. We think like machines 'made of sunshine', she says. 'Cyborgs' have no history. They are truly children of the modern world, a world that has become a feminist utopia, in that they don't look for a future of coupledom, and they don't have fathers. They are neither male nor female.

In one sense, Haraway's cyborgs are true post-modern people, with none of the definitions of authenticity. They don't look for community. They are disconnected from the previous generation and the one following. But in another sense, they do *need* connection – with each other. And in the essay's most famous line, she lists all those things that big corporation artificial intelligence can never be: 'The cyborg is resolutely committed to partiality, irony, intimacy and perversity.'

There is a fatalism to this debate – as if those who believe there is no difference between real and virtual, being alive and being 'better than well', and no such thing as irony or intimacy or partiality, are somehow bound to win. We've lived through the dot.com world, where the entire resources of government and corporate wealth seemed at their feet. And yet we have retained enough of a sense of ourselves to feel nostalgic about the idea of real relationships, real sex, real passion, real bank managers, face-to-face public services, that we have created an underground backlash in their favour.

Artificial intelligence is just that: it's artificial. 'Intelligence' has become just a metaphor – and the prophets of AI are like religious fundamentalists in the way they mistake their metaphors for real descriptions of the world. AI won't be taking us over any time soon. But some of the best minds in the world are going to be trying to achieve that – and who knows, they might surprise us all. Either way, the effect is going to be the same: people are reacting against this kind of reductionism. The closer the AI people get, the more authenticity becomes the critical concept at the heart of culture.

The result is nostalgia for real communities, a small but growing determination that – despite the possibilities of cosmetic pharmacology, despite the conveniences of virtual communities or the demands of the market – the possibility of inconveniently human relationships with real people won't somehow slip unnoticed out of our lives.

It never happened . . .

'The geriatric robot is wonderful. It isn't hanging about in the hopes of inheriting your money – nor of course will it slip you a little something to speed the inevitable . . . It's there because it's yours. It doesn't just bathe you and feed you and wheel you out into the sun when you crave fresh air and a change of scene, though of course it does all those things. The very best thing about the geriatric robot is that it listens. "Tell me again," it says, "about how wonderful/dreadful your children are to you. Tell me again that fascinating tale of the coup of '63 . . ." And it means it.'

Pamela McCorduck, *The Fifth Generation*, 1983

9

FAKE REAL #4: Pinning it Down

'In the years ahead, we must get beyond numbers and the language of mathematics to understand, evaluate and account for such intangibles as learning, intellectual capital, community, beliefs and principles, or the stories we tell of our tribe's values and prosperity will be increasingly false.'

Dee Hock, founder of the Visa network

'Emerson warned against the tendency to believe something just because it is written down. How much greater the danger when it is also boiled down.'

Thomas Stewart attacking Microsoft PowerPoint, *Fortune*, 5 February 2001

The world of customer service has undergone a revolution over the past decade, with customer-relationship-management software that tracks contact with you – so that call centre staff can pick up with you where the last one left off. And with the turnover of staff the call centres have, that's pretty important. But the oddest aspect of it all is that, next time you're talking to your insurance company or electricity supplier, they might actually be in India.

In itself, this is just a symptom of globalization. What makes it an authenticity issue is the illusion of Britishness. Call centres in Bombay, Delhi and Bangalore often have a clock showing UK time, so that the people on the phones say 'good afternoon' rather than the 'good evening' they might say if they looked out of the window. At some call centres, the temperature in the UK is shown on their computer screens. Staff will also have undergone a twenty-hour course in British culture – including the niceties of *EastEnders*, *The Bill*, Yorkshire pudding and Robbie Williams, a two-hour seminar on the royal family and a special session on the weather.

The staff are often highly motivated graduates, quite up to gossiping about what's happening on *Emmerdale Farm*. In fact, the presence of so many unemployed graduates in India is making it one of the call centre capitals of the world. The various accents are tougher. 'We borrow tapes from the British Council, but even after listening to them, there are about 20 per cent of callers who don't make any sense at all,' the vice-president of one Delhi call centre told the *Guardian*.

Of course, nobody is pretending they are *actually* in the UK. The peculiarity is that companies feel call centres can improve their relationship with customers. There's no doubt that dedicated staff who can deal with the majority of simple problems do a better job than a hassled salesperson in a showroom, however real – and that's probably why call centre staff now make up as much as 2 per cent of the entire UK workforce. There's also no doubt that there are call centres, like those run by the phone bank First Direct, that really do make a difference. The problem is the rest of them, who pay lip service to serving customers but actually measure their success in terms of how quickly they can finish the conversation.

That's the 'lie' and that's the other problem. Aided and abetted by a whole army of management consultants and accountants, the managers of call centres are encouraged to believe that because they can measure these things – because they can put a number to this aspect of their work – their management is somehow real, serious and respectable at a boardroom table. Then they wonder why the customers of their clients, the poor benighted consumers, are so frustrated, and why their staff have such a high burn-out rate. With a few notable exceptions, UK call centres have a turnover of staff between 60 and 80 per cent every year and actually succeed in making the relations between companies and customers even worse than before. And the main reason is that – because of all that IT equipment – every moment of staff time can be measured.

Building customer loyalty is hard to quantify, so what gets measured is how quickly staff can get callers off the phone. That's the bottom line: many call centres now try to get it down to just seven seconds per call. Even the few seconds between calls – known in the industry as 'post-call-wrap time' – get measured and logged. And then companies wonder why their customers hate them.

Call centre managers aren't the only ones in the grip of this particular 'authenticity game'. Most of our leaders, top bureaucrats and leading businesspeople are under the illusion that only by measuring, by transforming ideas into hard scientific numbers, can we get anywhere near the truth. Numbers are real, in other words – or so the thinking goes; anything that can't be measured is romantic tosh. It's the great myth of what the economist John Maynard Keynes used to dismiss as 'plain men'.

It is a very modern idea: we can reduce what doctors or teachers do to numbers, compare them using league tables, make the results public, and all in the name of democratic accountability. We can transform all this so-called professionalism, all those pompous professional airs, these claims to special knowledge into hard, measurable packets that we can pin down into something we can study and maybe reproduce – not just in streams of statistics, but into checklists and tick-boxes, or into computerized expert systems so that computers can do the same.

It's hard-edged, unambiguous and real. It's authentic – or it is if you believe all this.

But people do believe it, because our lives have been overwhelmed by numbers and calculations – and somehow especially the men among us. It's usually men who can reel off sports scores right back through the decades, or school league tables, voting figures, inflation rates and other bizarre facts. As a man, I know that the average Briton spends forty-five hours on hold on the phone every year, that 3.7 million Americans claim to have been abducted by aliens. I know that my average fellow British nationals have sex 2,580 times in their life, with five different people. I also know these figures sound hard-nosed and authentic, but yet mean almost nothing. It gives the impression that somebody has scientifically pinned down a truth we had always wondered at: forty-five hours on hold, eh? Well, I never knew that.

We are all of us – men and women – increasingly controlled by numerical targets. As employees, there are performance figures on the walls in every office, under every clock and in every lunch room. As consumers, we're counted every time we buy anything. The Blair government has also introduced about 8,000 new targets or numerical indicators of success since 1997 – and recently added 150 new environmental targets to the pot. They measure everything from the state of sailors' teeth to the number of specimens collected at Kew.

Then we have the ludicrous example of the European Commission locked in mortal combat with Campbell's soup, because they define the difference between a soup and a sauce by counting the bits in it.

Accountancy firms cream off up to 10 per cent of British graduates to do all this counting. Whole armies of number-crunchers are out there, boosting the cost of running transport, the NHS or social services. As Professor Michael Power of the London School of Economics puts it, this is in fact a 'gigantic experiment in public management'.*

In some ways, we've been here before – especially in periods of great social hope such as the 1830s, when Jeremy Bentham's followers rushed across the country in stage-coaches, armed with great bundles of tabular data, measuring everything they thought was important. They measured the number of cesspits (which they saw as an indicator of ill-health), or pubs (an indicator of immorality), or – to find out how religious children were – they tested the number of hymns they could recite from memory.

We're not in that kind of world now, though in increasing danger of a related one. What makes it different is that, because we expect more from our measurements, we're applying the same idea – that we can control things if we count them – to more and more elusive, but vital, areas of life. Doctors and psychiatrists are encouraged to diagnose patients according to numerical checklists because it seems more 'open and scientific'. Companies are exploring the idea of microchip implants for their workforce to measure their timekeeping. The frightening thing is that, simply because computers *can* count and measure nearly everything, then we do.

There was a time when we could trust our own judgement, common sense and intuition, but now we're unable to do anything without it being measured first because of a delusion that somehow that kind of information isn't 'real'. I don't just mean

* If you want to read more about it, I explore this phenomenon in my book *The Tyranny of Numbers.*

politicians who can't move without checking the polling data. I mean those expensive academic surveys that confirm what we already knew. Such as the recent discovery that the death of a parent can scar a child for life, or that alcoholics have an unusually high depression rate. Surprise, surprise. But if statistics are the only reality, it gets hard to act without them.

Large corporate organizations – government and business – are responding to this demand for the authentic by trying to benchmark and measure their progress further. They believe it gives them control over events – by turning the organization into machines with dials that can be read. Politicians look serious when they use statistics – it doesn't matter that most are what George W. Bush called 'fuzzy math'. Managers look tough when they measure. They look real.

Where did we get this idea, that only what can be measured is real? It borrows from a philosophical position at its most extreme, known as Logical Positivism: that statements that can't be verified are meaningless – and somehow that idea has filtered into our everyday lives in a bowdlerized form. And it meshes there nicely with the opposite idea that somehow mathematics and logic are purer and more authentic – that, as the philosopher Bertrand Russell put it – 'the objects of thought [are] more real than those of sense perceptions'.

We are surrounded by economists, sociologists and anthropologists longing for their discipline to be a science, because their status would seem higher. There is the same general bias in every area of life: that real knowledge is found in quantitative data, mathematical formulations and laws. It was the great dream of the early nineteenth century – providing the motivation for Jeremy Bentham to dream up utilitarianism – that this higher 'science' could somehow replace human judgement altogether.

Over the past two centuries that idea has become pretty

flyblown. Where cost-benefit analysis has been used to make decisions, it's been revealed that what is required is just as much judgement, common sense and human fallibility as anything else. The great insight of our own post-modern generation was to see through the dream and reveal it for what it was.

But for some reason we have come full circle, and belief in numbers is back with a vengeance. The watchword of the powerful management consultancy McKinseys – 'Everything can be measured and what can be measured can be managed' – is now being brought into the heart of government. As I write, McKinseys partner Nick Lovegrove has been brought into the British government to advise Chancellor of the Exchequer Gordon Brown on productivity, and the Culture Secretary Tessa Jowell on IT policy. Another McKinseys recruit has been appointed to advise the Prime Minister's office on transport policy. No wonder government has been in a measuring flurry.

It's the same story in business. Thanks to the efforts, a century ago, of the great pioneering duo of time and motion study in factories, Frederick Winslow Taylor and his stopwatch – Taylor actually died winding his watch – a similar idea took charge in industry for much of the twentieth century. Every factory and office function was meticulously timed and measured. Simple numbers were used to judge the success of the enterprise: originally the bottom line, and more recently – in the Enron era – a range of other different measures including stock price and earnings per share. A generation ago, one large American corporation issued all its executives with underpants bearing the slogan '20% ROI' – to remind them that nothing was worth it unless they could get that kind of return on their investment.

But the insights of modern management writers had weaned companies away from single bottom lines and the soulless, obsessive measuring of staff. The first great management guru Peter

Drucker hailed Taylor as the first knowledge worker, but exposed his fatal flaw – he was only using one simple, measurable part of the worker, ignoring their imagination and initiative. Taylor wanted his workers 'stupid and phlegmatic': in the end, even just in business terms, it was such a waste.

But then business came full circle too. The key to business success may be increasingly abstract – intellectual capital, reputation, customer loyalty – but Wall Street and the City of London wanted it measured. It didn't matter that this wasn't possible. If your competitors were going to do it, and create an edge for themselves by doing so, then it had to be done. So we have the Global Reporting Initiative, Calculated Intangible Value, Customer Value Management and much else besides.

The trouble with this is that, although putting things into numbers, targets or indicators looks hard-nosed and real, what's really important in life or business can't be measured. Love, loyalty, happiness, devotion, reputation are just not susceptible to figures, and the more you try to make them so, the more they slip through your fingers. Measuring may have brought a whiff of authenticity to the business of management, but it's a delusion.

Numbers and targets are the stuff of empire – the idea that a central authority, big corporation or government can organize every detail of what goes on by setting targets and measuring people's achievements. That every job can be broken down into measurable parts – Frederick Taylor's fantasy of time and motion – and every decision taken in full view of the auditors and the public.

But this is a technocratic dream that breaks down in practice. Big hospitals or schools seem efficient when you look at the figures. In practice, monster hospitals are bureaucratic, inhumane, mistake-prone and harbour fearsome infections – features economists try to defuse by calling them externalities. Meanwhile factory schools churn out alienated children who can't read. For All this measuring doesn't help us pin down reality at all, because numbers can't grasp the complex – and genuinely authentic – human factor.

'It may work fine in practice,' goes a joke the French make at their own expense. 'The trouble is, it just doesn't work in theory.' Anyone who has sat through conferences in Paris will know all about the French love of theory, in contrast to the nuts and bolts obsession of Anglo-Saxons about whether things will actually work. So it's paradoxical that Paris has become the birthplace of an unusual revolt against the pre-eminence of theory over practice, or economic abstractions over reality and of statistics over real life.

Calling themselves 'Post-Autistic Economic' – 'autistic' intended to imply an obsessive preoccupation with numbers – the movement soon spread to other universities in Britain and America. The movement's leaders at the Sorbonne – Giles Raveaud, Olivier Vaury and Ioana Marinescu – may not have had much of an impact outside academia, beyond causing mild consternation among econometricians. But their efforts marked something important: a growing disenchantment with the cult of measurement, statistics, targets and indicators.

Their campaign began with a web petition in June 2000, which protested against the dogmatic teaching of neo-classical economics to the exclusion of other points of view, and the 'uncontrolled use' of mathematics as 'an end in itself'. Within two weeks, the petition had 150 signatures, many from France's most prestigious universities, and *Le Monde* had launched a public debate. The call was taken up by students across France, and by the autumn the education minister Jack Lang had announced that he took the criticisms seriously, appointing the respected economist Jean-Paul Fitoussi to head a commission of inquiry.

By the time he had made his report, recommending sweeping changes in the way economics is taught, there had also been a vitriolic exchange of articles by French and American economists, a counter-petition launched by MIT and a peculiar Post-Autistic petition in Britain from Cambridge PhD students – although most of the signatories were too scared for their future careers to put their real names to it.

Economics is a discipline that appears more hard-nosed and authentic when it blurs into econometrics, and when it uses mathematical formulae to predict the future or explain the past. The trouble is that the formulae don't describe real life very well. 'The central ideas of economic theory are very simple,' wrote the economist Paul Krugman. 'They boil down to little more than the proposition that people will usually take advantage of opportunities.' This is absolutely true, but it can't be transformed into some kind of mathematical law, and anyone with their feet in the real world knows that people don't always maximize their monetary benefits. They may feel it's immoral to do so. They may downshift. They may just not feel like it. It isn't surprising, in these circumstances, that economists have been proved wrong so often when they cling to their favourite economic formula.

The phrase 'post-autistic' has a touch of Gallic facetiousness, but there was real anger underlying their campaign. It wasn't just that economics students were being brainwashed rather than educated, that whole aspects of life were being ignored because they were inconvenient to the prevailing theory. It was the creeping sense that they were actually being cut off from reality by the accelerating plethora of figures.

Shortly after the launch of the first Post-Autistic Economics petition, the world's faith in figures was severely dented by the bizarre goings-on in Florida during the American presidential election between George W. Bush and Al Gore. Because of all the counting processes, elections were supposed to be an exact representation of the will of The People. Heavens, you could count the ballots.

But this time it didn't seem to work like that. The precise result seemed to depend entirely on a judgement call about the ballot cards, and whether the little holes had been adequately punched through. At the height of the stand-off, one counting agent was even accused of swallowing the little bits of cardboard, which were evidence that someone had tried to make the ballots more unambiguous. Counting didn't decide the election, as we know. The Supreme Court stepped in, and used their very human wisdom – all too human, according to some – to break the deadlock.

Back in France, Fitoussi's 'Post-Autistic' commission was the subject of heavy lobbying from the International Economics Association and others, fearful that its findings would have ripples beyond France and beyond economics. And sure enough, the beginnings of a disenchantment with the idea that only measurement makes things authentic were beginning to appear.

For one thing, it was all too obvious that people can work around almost any numerical target to make it look good. They work to the target, not the task as a whole. In Britain, school league tables made teachers concentrate on getting borderline pupils through at the expense of their weaker classmates. Hospital waiting-list targets meant NHS managers preferred to treat simple problems and ignore more serious complaints.

The problem was that people are expected to do what the targets tell them, rather than what is actually necessary. That's why, for example, more expensive trolleys are now being ordered by British hospitals and reclassified as 'mobile beds', to sidestep the target that no patient should stay on a hospital trolley for more than four hours. Scotland Yard figures which showed they had recruited 218 people from ethnic minorities between April and September 2000 had broadened the scope of the term to include Irish, New Zealanders and Australians. The useful figure was four.

When one British MP demanded angrily why his local education authority was bottom of the league for getting rid of outside toilets in their schools, he discovered it was because they had actually replaced them twenty years before. Being bottom of the league, in this case, actually meant they were way ahead of the rest – something the numbers were too crude to pick up.

The consequences of pinning down the wrong factor are severe, as the Pentagon discovered in the Vietnam war, when they audited the success of military units by the body count they achieved. Result: terrible loss of life among the Vietnamese, but no American victory. It was the same measuring the success of train companies at keeping to the timetable. Result: they simply lengthened the journey times. Or with judging schools by exam results and homework. Result: ignorant, exhausted kids with brilliant CVs.

When the old Soviet authorities measured the output of their glass factories in tons, they made glass that was too thick. When they measured them according to square metres, they made it too thin. It's what is known as Goodhart's Law – after a former chief advisor to the Bank of England – that any statistic will become distorted if used by authorities to control the way people behave. It's the same mistake the calls centres make.

Another difficulty was that the target-setting business was becoming a political liability. It is, after all, enormously expensive. According to the US National Commission on Testing and Public

Policy, compulsory school testing probably takes up 20 million school days and costs anything up to $900 million. It's also increasingly unpopular among public service professionals, who sense that the measuring culture doesn't just ignore their professional knowledge and judgement – the aspects of their job that can't be reduced to figures – but may be one of the reasons why services remain so inefficient.

But there is the glimmer of a recovering sense of what is truly authentic: the growing idea that measurement culture – very narrow bottom lines, financial and otherwise – might be behind the failure of so many privatized businesses to show the imagination and verve expected of them. According to a speech in 2001 by National Portrait Gallery director Charles Saumarez Smith, measuring fever actually causes inefficiency – by 'aping the form rather than the content' of the private sector, and 'assuming that measurement is what is important and not intelligence and achievement'.

'Not once in the past seven years as director of a public institution do I recollect a single policy initiative that might adhere in any way to a belief that the best way of running the public sector might be through the recruitment of the best possible staff and allowing them a degree of autonomy,' he said, characterizing the modern public sector as embodying 'a belief that the system is more important than the individual, that accountability is more important than intelligence or creativity, with the result that the public sector is likely to continue to limp along impotently and inefficiently as long as it holds a low sense of its own political valuation and public esteem'.

It was even worse for those champions of measurement and auditing, the government of Tony Blair. Having set their targets with a loud political fanfare, the consequences are severe when they fail to meet them. They set themselves a target to cut truancy from 0.7 per cent of half days missed to 0.5 per cent. But by the 2002 deadline, the number of half days missed had actually risen to 1.1 per cent. They had also set a target to change the relationship between Britain and continental Europe and boasted a 40 per cent rise in ministerial contacts with their opposite numbers on the continent. Yet, at the same time, the popularity of the EU in Britain had slumped to an all-time low.

That was the problem. If you set targets you have some kind of control over, all you do is measure the activity of bureaucrats. If you measure progress towards what you really want to achieve – even if it's just a tiny fragment of a bigger picture – you find you don't actually seem to have quite the same level of control over it that you thought you did. Britain's Environment Agency set itself the very ambitious target of keeping down the rise in sea levels. This is an important thing to measure, but something over which they have very little control – as King Canute demonstrated when he used a similar indicator himself. That's the trouble with numbers: they sound toughest and most authentic just when they miss the point the most.

And so the resistance to this kind of fake authenticity grew. Britain's Health Secretary Alan Milburn apologized to anyone who had suffered because of the government's waiting-list targets, promising priority to patients with the most serious conditions. School league tables were scrapped in Northern Ireland after three quarters of the responses to a consultation by the Northern Ireland education minister Martin McGuinness had urged that they go. In the USA in 2000, pupils in Massachusetts and Denver refused to take their annual tests. Louisiana parents went to court to prevent them taking place at all. And in Massachusetts in 1998, so many trainee teachers failed (56 per cent) the latest bout of testing fever that the state education board had to reduce the pass mark.

While government doubts were growing, the authenticity of the accountancy profession was coming under renewed scrutiny. 'I believe there is a crisis of confidence in our profession,' Arthur Andersen chief executive Joseph Berardino told the US Congress in December, after the unexpected bankruptcy of their client Enron, whose accounts they had signed and to whom they had also been giving consultancy advice. Nor was Enron the first problem: accountancy failures over the six years before may have cost anything up to $100 billion, according to the former chief accountant at the Securities and Exchange Commission, Lynn Turner.

It's one of those strange paradoxes that – as Michael Power put it – whenever there's an accountancy scandal, whether it's Robert Maxwell or BCCI or Long-Term Asset Management, the solution is always *more* accountancy and tougher rules. The accountants are dead, long live the accountants. The idea that accountancy is an inexact profession doesn't seem to occur to the world.

Yet, in truth, there are different ways of going about it, and they are symbolized in the difference between accountancy ideals on opposite sides of the Atlantic. The idea of setting out general accounting principles – interested in the intentions of managers as well as what they actually do – is at the heart of European standards. American regulatory officials insist that their own Generally Accepted Accounting Principles (GAAP) are more authentic and more rigorous, because they use a tick-box style: did they or didn't they? As with all counting, GAAP may well be more effective at digging out malpractice that somehow gets hidden by cultural differences. But they didn't pick up the Enron scandal – maybe another example of how people will always get round the numbers.

And if you go back to the dawn of the accountancy profession, even in America, you will find the same commitment to principles rather than numbers – because that is where the truth lies. 'Use figures as little as you can,' said American accountant, James Anyon, giving advice to the next generation in 1912. 'Remember your client doesn't like or want them, he wants brains. Think and act upon facts, truths and principles and regard figures only as things to express these, and so proceeding you are likely to become a great accountant and a credit to one of the truest and finest professions in the land.'

Most of us who have applied for jobs over the past decade will have been introduced to the Myers-Briggs personality tests, the personality categories loosely based on Carl Jung's work on personality types. Often the interviewers will look playful as they introduce the idea, urging you to have a go – these tests are really just for fun, they assure you. They're not at all – nobody sets interview tests for fun – it's just that there remains some unease about the idea of reducing your personality to some kind of numerical or alphabetic code, so they can see if you could fit in with their existing team. Deep down, even the interviewers are embarrassed by this piece of reductionism.

It is because the thought of either recruiting or rejecting anyone on the basis of such an approximation, which boils down all nuance, all contradiction, all mood, all paradox – rendering us as simple individuals that can be classified – smacks a little of zoo-keeping. Even of eugenics. And yet personnel managers take these things seriously. One company in Virginia even makes its staff wear name badges that are colour-coded according to a Myers-Briggs personality classification, so that people know how to behave with them.

It seems equally peculiar to classify people by a numerical approximation of their intelligence. The controversy over IQ has been raging for most of the past century, catalogued in Stephen Jay Gould's *The Mismeasure of Man* (1981), over the way the figures are used – as if they measured something fixed about people, or worse that they could measure 'worth'. IQ tests clearly do have some kind of baseline role, but the truth is – as Howard Gardner pointed out in *Frames of Mind* (1983) – there are actually many different kinds of intelligence, and each of them should be measured in different ways.

If, of course, they are measurable at all. There are people with good mechanical intelligence, good mathematical intelligence, good linguistic intelligence. But there are also people with intelligences that aren't academic but practical – sporting geniuses, design geniuses, taste geniuses, even people with a low conventional IQ who have reached genius level at bringing up children, or looking after old people.

That's the difficulty with artificial intelligence. 'You can measure speed. But if you want to engineer a device to maximize its beauty, you no longer have a measurement device,' Jaron Lanier says. 'It becomes subjective. Artificial intelligence is like that. When you talk to a person, there's an element of faith on your part that there really is somebody at home.' Why should we show this faith to a computer – when intelligence is such a complex multifaceted idea?

It's bad enough to pin down intelligence in figures in the name of authenticity, and narrow its definition just to make it measurable. But it would be much worse if genetics researchers, in their search for a single 'intelligence gene', took narrow measurements like these as their specification – believing that they were authentic because they could be measured. The danger then is starting to breed the human race to encourage this so-called intelligence gene – only to find a century later that we have a world population brilliant at passing arithmetic exams but somehow devoid of all those other creative and family intelligences that we used to rely on.

That's the great fear: that in the end those who think reality lies in the numbers will recreate the world as if nothing else matters. We forget those aspects of life – the most important ones – that can't be measured, then forget we've forgotten them. You can already see this process starting with education and economics. If exams or other test scores are the only things that matter, then that's all education becomes. Only what is immediately relevant to get through the tests – sometimes no more subtle than multiple choice – gets taught. Soon we can barely remember the days when school included anything else – and an education in doubt, or argument, or beauty, or creativity gets swept away.

If we only measure success by Gross Domestic Product or the single bottom line of money running through the economy, then we also drive out all those things that can't be measured. The environment gets sacrificed without our even seeing it, and soon we have created a world where the numbers really *do* measure the world accurately, because everything else has been factored out. Imagine watching *It's a Wonderful Life*, hearing poor old George Bailey being described by his brother as the 'richest man in town' and not understanding what on earth he was talking about. Surely Mr Potter was the richest man in town? Is this some strange, medieval metaphor?

And that's the fate that awaits us if we believe that reality consists only of what can be measured. Because reality is complicated. Layers of inconvenient meaning mess up the neat metrics of managers and technocrats. If you really want things to be real, you have to let in these shades of meaning, these meanings within meanings, these paradoxes and contradictions about life, and face them head on. Just as diversity is the basis for life, so complexity is the basis for authenticity.

Reducing things to numbers goes hand in hand with reducing them to checklists, computer programs or bullet points. The ultimate boiling down was the prediction by a General Electric executive, Dr G. L. Haller, who, three decades ago, said that we should soon be speaking a 'precise' machine language, in which Juliet may say of Romeo: 'Delta symbol not imply delta referent attribute end.'

Haller is wrong so far – though, to give him credit, he timed this change half a century after he was writing, so we still have twenty years to go. But his example goes some way to show how, in the search for authenticity, counting, measuring and pinning things down are a dead end. His quotation from Computer-Shakespeare may have been precise, but proves that when you remove the ambiguity of human meaning, and the richness of the language, it actually doesn't mean much at all.

The same is true of medicine. You can reduce what doctors do to numbers, or programmable criteria, but something gets lost in translation. Exactly what is still the subject of a key debate between the advocates of evidence-based medicine – that diagnosis is better formalized, checklisted and computerized – and the advocates of narrative-based medicine who don't agree. For the latter, like Dr Trisha Greenhalgh from the Royal Free Hospital in London, doctors have an ability that can't be picked up by cold, logical analysis. They can listen to stories, which have a richness about them.

There's nothing wrong with checklists, or using computers as an aid to diagnosis, any more than there is with measuring and counting things. Quite the reverse. They remind even the best of us what we've missed. They let us take situations unawares and see through our own prejudices. The danger is when in the name of authenticity – but actually of centralized control – we forget that checklist doctoring misses out those diagnostic tools that go beyond simple facts: doctors' intuition, judgement, experience and common sense.

Checklist doctoring, like checklist accountancy or checklist customer services, is a fearsome thing. And it takes us back to call centres again. Try asking for something from your bank's customer service centre if they don't happen to have a space on their computerized report forms to describe it. It's a frustrating business. Try booking a train journey into central Europe through a travel agent these days, as I did recently. They can't do it because their software refuses to believe that anyone would want to go by train to the Croatian coast. It makes you long for the old days when a 'real' travel agent could look these things up in dusty directories.

We know it's impossible to run a successful business just with numbers because people aren't predictable. We have to work with complex people, bring out the best in them, make them feel secure, encourage their creativity, inspire them to take responsibility when all the rules and metrics point the other way – those flashes of brilliant disobedience that the Royal Navy knows as 'The Nelson Touch'. Management is about people after all, which is why Tom Peters's concept of MBWA (Management By Walking Around) works and why, as Richard Branson reveals in his autobiography, he relies on 'gut instinct' rather than statistics when deciding on investments.

Business writer Thomas Stewart, author of *Intellectual Capital*, devoted his *Fortune* column in February 2001 to a similar critique of Microsoft's PowerPoint computer program. The spread of PowerPoint means that almost every presentation at every business conference includes those neat encapsulations of complicated ideas boiled down into three bullet points. They look neat, but of course they are also simplistic, because – normally anyway – truth is anything but neat. It's sometimes breathtakingly simple, but it needs explaining. Google's Peter Norvig actually wrote a PowerPoint version of Lincoln's Gettysburg Address, complete with impressively irrelevant graphs about the USA 'four score and seven years ago'. Tellingly, the only place you don't see PowerPoint is at those elite conferences of chief executives, because – as Stewart put it – 'captains of industry like to see a speaker think, not watch him read'.

The obsession with measuring attempts to pin down authenticity by reaching back before all those postmodern ideas about relative truth and social context. Relativity applies as much to scientists as to businesspeople and politicians: since quantum mechanics and the Uncertainty Theorem, we've had difficulty with truth. In his play *Copenhagen*, Michael Frayn has the nuclear pioneer Niels Bohr put the case like this:

> It starts with Einstein. He shows that measurement – measurement, on which the whole possibility of science depends – measurement is not an impersonal event that occurs with impartial universality. It's a human act, carried out from a specific point of view in time and space, from the one particular viewpoint of a possible observer. Then, here, in Copenhagen in those years in the mid-twenties we discover there is no precisely determinable objective universe. That the universe exists only as a series of approximations. Only within the limits determined by our relationship with it. Only through the understanding lodged inside the human head.

That's the problem, and the defining discovery that has shaped our age. It is hardly surprising that, in their search for authenticity, people try to go back before this modern eating of the apple of the Tree of Knowledge. We have been thrown out of the Garden of Certainty – of course we want to measure things. But we can't go back to the days of innocence, any more than Adam and Eve were able to.

Again, the search for authenticity isn't a conservative phenomenon. It can't be backward-looking, because we know the old world of Newtonian mechanics and measurement in numbers can't provide it. The search for what's real and authentic has to continue in the face of overwhelming relativism. It is underpinned by a kind of faith that there *is* a reality – even if we can't necessarily perceive it with absolute certainty.

The touching faith of the New Realists goes hand in hand with another faith. Despite the philosophical difficulties in perception, despite virtual reality, deconstruction and all the other tenets of postmodernism, we are not alone. We don't live in a separate universe. We may not be able to understand the complexity of the people around us – even those closest to us – but their complexity is what makes them real. We can't measure them, sum them up on PowerPoint, reduce them to numbers, statistics or targets, or control them with formulae, because they will always slip through our fingers. That's the basis of the new authenticity: reality is human.

It never happened . . .

'Sonic cleaning devices and air-filtering systems will banish dirt and just about eliminate dusting, scrubbing and vacuuming. Combination freezer-microwave ovens will take care of the cooking automatically. Dishwashing will be a thing of the past, since disposable dishes will be made of powdered plastic for each meal by a machine in the kitchen.'

Wall Street Journal, 'The shape of the future', 6 February 1967

10

Real Politics

> **'Is it politically reprehensible, while we are groaning under the shackles of the capitalist system, to point out that life is frequently worth living because of a blackbird's song, a yellow elm tree in October, or some other natural phenomenon which does not cost money and does not have what the editors of the left wing newspapers call a class angle?'**
>
> George Orwell

> **' "It was as true," said Mr Barkis, ". . . as taxes is. And nothing's truer than them." '**
>
> Charles Dickens, *David Copperfield*

As I stood in my own election count, at the end of the 2001 general election – sweat pouring down my face both from humidity and worry – it struck me what an emotional business politics is. The public image of politicians is of petulant, rather than emotional figures. But they're not really different from anyone else, although they do tend to be angrier – that's what drives them to do peculiar things like standing for Parliament or running for office. Still I have to confess, before I embark on a discussion of real politics, that I am one of them.

In a small way of course. The voters of Regent's Park and

Kensington North – which stretches from Notting Hill to London Zoo – provided me with a small swing that left the Liberal Democrats exactly where they were before the election, namely third. The high point of the campaign for me was an hour canvassing a closed order of Carmelite nuns ('Can't we get back to the subject of abortion again?' said the Mother Superior). The low point was the moment during the count when I was called over to see one spoiled ballot paper scrawled with the words 'Would never vote for Boyle'.

For the people taking part, politics can be as emotional as a football match – in the fleeting connections with people, the rollercoaster hopes and disappointments, and the passionate partisanship and camaraderie. 'There is nothing more emotional than a political campaign,' said political consultant David Garth, one of the team behind Michael Bloomberg's campaign to be Mayor of New York. But most people don't see it like that. From the outside, the whole business seems dull, stolid and irritable; and in a way, politicians and economists collude to encourage that idea. They want to seem in control, and that means being hard-headed and rational. They are fearful of emotion, preferring to stick to tough measures like unemployment figures or retail price indices rather than well-being, dignity or joy. They get scared when people take to the streets weeping, as they did after the death of Princess Diana.

If there can be such a thing as real politics, this lingering untruth might offer a clue where to look for it. The trouble is that – unlike real business, or real food, or real culture – very little has emerged that could possibly be given the label 'real politics'. There are hints and phrases. There's certainly longing for a politics more based on ethics or which decentralizes power, handing it either to business (the right) or local people (both right and left). There's a growing horror of spin-doctoring and political campaigning of any kind. There's certainly a hunger for real politics. But if it exists at all, it hasn't emerged much from its chrysalis.

The demand for it is all too obvious, in the depressing cynicism among voters about the lying, spin, corruption and bizarre, irrelevant TV rituals that dominate politics across the world. Individual politicians are respected, even occasionally loved, but as a group they're a big turn-off. And fascinated as I remain by politics, I can see why: the excruciating dullness of most political meetings; the party conferences that have remained much the same shape since 1918; the re-heated rhetoric of the 1940s – 'education for all', 'fairness for all' – long since sucked dry of any meaning and which now just sound patronizing. The public watch anything up to 10,000 TV advertisements a year, created by the best marketing imaginations in the world: they are extremely adept at seeing through a sales pitch. And they just don't buy it. Negative campaigning can undermine a vote, but it very rarely manages to encourage one.

Every so often a politician manages to break through this foggy language to express what people feel. Tony Blair managed this in 1995 with the phrase 'I want us to be a young country again', which put into words people's sense that they needed renewal. But for one phrase that captures the imagination or the zeitgeist, we have to put up with tens of thousands of carefully manufactured sound bites on press releases, full of righteous and bogus indignation.

We also have to put up with a jumble of arbitrary buzzwords provided by focus groups. 'He might equally have said "the government of my passion",' wrote the *Times* columnist Matthew Parris after one of Blair's early verbless speeches, 'or "the vision of my consensus", "a young vision, flexible, multi-facilitated and committed". "New compassion", "mission with opportunity".

"Justice with social ambition".' Just as the New Realists react against the sense that they are being manipulated by marketing, so they react against political manipulation too – especially against ads with the word 'rats' flashed for one thirtieth of a second as the Bush broadcasts had in 2000.

Worse, once they become governments their language strips itself of meaning, swallowing technocrat-speak – the insider language of double-think, of 'spreading excellence' and other empty phrases, of people who are sheltering from the truth of their own complete powerlessness. Another political columnist, Simon Carr, said that listening to it made him realize why people vote for Jean-Marie Le Pen. 'It's the language these ignorant, arrogant, clapped-out, over-promoted, jargon-jabbering, morally incompetent, intellectually fetid, Paul-paying, Peter-robbing hucksters use as they administer the biggest budget in the British economy.' Many would agree.

The result is that the last UK election (2001) managed to enthuse just 59 per cent of voters into the polling booths. The current leader of the free world was elected by the votes of just 25 per cent of registered voters (though, luckily for George W. Bush, five out of nine Supreme Court justices). Nine million people voted in the TV poll for *Pop Idol* – getting on for a third of the number who voted in the general election a few months before.

Studies by the Hansard Society and the BBC show the problem is even worse, that only four in ten young people voted and only one in three of the most civic-minded group in the whole population – women over fifty-five. Research also seems to show that this isn't to do with apathy. People are very interested in politics generally – pressure groups, environmental campaigns and single-issue lobby groups – but they actively disapprove of the clubby conspiracy with political journalists, the arcane rules, the obscure arguments and the tortoise speed of political change.

It's a little unfair to compare this with the speed and informality of decision-making in business, because there is just as much in-fighting and personal politicking there. It's just that it isn't slowed down by being carried on in the full glare of the media spotlight. But still, politicians are 'like parents who tell you what time to go to bed but can't put your breakfast on the table', says Matthew Taylor from the think-tank IPPR – and he's right that the combination of arrogance, viciousness and powerlessness really is a turn-off.

I confirmed this, to myself at least, when canvassing a small estate in Romsey in another by-election in 2000, where everybody was in but where, without exception, nobody was voting. 'On principle,' they said smugly, which seemed to me to make it even worse. They *could* be bothered: but they had moral objections to it.

But politicians are just as fed up as the public. Margaret Thatcher's guru Sir Keith Joseph famously described his impatience to get his fingers on the levers of power when he took office in the early 1960s, only to discover 'they weren't connected to anything'. This is much more the case today forty years on. National parliaments achieve so much less than international bodies and local authorities. Yet the more powerless they become, the more jealously they guard their privileges, and the more pompous the debates become on issues they can't possibly do anything about.

National politicians in Westminster, Paris or Berlin have yet to realize that almost their sole power is now to cajole, imagine, inspire and coordinate. But until they realize it, they can't even manage that. And meanwhile they sit bemused as the giant organizations that used to manage our lives – the health systems, the social security bureaucracies, the education systems – grind to a halt through their sheer complexity.

Because of this, politicians tend to be angry enthusiasts,

trapped in a Machiavellian world of cynicism that makes it hard for them to grasp new thinking – except as far as it helps them navigate the very narrow problems they set for themselves; or except as far as it's possible to imagine it inside current administrative arrangements; or except as far as they fit into traditional party allegiances. Both major parties in the USA, for example, back the controversial American Channel One network, discussed at the beginning of this book – beaming programmes into schools on condition the pupils are forced to watch their advertising as well. Republicans like it because these are education resources which aren't funded by taxation. Democrats like it because they give teachers a break from teaching children. The growing sector of voters who want a more authentic kind of education find themselves with nowhere to go in the overwhelmingly technocratic political mainstream.

Still, the descent of politics into hopelessly fake isn't all the politicians' fault. Individual politicians are often manically hard-working, idealistic people with a determination to make things happen for those they represent, individually and collectively. But they are often also twisted by political reporting into behaving like carefully choreographed automatons, terrified that any word out of place could be pounced on by the press.

The truth is that politicians are locked into a mutually destructive relationship with political journalists, especially broadcasters. The literature and speeches have never been so bright and user-friendly – the days when Gladstone would address a public rally for ninety minutes in the drizzle have long gone. But both are aware of the dwindling public interest in party politics, as politicians keep ever more rigorously on-message while the broadcasters treat them with a mixture of private respect and on-air contempt. The results are obvious.

So this has been a difficult chapter for me to write. I enjoy party political events. I strongly believe in what my own party stands for and respect the enormous efforts that its activists make – I even feel inspired at the rallies I go to. I certainly believe that, if anyone deserves power, then it's us. But, at the same time, I find myself catching sight of us as the vast majority of potential voters see us – and being only too aware how little politicians, as a breed, are able to achieve. Running for office myself, even in a small way, allowed me to see for myself how easy it is for politicians to forget their own irrelevance. Simply because people are friendly when you meet them, and because – while you may not be able to change the world – you can sometimes provide real help to individuals, you imagine that all remains pretty much right in the world of politics.

The result of all this is that political debate has become an undemanding mush. Politicians tend to debate designated political issues – usually the ones that fit neatly into the accepted divisions between government departments – while the more awkward ones, often the things that people discuss at home or worry about the most, don't get a mention. They tend to debate what differentiates themselves traditionally from other parties, but steer clear of areas where their opponents have no track record. Or they debate what they have the power to do something about, oblivious of the way that globalization has swept away that power – and collude with political journalists by pretending that the recent boom or bust was caused by the government in office, rather than the hurricanes of world finance.

This makes for a strange categorization of issues. Politicians debate the size of school classes endlessly, but for some reason not the size of schools. They debate the mistakes in hospitals endlessly, but not the obsession with pills and gizmos. They debate public-sector borrowing but not the way money is created in the first place. It's frustrating getting to grips with issues when some of the basic assumptions seem to be beyond discussion.

Yet meanwhile, many voters find themselves commuting for four hours a day, while almost half of their marriages unravel, and they look forward to miserable, meaningless deaths attached to tubes in hospitals – and about all this, their politicians have nothing to say.

And quite right too, say the politicians – I've had these discussions – because we shouldn't be interfering in these aspects of people's lives. That would be absolutely right and admirable were it not for the fact that – unnoticed by the majority of our elected representatives at a national level – they have almost no power to interfere in most of the traditional areas either.

One way or another, politics doesn't challenge basic assumptions or – for example – pick up on the issues in this book. Real food? A fad. Real business? Isn't business just about making a profit? Real relationships? Well, it's a matter of administrative efficiency. The idea of authenticity is hard to grasp because the whole political world is fixated on the idea that human beings are cogs that can be run well if you oil the machinery of state. That's what happens when you leave out real emotions.

The American philosopher Charlene Spretnak tells of a revealing visit she made to Slovakia in 1993. As she drove with members of Slovakia's Green Party from Vienna airport to Bratislava, the driver gestured towards the soulless high-rise flats – familiar to anyone in the Western world as well as the East – and said: 'That's socialism.'

In reply, she reeled off a list of the assumptions of modern politics to him – that people are simply economic beings; that you 'can't stand in the way of progress'; that giant centralized organizations are somehow more efficient. 'This is what you were taught in school, right?' she asked. 'It's what I was taught in school too. Even though we were assured in the strongest possible terms that our two systems were almost unimaginably alien to one another!'

The 2001 general election unleashed a flurry of interest by politicians in the art of authenticity. The government's spinner-in-chief Alastair Campbell even agreed that politician 'spinning' had become an arcane game between politicians and press: 'The victims are the public who don't think it has anything to do with them whatsoever.' But by the time Campbell had abolished the lobby system of journalists, the search for real politics had become a trend.

It had begun in the days immediately after the election spearheaded by an unusually honest article by the trade secretary Patricia Hewitt, where she recognized people's frustration and called for a more grown-up style of politics – identifying it in the style of one of her opponents. 'Lib Dem leader Charles Kennedy showed us what was possible during the election campaign,' she wrote. 'Being right is more important than being "on message" if the message conceals more than it reveals. We will have to find a different way of campaigning, a different kind of conversation with the voters.'

The same idea was already appearing in mainstream American politics. During the presidential primaries in 2000, both Al Gore and George W. Bush – both with obsessively constructed images – came up against difficult challengers who seemed more genuine and more authentic. 'Before this setback, George W.'s every move and utterance was carefully scripted in advance, tested by focus groups, polished by political consultants,' wrote Bill Clinton's former Labour Secretary Robert Reich after a presidential primary rebuff:

> See him once, he's charming. See him a second time, he's still charming. This wouldn't have been a problem were it not for John McCain, who's so utterly natural he's made Bush's potted charm seem as artificial as a metallic Christmas tree. McCain is the Real Thing. Bush is losing in New Hampshire, and it's finally dawning on his handlers that no number of slick TV ads will fix the basic flaw, which is the appearance of slickness.

Bush clawed his way back against McCain, just as Gore did against the more genuine style of Bill Bradley, using the weapons of carefully scripted 'authentic moments' and TV ads which were more like documentaries. But then, as Reich pointed out, even sincerity can be faked: 'Bill Clinton's passionate "I did not . . . with that woman" runs repeatedly through the public mind like some monstrously cynical continuous loop, warning against trusting anyone in public life to mean what they say no matter how sincerely they appear to say it.'

That is the problem underlying the whole idea of 'authentic politicians'. Authenticity soon breaks down if politicians start believing their own 'we can do it' rhetoric. Or if they are lulled into complacency by the deference of those around them. Or if they are surrounded by a party machine dedicated to something very different.

Because, although I am an active member of a political party myself, I am forced to recognize the truth in what one political commentator said to me – that political parties are dying. In their current form as indivisible, controlling monoliths, that's probably true. They're not providing a service that anybody wants: their staggering failure to achieve real change is hanging like an albatross around their necks – though they are blind to it themselves. The combined membership of political parties in the UK is only the same as the circulation of a moderately successful women's magazine. They may even be dead already.

Real politics demands that political parties should be on people's side. It demands a generosity at the heart of their activities that seems so often absent. Political parties now look hopelessly preoccupied with themselves. They're not even partisan, exactly: they give – or seem to give – their attention to those who donate money to them. They give their loyalty to individuals who are loyal and useful to them. If we were to imagine the kind of political party of the future with some chance of regaining a mass following, then they would need to find some generosity of spirit – perhaps by turning themselves into training organizations dedicated to spreading the techniques of getting what you want. Parties whose central task is just winning elections look cheap. In the long run, you win as a by-product of what you do and what you are.

The pioneers of this kind of politics go back to the idea of 'community politics', formally adopted by the Liberal Party in 1970. Community politics was always more than just news-sheets delivered through every local letterbox. It was a genuine attempt to turn politics on its head, working with local organizations, tenants' groups and amenity campaigns to help them achieve their aims. The community politicians used the slogan 'if we win – you win!' – and they meant it. They had to mean it, or the whole thing would mean nothing.

Now that every politician claims to be a community politician, and the news-sheet style has descended all too often into diatribes against rival politicians, the technique can't provide the enormous political advantages that it did in the 1970s. The days when local politicians can get behind neighbourhood associations and put themselves at their disposal have gone. People are just too cynical these days; politicians are much too busy. But they have to respond somehow, otherwise enough of the electorate will turn to demagogues pedalling fake real solutions, like Jean-Marie Le Pen. And if Le-Pen-style politicians are the only ones claiming to stand up against 'global technocracy', then the old parties only have themselves to blame if monsters like him get elected. 'Global technocracy' is precisely what many New Realists regard themselves as being against.

So politics hasn't quite embraced authenticity, but you can see it emerging in the mainstream trend towards decentralizing power. You can see it in the brief attempt to create an 'ethical foreign policy' for Britain, however difficult to follow through, and in the hunger for campaign-finance reform in the shape of the Shays-Meehan Bill that banned 'soft money' donations to political parties in the USA – an attempt to tackle the sense that policy-making had become what the *New York Times* called 'duelling donations' from competitive interest groups. You can see it in the four US states that have opted for 'clean elections' with strict public-spending limits and public campaign funding, and in the new Parliamentary Standards Committee in the House of Commons.

You can see 'real politics' emerging outside conventional politics altogether, in ambitious projects like Imagine Chicago, where people are being involved in the long-term planning of cities. Or in projects to put modern concerns like 'self-esteem' or 'emotional literacy' at the heart of politics. Or in the New Economics Foundation's 'democs': new ways of reaching consensus on difficult issues.

I'm excited by the arrival of real politics – with all its dangers, of which more later. We might still spend an inspired evening listening to old-fashioned political speeches, or planning new ways of taking over the so-called reins of power. But then we could spend a few hours waiting in one of the technocratic bureaucracies born of modern politics – the wildly inefficient monster hospitals of the British NHS. Or we could pass a day with farmers in Cumbria who had their whole flocks and family pets slaughtered because a government computer program suggested this was the quickest way of eradicating Foot and Mouth Disease, against which almost no precautions had been taken for over thirty years.

Then we turn on the television, and watch politicians getting into a lather about whether or not a Secretary of State said an obscure sentence to his officials, and you watch all those prodigious reserves of wit and rhetoric being directed towards some miserable cross-party put-down on the floor of the House of Commons. And we think: there must be a better way.

Was there ever anyone who advocated 'fake' politics? Put like that, it's ludicrous. And yet, in a sense, periods of great social hope are often accompanied by the idea that we can somehow do away with political debate, with the inconveniences of ideology, and that decisions can be somehow 'measured' automatically – rather along the lines of the last chapter. This is a dream of running politics by numbers, and we are living through the dream now. It's one of the key reasons politics looks so fake – because its key players don't really believe much of the charade either. Real politics would mean putting this disastrous dream aside.

It began with the rise of the statisticians – then known as *statists* – in the early nineteenth century, briefly suppressed by Napoleon and flourishing in the 1830s, driven by the idea that the chaos of politics could be replaced by an orderly rule by facts alone. It was an idea that also originated with the philosopher Jeremy Bentham, who nearly bankrupted himself persuading the

British government to build a revolutionary new prison on the site now occupied by the Tate Britain. His Panopticon was based on the idea of one guard being able to watch all the prisoners simultaneously and a regime of work that – as he put it – would 'grind rogues honest'. After initial enthusiasm, the government backed out of the project.

It later transpired that the reason he had been so messed around – enough for the government to pay him damages of £23,000 – was that the site was right next to land belonging to the powerful politician Earl Spencer. If a project of enormous public benefit like this one could be held up by the whims of one man, he thought, then a new system of government was urgently needed that could edit out such inconveniences of personality and prejudice. Hence the idea of Utilitarianism, the 'greatest good of the greatest number' – that somehow the correct policy could be simply calculated, without the need for irritating debate.

Britain has almost swallowed Bentham's idea nearly two centuries later. The Blair government announced nearly 8,000 new numerical measurements of success in its first four years of office, and the whole concept of ideology seems to have been banished from political discourse. The big parties often seem identical in outlook, resorting to a depressing series of diatribes attacking each other for incompetence and corruption instead. The key issues of the day on both sides of the Atlantic – globalization, the causes of terrorism, trade and the environment – survive somehow in the newspapers without debate by politicians. Ironically, both too much ideology and its complete absence can disconnect politicians from real life.

The measuring idea is a dream of politicians as machines that take no notice of individual difference – the masters of the great Machinery of State, grinding out housing, prisons, health or justice. 'A bedpan isn't dropped without me knowing about it in Whitehall,' said Labour's health minister Aneurin Bevan after the creation of the National Health Service. These are politicians caught in a trap of their own myth making – responsible for everything, capable of anything. It's a model that goes back to Niccolo Machiavelli's *The Prince* and its the idea that statecraft was somehow a science that could be mastered.

Any politician might smile secretly at the idea that they could be described as Machiavellian, but the whole idea is rapidly shrivelling before our eyes – partly because it fails to deliver much for our complex modern world. And partly because people are not the predictable machines that politicians and economists say they are – put in tax cuts, get votes.

Modern politicians who cling to the idea – as the vast majority of them do – find themselves locked into a producer–consumer paradigm. We are powerful, you are powerless – we will provide, they say. Of course things aren't as bad as they were a quarter of a century ago, when the Lewisham Labour councillor Nicholas Taylor, then chair of the housing committee, was astonished to find his colleagues fighting tooth and nail against the idea that people should be allowed to build their own council houses. 'If Lewisham Labour group has a fault,' said the borough architect at the time, 'it is the conviction that if a thing is worth doing at all, it is worth the council doing it for you.'

'Centralism runs in the DNA of all Westminster politicians,' according to Simon Jenkins. This is even more true at the level of the European Union, which – in the name of free trade – regulates the maximum length of buses, the time worked by doctors and the level of street noise.

But we also know now that centralized government can't work any more. It failed to deliver behind the Iron Curtain, just as it failed to work for business a generation ago, because it was so inefficient – it confused information in the slow trickle-down from hierarchic level to level, and it failed to use the imagination and initiative of the highly skilled people on the ground. Yet politicians still cling to the idea – not so much of centralized power but of themselves as providers – because they can't bear to accept their own powerlessness.

But of course that's only half true. Politicians who work at an international level are able to tackle international problems – the greenhouse effect, nuclear safety, terrorism – because they know that only by sharing power can they make any difference. It's the same for those working at local level, again with the proviso that they are able to let go enough to share power with the people who live and work there. 'There go my people,' said Gandhi, 'and I must run to catch up with them, for I am their leader.'

The politicians who are most rudderless are those who cling most fervently to the idea that they have the power to change things: those in national parliaments and those who aspire to be there. Trust me on this: I am one.

They can pass laws which will have an effect, but it isn't clear whether – simply by passing laws – they can provide health-service systems that work, educate children, protect the planet or make the economy hum. They can certainly undermine it, they can make things worse – but only by sharing power can they make things better. The larger countries whose laws are bound to have most effect – the USA and China – may find this out last of all, but it's true nonetheless.

The implication of admitting this is that politicians must start the process of transferring their powers on to levels of government that can actually make things happen. It means passing power down to regions, cities or communities – the opposite process to globalization. Real politics is about local pride, and recognizes that we all come from all these levels. I'm European, English, and simultaneously from London and Crystal Palace – and I'm proud of them all. Real politics is concerned about identity without over-emphasizing one factor in particular as the source of all good.

Real politics explains the sudden appearance of community newspapers and local (virtual real) news on the web, like Paddington's Newspad, and the other twenty-five websites linked together as London Independent Online, and the innovative and ambitious E-tropolis project in Evanston, Illinois. It explains the resurgence of small languages like Welsh, Manx and Gaelic, and the commitment to defending small nations like East Timor.

The idea of small units of nationality goes back to the 1960s, when the author of *The Breakdown of Nations*, Leopold Kohr, found himself asked to put his ideas into practice for the government of the tiny Caribbean island of Anguilla – which was refusing to be lumped in with St Kitts as part of its independence deal from Britain. The British colonial authorities refused to believe that somewhere so small could go it alone, and tried to undermine the revolt by invading the island – not with marines, which was considered too provocative, but with London policemen. The headline in the *New York Times* summed up the situation with the phrase: 'The Lion that Miaowed'.

Forty years later, it's fascinating to see how differently we regard these issues. Small nations have a right to exist – in fact we've gone in war in defence of the Falklands, Kosovo and Kuwait to enforce that right. There are no more beach invasions in favour of conglomerates. Quite the reverse: Freddie Heineken, the late, brilliant master of the beer empire, proposed to guarantee peace in Europe by breaking up the EU into seventy-five nation states with no more than 10 million people in each.

Decentralizing power inside countries and companies has increasingly become the civilized option for enlightened governments. GE's Jack Welch said 'Think Small' was his watchword for the 1990s. All education is managed locally in Denmark. Health and even energy are organized by cities in Sweden. Even highly centralized France is now undergoing an enormous process of decentralizing power to regions, departments and communes. In Britain, power has been devolved to parliaments in Scotland, Wales and Northern Ireland.

Breaking yourself up into tiny pieces isn't necessarily the highest goal of real politics, but it is a symptom that a new idea is out there and that people can somehow share sovereignty and govern themselves. It's human and it's a matter of taking responsibility, and that seems to me to be authentic.

But it isn't enough. You can't fully decentralize political power because it leaves everyone vulnerable to global economic power. It proves yet another example of the progression that New Realists seem to undertake, finding they're just not satisfied by partial authenticity and adding to the pressure to exercise some control over global business. This progression also means that real politicians are emerging in other ways, outside conventional politics altogether.

Michael Clark has been, among all the other things in his life, a successful stand-up comedian. His busiest period was in the late 1980s and early 1990s pretending to be Bob Dole – until Dole torpedoed this aspect of his career by failing to beat Bill Clinton and bowing out of frontline politics. Clark would conduct his performances like impromptu press conferences, portraying Dole as a free-market maverick. Why do we need the federal government to run air-traffic control? he would ask. Why can't people just land where they like? That's the American way.

But on the other side of his life, Clark was managing a small political revolution of his own as president of the Citizens Committee of New York City. The organization is almost unique on either side of the Atlantic, although smaller outfits have attempted to manage the same thing. But this hasn't been a political revolution organized through the government in Washington, DC, still less the state capital in Albany or City Hall. It has overseen the emergence of thousands of tiny block associations dedicated to improving the life and environment of their neighbourhood – sometimes against enormous bureaucratic and criminal obstacles.

From just over 3,000 a quarter of a century ago, there are now 12,000 in New York City – a fourfold increase. Their success, often in difficult neighbourhoods plagued by racial tension, prostitution and drug culture, has achieved as much as anything in the city's successful battle against crime. As many as a million New Yorkers are out in their neighbourhoods every week, volunteering, organizing and doing the things that politicians had promised them but failed to achieve.

Their achievement flies in the face of all those suggestions that people are actually just disappearing inside their computers, turning away from geographical neighbourhoods and disengaging from all kinds of politics. On the contrary, in New York at least, people are prepared to put their time into making things happen – and this is a city where, as Michael Clark puts it, 'people's scarcest commodity is time'.

'I believe this is the great story of civic society over the past twenty-five years, if you think voluntary time is a kind of investment,' he told me. 'People have withdrawn from government and from large bureaucratic organizations. They don't really believe that government or big facilities or conglomerates can deliver. They have decided instead that they want to see and touch and feel the places they put their voluntary time.'

Although Rudolph Giuliani took much of the credit for the enormous cut in crime in New York, the story actually goes much further back – and involves the kind of collaborative local problem-solving that got police and communities talking to each other again, and then working together.

The idea of zero-tolerance – though no police force in the world can actually afford to have literally no tolerance at all – goes back to an article that George Kelling co-wrote in *Atlantic Monthly* in 1981. Now at Rutgers University, in his article 'Broken Windows' Kelling made public detailed research in the South Bronx area of New York. If you broke one window there in a deserted block and mended it the following morning, the building would stay intact. But if you didn't mend it, every window would be broken within seventy-two hours.

This discovery provided the theoretical basis for the policy that the New York police put into effect in the 1990s. 'It was that the little things matter enormously,' said Clark, and that meant that police and neighbourhoods simply had to work together. In 1984, the police asked the Citizens Committee to pilot new ways of dealing with drug-dealing. When the first few meetings with local people degenerated into screaming battles very quickly, Clark was forced to find more innovative ways to get both sides talking. When they did, it quickly became clear that each side wanted very much the same thing, but had believed the other side didn't care. Police and locals combined were able to make a difference to the little things like loitering, graffiti, and petty theft, and the little things made a big difference – as we know.

This approach involves issues across the political spectrum, but does seem to deliver real improvements – which is why Clark has been working with the Police Service of Northern Ireland to underpin a similar revolution over there. But it means a completely new role for politicians, as the convenors rather than the managers of change. 'Government imagines itself like Mighty Mouse,' says Clark. 'They never talk to people in neighbourhoods. Instead they see themselves as public servants who bring the stuff that local people want, sprinkle something like fairy dust while everyone applauds.'

It doesn't work. 'Politicians gargle with the word community, but they spit it out as soon as they walk offstage,' says David Morris of the influential Institute for Local Self-Reliance. Politicians can't make a difference until they accept their own powerlessness. If they don't, they get overtaken by grassroots groups who don't need politicians in quite the same way any more. Tackling the little things that make a real difference also recaptures some of the passionate connection that politicians get from standing for election. It's emotional because it's a joint endeavour.

Clark's committee has become a model for a new generation of community-level campaigns in Europe too, like TELCO – the East London alliance of multi-ethnic organizations under the chairmanship of the local priest. I first realized TELCO was something different when I went to a meeting they organized at the Whitechapel Art Gallery about the disappearance of bank branches and cashpoints. It was a meeting that restored my faith in the idea of community activism. It was packed with 200 men, women and children, all cheering loudly – brought together by TELCO's partners around the UK in the Citizen Organization Foundation Institute.

I couldn't decide what was most impressive. Perhaps it was the intelligent – not to say enthusiastic – interest taken in the proceedings by the very diverse audience. Maybe it was the fact that they managed to squeeze twenty-one speakers into an hour by the rigorous use of the stopwatch, wielded by a determined lady from Sheffield. But there's no doubt that the icing on the cake was managing to attract to the meeting, not just the chief executive of the new Financial Services Agency, but the Governor of the Bank of England.

Both sat throughout the hour and a half, listening to an elderly Asian lady who wielded a large map to pinpoint the five banks which had been in Canning Town five years before, all now disappeared, or the four-hour bus ride to get to the nearest cashpoint. Or a speaker from Liverpool, describing the gathering of loan sharks and their minders outside one DSS office every morning, ready to lend their clients' social-security books back to them temporarily so they could withdraw their latest loan repayment.

Neither Davies nor George signed up to TELCO's banking demands, but they have supported the campaign for community banking ever since. It was astonishingly effective.

These local organizations have a parallel in crisis-ridden Argentina, where thousands of 'self-convened neighbourhood assemblies' have emerged after the collapse of their economy together with most people's faith in elected politicians. What sickened the Argentines was just how much the financial classes had enriched themselves while the economy spun out of control – and worse, the vast sums salted away outside the country by Western banks who had lent them the money and those who had arranged the loans. The last massive borrowing deal in June 2001 increased Argentina's debt by a disastrous $55 billion and earned £150 million in commission for those who arranged it.

Six months later, street demonstrations forced Fernando de la Rúa to resign the presidency, and people from all over the cities celebrated, coming out of their houses, banging pots and pans. Despite the uneasy tradition of political involvement in

Argentina – under the military dictatorship, teenagers would disappear just for distributing mildly dissenting leaflets – the pot-bangers have stayed involved. There are now assemblies in most neighbourhoods in Buenos Aires and all over the rest of the country. They remain deliberately informal, often with their own websites.

The problem is that the assemblies often want very different things. A major gathering at the Parque del Centenario at the end of January 2002 could agree on little – except that their existence was due to a moral crisis in the country. 'We have been asleep for far too long and it's about time we woke up,' Noemi de Marco, bankrupt proprietor of a biscuit shop, told the *New York Times*. 'Through our own indifference, we have allowed the country to be stolen from us by corrupt politicians who have no respect for the law or their fellow citizens and who see the state only as a tool to enrich themselves.'

It's a frightening atmosphere. The moral crisis is a sign of people demanding ethical politics, but this is a mood, taken together with the banging pots, that can easily get out of hand. One leading Argentinian business newspaper called the self-organizing assemblies 'soviets'. A leading sociologist said that they 'reeked of fascism'. Both were right, but that somehow also missed the point. They were also an example of ordinary people deciding to build on the wreckage of what had once been productive politics.

You don't get there in one bound, of course. But it's interesting that so much 'real politics' seems to start with conversations. 'The kind of conversation I'm interested in is one in which you start with a willingness to become a slightly different person,' wrote the historian Theodore Zeldin – and that's the key to it. These are conversations that open the possibility of changing your mind. Perhaps that's why so many new experiments have the word 'café' in their titles. Like Channel 4's Café Society, Café Scientifique – just arrived in the UK – or Vicki Rubin's 'conversation cafés' in Seattle.

Conversations that change the world often result in yet more 'non-governmental organizations'. There are now at least 100,000 NGOs working on green issues alone all over the world. Some of them are persecuted and embattled; others are increasingly powerful. One question from Greenpeace by fax to a food manufacturer in 1999 was enough for them to take GM ingredients out of baby food. Indonesian NGOs helped bring down the dictator President Suharto.

This is a different kind of politics, often focused on a single issue, often uncompromisingly ethical. But then, authentic politics is a call for morality – or at least ethics and objectives that are consistent, what Tony Blair used to call 'joined-up government'. The emergence of real politics is heralded by an impatience with simple pragmatism, and – except perhaps during serious national crises like 9/11 – a demand that principles should be put into practice everywhere. If bombing innocent people is evil, then it remains evil whoever does it. If free trade is the right way forward, then that applies to the USA as much as to India or France. Suddenly hypocrisy is a major political story, when the old pragmatic politics had made it a way of life. Real politics does not mean *realpolitik*.

Let's not pretend that any of this is risk-free. Argentina's neighbourhood assemblies could well become the focus for intolerance and repression from both the right or the left. The increasing power of unelected NGOs like Greenpeace or Oxfam is going to remain controversial as long as they avoid the issue of who decides what they do. You can see the dangers, too, in the way some people cling to 'real' versions of long-dead ideologies, like Roy Hattersley's Campaign for Real Labour. Or much more dangerously, clinging to old imperial whites-only nationalism. Equally dangerous is the search for an element of faith in modern politics, the heady mixtures of nationalism and religion, the Al-Qaedas, the IRAs, the Moral Majority in the USA – all in their very different ways searching for authoritarian reality through the shifting compromises of modern politics.

But the biggest dangers are probably in the most hopeful aspects of real politics – the drive towards regionalism and what Charlene Spretnak calls 're-localization'. Defending yourself against the homogeneity of mass culture can often look nationalistic: regionalism in Ireland, Bosnia, Kosovo and the Basque country has already demonstrated that the mistaken byways of authenticity can kill – especially when it's emotional. You can see why the whole idea of authentic politics seems so dangerous to modern politicians and journalists.

All of these aspects of real politics – decentralization and the rise of NGOs – are reactions against the failure of politicians to deliver, at a time when change and whether change is possible, personally or politically, has become one of the key issues of the age. Finding ways that politicians can make things happen despite the complexity of the modern world requires first – like an Alcoholics Anonymous meeting – that they must admit their own powerlessness. It means rejecting the old producer–consumer paradigm, and finding new kinds of leadership that can pull resources together.

It also means facing up to the central, paradoxical nature of change. Most of us know, deep down, that change happens in a crab-like way. We snatch victory from the jaws of defeat. Great failures, great disasters drive great successes. 'Men fight and lose the battle,' William Morris wrote in *A Dream of John Ball*, 'and the thing that they fought for comes about in spite of their defeat, and when it comes turns out not to be what they meant, and other men have to fight for what they meant under another name.'

But politicians seem to forget that. Excited when they win, they are miserable when they lose. They blind themselves to the way that victory makes failure possible and vice versa, losing touch with the paradoxical grammar of change, and can't then use what levers are available. It isn't any wonder that people look at politicians, in all their pomposity, as if they have missed some basic moral truth.

Then they look at the rest of politics – the spin, the half-truths, the compromise – and long for something real, even if they can't quite put their finger on what that might be. For some New Realists, real politics means something more than just politicians acting authentically or people taking back power. They wonder whether there isn't something much more fundamental missing.

Embroiled in her hopeless bid to sort out the health-care system, Hillary Clinton – First Lady and future New York senator – puzzled American political commentators in April 1993 with the heady phrase the 'politics of meaning'. 'If we ask, why is it that in a country as wealthy as we are, that there is this undercurrent of discontent, we realize that somehow economic growth and prosperity, political democracy and freedom are not enough – that we lack meaning in our individual lives and meaning collectively,' she told the audience in Austin, Texas. 'We lack a sense that our lives are part of some greater effort, that we are connected to one another.'

It did seem at the time to people who – like me – fastened onto the phrase without quite knowing what it meant, that this was a chink of light in the futile debate about the future of politics, low electoral turn-outs and general fatalism about politics and their elected representatives.

The 'politics of meaning' phrase emerged out of detailed research by a group of psychologists and social workers in Oakland, California starting in 1976 – one of whom was Rabbi Michael Lerner. Their motivation was to understand the psychology of blue-collar workers better, and find out in particular why they seemed to be moving politically to the right – dramatically delivering the presidency to Ronald Reagan four years later.

The basis of the research was a new stress clinic in the city, and it quickly became clear that the assumptions of the researchers were going to be proved seriously inadequate – even elitist. They found that the overwhelming reason their clients were under such stress wasn't among the conventional reasons – juggling roles, complex high-pressure lives and low pay. It was because they regarded themselves as wasting their lives on meaningless, pointless work. They tended to have a deep desire for meaningful work for the common good and they blamed themselves for what they saw as their own mediocrity.

These were not the findings Lerner and his team were intended to uncover. The researchers were even told by the National Institute for Mental Health that there were no official categories that could understand the concept of meaninglessness, and even that the findings might lead to a reduction of funding in the future.

But Lerner ran with the idea, arguing in his book *The Politics of Meaning* that we have competing internal voices in our heads – one that dares to hope for meaning, and the other which ridicules the whole idea. 'Most Americans hunger for meaning and purpose in life,' he said 'yet we are caught within a web of cynicism that makes us a question whether there could be any higher purpose besides material self-interest, and looking out for number one.'

When Hillary Clinton used the term in 1993, the media briefly dubbed Lerner as a White House 'guru'. The 'shock jock' Rush Limbaugh devoted a whole chapter of his book *See, I Told You So* to attacking him. But Lerner complained later that Hillary Clinton had actually misused the term. Her language misappropriated the Politics of Meaning, he said – 'instead she hyped the rhetoric of caring'.

It was the same old story: politicians failing to understand that the days when they could simply deliver guidance to a grateful public have long gone. It isn't that caring is somehow unimportant, but that any politics which undermines people's ability to deliver for themselves simply increases their sense of powerlessness. 'Powerlessness corrupts,' says Lerner. 'When people feel themselves powerless to change fundamental aspects of their world, they begin to make accommodation with the "realities" that they actually detest.'

Since his brush with the White House, Lerner has made a name for himself as editor of the radical Jewish magazine *Tikkun* (*tikkun olam*: healing the world) – and has taken these ideas of a new kind of spiritual politics onto a wider international stage, launching the multi-faith Tikkun movement in New York in January 2002. It's a movement with its roots in the left, although not the traditional left – which he regards as just about inclusion and equal opportunities, but which fails to recognize people's hunger for meaning and spiritual vision. And in the weeks after 9/11, when people looked for hope and idealism, Lerner was there to provide it – arguing for a real politics that rejects what he called 'realism', by which he meant lowering your hopes to a 'realistic' level. 'Realism is inherently unrealistic,' he says – urging people to stop voting for the least bad option on the ballot, 'because it never understands the possibility of transformation.'

And at the heart of the new real politics, Lerner urges a 'new definition of productivity, efficiency and reality, a new bottom line – a measuring rod of human beings created in the image of God'.

This kind of talk has certainly made him enemies, especially in the hawkish wing of Zionism that took exception to his campaign to make Isreal withdraw from the West Bank. He was unperturbed by regular emails saying things like 'You sub-human leftists should all be exterminated'. But when a website identified him as one of three of America's 'self-hating Jews' (the others were Woody Allen and Noam Chomsky), condemned him as a traitor and published instructions about how to get to his home in California, he called in the FBI. Real politics isn't a cosy business.

Optimism, and certainly hope, do seem to be requirements for any kind of real politics – though not to the extent of withdrawing into a dreamworld. But Lerner has a reply to people who accuse him of doing just that. He points to the success of the women's movement over the past four decades. 'In a very short period of time they have achieved revolutionary change, and they also began with little groups struggling away,' he said. 'They were also accused of being utopian fools, and they were also asked if they could come up with any examples at all of women's equality in the past 10,000 years – "show me a single place where women share power with men," they were asked – yet look how they've changed the world.'

What's more, the disaster at the World Trade Center has meant that more people have been thinking about the meaning of their lives, and what they really believe in. Despite the rage and the revenge, the 9/11 tragedy caused many thousands of police, firefighters and ordinary people to reveal that people might, after all, have what Lerner calls 'a deep destiny to care for and show love to human beings'.

Moments of disaster are also moments when the hopeful inner voice can break through the cynical one. But then, real politics is paradoxical. Disasters are moments that are 'pregnant with possibility', says Lerner. And it's true that the same thing happened during the London Blitz in 1940, when – despite the terrible loss of life – an inspiring glimpse of a caring, committed and united society emerged. As early as 1944, the writer John Lehmann was describing a myth of healing wholeness, 'between past and present, between one class and another . . . a myth which we in England felt we were about to recapture for one moment of astonishing intensity in 1940, when everything seemed to be falling into place'. It seems strange to us, knowing that most of what was falling at the time was actually high explosive.

Lerner is 'realistic' enough to see that this kind of revolution is not going to be brought about by an old-fashioned hero. 'Social transformation is going to be done by deeply scarred people, not the embodiment of their own highest ideals. Broken, screwed up egotists – because that's all there is on the planet.'

New visions of politics are rare, so we shouldn't dismiss Michael Lerner just because his vision seems hard to achieve. All revolutions are unlikely, and it is pretty clear that the old way of doing politics is going to have to change. People are demanding it, and in democracies, what they want they eventually get. Whether it turns out to be what they actually wanted is another matter: often that has to be fought for again under another name.

And though he comes from a very different kind of world, Lerner's idea of spiritual politics with human beings as the bottom line is reflected in the inspirational speeches of Czech playwright-turned-president Vaclav Havel. Apart from the miraculous transfer of power to majority rule in South Africa, one of the most hopeful examples of real politics in the late twentieth century was Czechoslovakia's so-called Velvet Revolution in 1989. Havel was widely credited with inspiring this peaceful transformation from a communist dictatorship to democracy.

He came to prominence a quarter of a century ago as one of the original three spokesman for Charter 77, an ambitious and humane document that demanded the rights of free expression in the darkest days of totalitarian rule. He spent four years in prison for this, before being released with broken health. During his imprisonment, the only thing he was allowed to write were regular letters to his wife – and only then about personal matters. If he wrote about anything else, the whole letter would be confiscated. And whenever he tried to stray into philosophy, for instance, once using the phrase 'order of being', he was told by the prison governor that 'the only order you can write about is prison order'. At one stage he was even banned from using exclamation marks.

Havel's speeches, often delivered by proxy because he was refused permission to travel outside the country, inspired people all over the world. And decades later, they prove that Havel was ahead of everyone else, tiptoeing towards some idea of how real politics might look. His central idea, right back to his earliest days as a dissident, was the idea of 'living in truth'.

Of course truth is vital when you face a secretive regime, where even language has been perverted into a dull kind of 'doubletalk'. In an essay written during Havel's trial in 1979, the novelist Milan Kundera called this a 'radical demystification of language' – demonstrating with many examples where words have no real meanings, or meanings that are really different from the way the politicians or marketeers are using them. 'Despite its modesty and fastidious legalism, the Charter attacks the very foundation of the regime to the extent that it is precisely a grandiose mystification of language that, without a doubt, has never known its equal in the history of humanity,' he wrote. A great deal of modern politics needs a bit of linguistic 'demystification'.

What makes Havel particularly interesting is that his rhetoric applied equally to West and East. Just as Lerner was preparing his study of blue-collar workers in Oakland, revealing them to be exhausted by their meaninglessness, Havel wrote to the communist leader of Czechoslovakia, Gustav Husak, that 'despair leads to apathy, apathy to conformity, conformity to routine performance'. The communist state prefers 'a cult of right-thinking mediocrity, bedded in hoary national self-satisfaction, guided by the principle that everything must be slick, trivial, pre-digested, and culminating in that false optimism which puts the drabbest interpretation on the dictum that "truth will prevail" '.

What was it about this 'consolidation' that the Czech government was feeling so proud of? Havel asked Husak in his 1975 letter.

> What if we take consolidation to mean something more, a genuine state of mind in society? Supposing we start to inquire after more durable, perhaps subtler and more imponderable, but none the less significant factors. What lies hidden behind all the figures by way of genuine, personal, human experience? Supposing we ask, for example, what has been done for the moral and spiritual revival of society, for the enhancement of the truly human dimensions of life, for the elevation of man to a higher degree of dignity, for his truly free and authentic assertion in this world?

These are questions that both East and West needed to face – though that's not to suggest moral equivalence between East and West during the Cold War. The West may have lied, supported hideous dictators, threatened to destroy the world in a nuclear holocaust, but the systematic destruction of people's lives by the totalitarian governments of the Soviet bloc was in another league of inhumanity. Even so, the basic mistakes both sides were making – muddling human beings and machines – were disturbingly similar, just as Charlene Spretnak discovered in Slovakia in 1993. Havel recognized this in his 1978 essay 'The Power of the Powerless':

> There is no real evidence that western democracy, that is democracy of the traditional parliamentary type, can offer solutions that are any more profound. It may even be said that the more room there is in the western democracies (compared to our world) for the genuine aims of life, the better the crisis is hidden from people and the more deeply do they become immersed in it.

For Havel, the crisis is spiritual, and no organizational plan without God can tackle it. Havel's bottom line is the same as Lerner's. It is human beings – and that seems to me to give us a clue about the meaning of New Realism and where it's going.

It never happened . . .

'The use of nuclear explosives for excavations and mining . . . permanent lunar excavations . . . artificial moons and other methods for lighting large areas at night . . . human hibernation for relatively extensive periods (months to years) . . . commercial extraction of oil from shale . . . effective desalination on a large scale . . . life expectancy extended to 150 years?'

Hermann Kahn and Anthony J. Wiener, *The Year 2000*, 1968

11

Authenticity Wars

'If you are advertising any product, never see the factory in which it was made . . . don't watch the people at work . . . because, you see, when you know the truth about anything, the real inner truth – it is very hard to write the surface fluff which sells it.'

Advertising copywriter Helen Woodward in the 1920s, quoted in Naomi Klein's *No Logo*

'When I retire from Madison Avenue, I am going to start a secret society of masked vigilantes who will travel around the world on silent motorcycles, chopping down posters at the dark of the moon.'

David Ogilvy, founder of the advertising giant Ogilvy & Mather, 1963

When I was growing up, the arrival of my copy of a comic called *TV21* on Thursdays was the high point of my week, and of my friends. I've still got piles of them in my roof. They're probably valuable by now. All the characters were from television programmes – but our television had been inherited from my great grandmother and looked as though it had been constructed by John Logie Baird himself. It certainly didn't get ITV, where most of these programmes resided. I had to get my taste of this futuristic *Thunderbirds* puppetry through the comic instead.

Inspired by the puppets of Gerry Anderson, *TV21* pretended to be published 100 years ahead, in a futuristic world of spaceships, missiles and hover-cars, most of which now exist in some form or another. These were the days of the Apollo missions and great technological hope – the days before the 1970s energy crisis, with scientists on the screen half the time, explaining the way life would be in the future.

But then I am of the generation brought up in the great age of technocracy. Harold Macmillan had made his speech with the famous sentence, 'Let's be frank about it: some of our people have never had it so good' almost exactly nine months before I was born. I'm not suggesting there was any connection, but it was an important moment nonetheless – the moment when the British suddenly found they weren't as poor as they thought. 'You've never had it so good' was also the Democratic Party slogan in the 1952 presidential election, and since then we have all been working out – at different speeds – what 'having it so good' might mean.

For most of that half century, it's meant consumer spending, foreign holidays, labour-saving devices – what Harold Wilson called 'the white heat of technological revolution'. We have been a generation obsessed with technology and its possibilities, our minds packed full of images of Thunderbird 1 and the Mysterons, but we have also witnessed many grand technological visions turning to dust.

We were told that traditional streetscapes were old-fashioned, and that we would soon be living in 'streets in the sky' – but we lived to witness the dramatic demolition of the high-rise flats, some even self-destructing, and a return to streetscapes. We were told that we were going through a pharmacological revolution that would mean we could all be permanently high or permanently sedated, according to taste – yet now a third of all Americans use Chinese or Indian herbs, medicines based on our body's ability to heal itself. We were told that the future of food was in tubes or pill form, but we lived to witness organic food, Nigella Lawson and all that. We were told that we were entering a new age of rational organization, managed by technocrats, only to witness the emergence of an ethical business sector that makes a nonsense of narrow economic rationality. Not to mention nuclear energy, supersonic air travel or Mars landings. I believe the period ahead will be one where the technological dream finally assumes its proper place.

Some technological dreams came true, of course. But I was six years old when the Rand Corporation predicted automated air traffic control by 1974, and teaching machines in general use and nuclear-propelled aircraft by 1975. I missed the last tram from British cities but I've witnessed their revival, together with a range of other things we were told had gone for good: real bricks, real buildings made of wood, real ice cream.

More recently, we have been told over and over again that globalization and virtualization are inevitable glimpses of the future – and maybe they are, but only part of it. The other meaning of the famous photo of the rabbi putting his mobile phone up to the Wailing Wall in Jerusalem, so that his New York relatives can pray at it – the most surprising recent image of globalization – is the survival of traditional ways of thinking.

At the same time, we have also seen the emergence of a growing articulate minority of the population who are rejecting the idea that progress means a fake, second-rate world and are demanding real human contact, real experience and real connection. They don't *just* want authenticity – this is no puritanical return: they enjoy drinking too much, they want fast food when it's convenient, and they certainly want to use the internet. But they don't want that to be their only choice. They want something authentic to go back to.

Their demand for reality has come partly in response to the failure of these technocratic dreams, but also partly because some of them have been so successful – the rise of personal computers, fast food and food additives, for example – that they worry about their grip on reality. They are the living embodiment of Robert Nozick's prediction: 'In a virtual world, we'll be longing for reality even more.'

The demand for authenticity is inevitable, and probably unstoppable, but it is also extremely dangerous. Unmet demands for something 'real' are emerging in some very scary forms – in fundamentalist interpretations of the Bible and the Koran, in bizarre new kinds of nationalism and authoritarianism, in brutal backlashes against women, asylum-seekers or outsiders. We have already seen how this yearning for some kind of connection, some kind of faith, can turn someone like Richard Reid – to name one of many – into a suicide bomber.

But authenticity is bigger than its own lunatic fringe. These ideas are not representative of the New Realists, who want to learn from the past, but not to go back there. Nor are fervent nationalism or fundamentalism always very authentic either – they sometimes turn out to be based on fictions: national boundaries with shallow historical roots, or strange intolerant interpretations of the Bible that reject two thousand years of theology. Either way, it's a fake authenticity if people are frustrated in their demand for the real stuff.

But most important of all, the demand is never static. New Realists are constantly dissatisfied with the whiffs of authenticity they're offered and want to move on to something less contradictory. They start by embracing the exotic new foods flown from around the world onto supermarket shelves, but the contradictions nag away at them and then they want their food organic or locally-grown too. They start by demanding that business gives something charitable back to society, but the contradictions nag away again, and soon want their money invested ethically and corporations to embrace a broader bottom line.

All too soon, the virtual real experience of watching *Big Brother* or *Changing Rooms* isn't enough and they wonder whether television can provide them with authenticity at all. New Realists are on a conveyor belt: that's why the mega-retailers who say that the authenticity revolution in food has gone as far as it's going are wrong – it's only just begun.

That is going to be hard for business, but it is no reason to deny that the process is happening. Nor does everyone want it. Not everyone agrees on the package of attributes – rooted, human, ethical – but enough people do to drag the world in their direction if they shout loudly enough.

In the meantime, the stage is set for conflict between these different demands, as the whole question of what is real becomes increasingly central to marketing, culture, politics and religion. Authenticity is fighting it out with the virtual real, fake real, faux faux and the downright fraudulent. The argument is developing already between global distributors and fresh, local food. Or between virtual customer service systems and real customers. Or between brand marketeers and those who want to drag them down – with Adbuster's culture-jammers already out there subverting hoardings, putting brochures in airline pockets advertising 'Deportation Class seating', or preparing fake company videos to prepare children to work in fast-food outlets.

You can already see the battle emerging in the argument over cyborgs, when the DigitalAngel company – selling implanted microchips to keep track of children – was slammed by US TV networks and Christian groups, forcing them to drop their predictions of $80 billion revenue. Or whether PlayStation can – as

NASA researchers claim – provide hyperactive kids with more 'optimal brainwave patterns'. You can see it in the way the proponents of global and virtual are beginning to take up the cudgels against the proponents of local and real, pouring scorn on each other's compromises – both failing to see how their lives are wrapped up in the trappings of the opposite side.

You can see the same arguments developing in the subtle differences between food and fabric technologists – for instance, the inventors of new fabrics that make you slim while you wear them – and defenders of traditional food and clothing. Or between the proponents of better-than-real technology and community economists who want to rebuild local supply – Mars, for example, has patented cocoa beans that tackle anything from hypertension to cancer, but can they provide growers with sustainable livelihoods? Or between fast-food outlets and communities, like Ocean Beach, California, which has fought off chainstores since the 1970s. These debates are already taking place on a symbolic level between real and virtual.

And in the end the sharpest conflict, and certainly the most subtle, is for the hearts and minds of young people now that the power of advertising is waning. Advert after advert urges them to rebel, to be themselves, to fight back by buying the advertised product, while the advertisers keep their fingers tightly crossed that they won't notice the contradiction.

Global corporations are going to such extreme lengths to defend the reputations of their brands because they really believe all the hype that brands are the new authenticity. The trouble is, because brands are not in the least authentic, they are actually extremely fragile. They can disappear before your very eyes like Enron or Worldcom.

More evidence of the struggle between real and unreal is the public obsession with fakeness. Hollywood seems to have picked up the zeitgeist enough to align itself firmly with the New Realists with films like *The Matrix* and *The Truman Show*, both of which are about people breaking out of virtual worlds. Even back in 1985, *Rocky IV* was spun as a conflict between fake and authentic. Sylvester Stallone was shown training for his latest boxing challenge in all-American authenticity, running in the snow, lifting carts on farms – while his robotic Soviet opponent worked out in a high-tech gym surrounded by scientists, wires and lethal-looking electronic devices. Those were the days before we realized the USSR couldn't afford much in the way of lethal-looking electronics.

But a different kind of defence is going on in the corporate world, with all the plotting and espionage of the Great Game – a term that originally referred to the subtle play and counterplay of British and Russian agents in the hills of Afghanistan at the end of the nineteenth century. Some are taking this to extreme lengths – like the twenty-year battle fought by McDonald's against an unfortunate man called Ronald McDonald who had been running the McDonald's Family Restaurant in Illinois since 1956. They have been defending their brand with similar battles against McAllan's sausages in Denmark and the McCoffee shop in San Francisco. At the same time, some electronics giants are making secret contacts with environmental groups, afraid that they may be forced to take responsibility for the disposal of toxic substances in their machines.

Other big companies, such as Coca-Cola, are employing 'internet police' to surf the web and stop people misusing their logo. 'Coke is about optimism and authenticity. It is never cynical or funky or moody,' wrote Steve Heyer, an adviser to the Coke chief executive, responding to a German advert which showed young people rubbing themselves erotically with Coke bottles. Too much postmodern irony can destroy a brand.

Some, like Gap and Nike, have been running intelligence operations on campuses to keep up to date with what their opponents are saying about them – and the stakes are high. When the student Jonah Peretti famously tried to get his Nike sneakers custom made with the word 'sweatshop' on them, the email exchange was forwarded to millions of people around the world. Some use a battery of fake names to run whispering campaigns on the internet in favour of GM foods, or polluting waterways or heavy forestry. Or, according to an investigation into the email campaign against Berkeley University researchers who had published a paper on GM contamination in Mexico, to denigrate their opponents.

These hidden battles for hearts and minds lead down some bizarre alleyways. It wasn't just Nike's offer of $25,000 to consumer champion Ralph Nader to appear in one of their ads, holding a pair of sneakers and complaining about 'another shameless attempt by Nike to sell shoes'. That's a complicated enough strategy: there are more subtle twists.

In 2001, a series of billboards appeared around Australia with the slogan: 'The most offensive boots we've ever made. 100% slave labour', which purported to be from an organization called Fans for Fairer Football – which in the end, it turned out to be Nike's own marketing department. The idea – it seems – was to try and unlock the cynicism of sneaker-buyers by overplaying the activists' hand, so that it became cool to dismiss the sweatshop accusation, so that activists would become a laughing stock to the world-weary young. Similar thinking may have been behind a recent Pot Noodle campaign to 'Save your local take-away'.

It is pretty extraordinary that a modern brand should make such accusations against itself – all to eke out just enough cynicism to make a few more sales, without manipulating it so that people care *too* much. In the battle for fake authenticity, postmodern knowingness can be an ally. But it's a Faustian bargain: in the end it breaks down belief.

The sweatshop campaign is a major symptom of New Realism, because, as Naomi Klein puts it, it's a 'head-on collision between image and reality'. When the US TV presenter Kathie Lee Gifford wept having been confronted on air with the fact that her named-brand clothes were being made by child labourers in Honduras, fake and authentic were face to face, and authentic won. It does win, in such situations.

That's why the key media story these days is hypocrisy. You can devastate great swathes of rainforest and newspapers and television alike ignore you, but if you make public commitments to avoid sweatshops and it transpires that you have broken your own codes, then all hell breaks loose. Consistency counts these days.

So when you hear experts telling you, as the advertising agency Young & Rubicam said in 2001, that 'brands are the new religion' – or that they 'spread meaning and purpose in life' with all the passion of the early Christians and Muslims – don't believe them. The design consultancy Fitch backs the idea by saying that more people visit Ikea on Sundays than go to church, that 12,000 people have been married at Disney World and goodness knows how many are now buried in Harley-Davidson branded coffins. But that really isn't the same thing – whoever got martyred for McDonald's, after all? But even if it were true, that mighty disappointment would fuel the demand for authenticity all the more.

One of the most bizarre symptoms of our growing obsession with authenticity was the *Titanic*-mania that swept the world after the success of the film. I have a brochure that offers an authentic floor tile from the Smoking Room of the *Titanic* – though not so authentic that it come from the seabed. I can buy an 'authentic' officer's cap from the *Titanic* and an authentic piece of the gantry used to construct liners in the same shipyard in Belfast where *Titanic* was made. To add to the sense of authenticity, the souvenirs are 'officially licensed' by the original shipbuilders, Harland & Wolff. And taking this kind of stuff to extreme lengths, two South African companies were reported to be building a $600 million replica of the doomed liner. Though this version had extra lifeboats hidden behind a screen (even authenticity has its limits).

Needless to say, the prospect of living in a world dominated by New Realists is a potential nightmare for business. It's increasingly difficult to palm them off with anything pretending to be real. Even virtual real solutions may only satisfy them for a while. And the more you encourage scepticism among the young, the more you urge them to throw off the shackles of puritanism and authority, the more they will end up turning that disillusion against you.

It is doubly difficult given that many people – probably even the majority – won't respond to the language of authenticity. One volume housebuilder in the 1980s was puzzled by why customers were snapping up identikit homes made out of the equivalent of ticky-tacky at twice the speed that they bought the individually designed ones – with real stone facing and pitch roofs. But their research showed that people perceived the fake ones as easier to buy and sell. To some people, authenticity still looks difficult and exclusive. The constant growth of the already massive skincare market, up 2 per cent in five years in the UK, is enough to prove there will still be money in artificial.

But subdividing the market to focus on those most responsive to your message, using new TV technology like TiVo and Replay, may just explode in your face. 'The formula for a field-hockey channel that sells only field-hockey equipment or a haemorrhoid that sells only haemorrhoid treatments is endlessly reproducible,' writes the business writer Michael Lewis. Maybe so, but many New Realists would rather expire on the spot than be categorized in this way, and if they ever suspect they are being categorized, they wreak a terrible revenge.

That's the problem for business. What people want they tend to get, but if they *do* succeed in getting it, the whole structure of how we organize business is going to have to change. And if they don't get it – either from business or politics – the chances are that the kind of revolt against globalization emerging in France is going to spread, and more New Realists may find themselves tempted by fake real in the shape of vicious and intolerant movements like Jean-Marie Le Pen's. It may be too late already.

In the meantime, business will have to work out how to deal with the growing clamour from the prophets of authenticity, some of them in unlikely guises like the American sociologist George Ritzer, coiner of the phrase 'McDonaldization' – like Dylan Thomas urging people to 'rage against the dying of the light'. Never go to stadiums with artificial grass, he said. And if you do go to McDonald's, subvert it by getting to know the staff and sitting around reading newspapers. 'Above all, people should avoid the routine and systematic use of McDonaldized systems. To avoid the iron cage, they must seek out non-rationalized alternatives wherever possible.'

So what can you do, as a business? Well, here are twenty guidelines for coping with the Age of Authenticity.

1: Put authenticity on your own corporate agenda

That means deconstructing the idea a little, and working out what it might mean for your company – in terms of ethics, honesty, sustainability, simplicity and rootedness. It means being aware that an increasing minority of your customers are looking for something with an emotional experience at its core – even something as simple as buying a dozen eggs. But bear in mind as well – and this is the bit the business manuals don't tell you – that the experience has to be rooted in something truthful and human. Otherwise it won't be recognized as a real experience at all. Look at the success of Lonely Planet and the Rough Guide series: successful business ideas will increasingly be those that enable people to create their own authentic experiences.

2: Make it personal

There's no doubt that there is a demand for products that are able to speak to people personally, and find new ways of fulfilling themselves personally too. The staggering success of Oprah Winfrey's magazine for women aged between twenty-five and forty-nine – these are not artificially segmented markets for people with haemorrhoids – is powerful evidence of this. *Oprah* Magazine, subtitled 'a personal growth guide', isn't filled with painfully thin models or shaming lists of what's fashionable and what's not, and it built a circulation of 2.5 million in its first twelve months. A third of those who bought the first edition subscribed on the spot. A slew of similar magazines followed, ranging from *Real Simple* in the USA to *Sotomoto* in Japan.

3: Maximize human contact

'Simple systems-based advice will be comparatively cheap; person-to-person advice will be comparatively expensive,' writes Robert Bruce, accountancy editor of *The Times*. This means that we have to find other ways to provide people with human faces – including new kinds of reciprocal systems like time banks. It's hard in these days of downsizing, where every indicator of corporate value seems to demand that you shed staff – but somehow you have to give people face-to-face contact. Not just between staff and customers, professionals and clients, but between managers and employees, and employees together. Human contact is the driving force of authenticity. The more you reduce things to internet connections or automated systems, the further you get away from what's real.

4: Split up the organization

The kind of face-to-face service that the New Realists are demanding can only be provided by organizations on a smaller scale, and controlled locally. The solution isn't hierarchies, which suppress imagination and innovation and feel impersonal and mechanical – because they are. We know that from bitter experience. Yet because governments and managers believe they can have more control through hierarchies – or through virtual hierarchies managed by batteries of numerical targets – these lessons are not put in place. The solution is networking between smaller organizations, which can provide the variety of service without the intractability. You have to be big but appear small to the customer, as the Henley Centre for Forecasting advised companies – but these demands really are contradictory. You simply have to be small.

5: Be yourself

This doesn't just mean being true to yourself in your dealings with those around you – that's hard enough. Your company also has to be itself, and that means being wise enough to track down the lies you tell each other about the company, facing up to them, and being honest about where you're failing. Consumers are quite sophisticated enough these days to sniff out a whiff of pretence from thousands of miles away – and it will always be more obvious to them than it is to you. The slightest doubt in the back of the mind of the CEO is like a megaphone in the mass media.

6: Beware of contradictions

It's easy to use the symbolic language of authenticity. We see it everywhere these days – 'real' frothing coffee machines at Starbucks or 'real' emotion on *Survivor*. But if there are contradictions between what looks authentic and the truth behind it, if it is actually based on an identikit formula from one side of the world to another, or if it's actually based on slave labour in some little-known Asian hellhole, then it looks fraudulent. And as people demand consistency and honesty in their search for the real, they are liable to turn against you.

7: Provide customers with a choice

The New Realists are not puritans, dedicated to removing anything in the least bit phoney from their lives. They like fast food and the internet sometimes: they just don't want that to be the only option – and they hate being lied to. They also appreciate authentic services as part of their existing service. Far from dividing into separate warring factions, the conventional and the complementary health sectors – for example – are actually coming together. Homeopathy, osteopathy, herbalism and acupuncture are increasingly available through conventional doctors' practices. That's the future in other sectors too.

8: Create real places

Shops, factories and offices can make an enormous difference to the places around them. Soulless concrete blocks, with nothing to look at for people at street level, can destroy a place – just as places with life, bustle and vigour, that enhance the environment, can create a place when there was just a desert before. But they have to feel permanent. Carlo Petrini's Slow Food movement has given birth to a Slow Cities campaign. Money tends to follow life, not the other way round, so this idea is likely to spread.

9: Provide people with space to be themselves

If you whittle experiences down to the lowest common denominator – whether the experiences of staff at work or of people interacting with your organization – you impoverish them. Sometimes counteracting this is going to mean simply letting them create their own options, fit into categories you've never imagined, and break out of definitions – blurring clients, customers, staff and volunteers in whole new ways. Sometimes it just means treating people with dignity, taking customer service beyond the perfunctory 'have a nice day'.

10: Encourage social innovation

Technological innovation is to some extent still driving the way we live. But the real challenges are social – not so much how we can save time by using fancy new machines, but how we can work in different patterns; how we can build a loyal customer base; how we can get on better together; be more creative; get ideas from customers; bring sworn enemies together in a new point of view. The real human challenges are about peace and wealth. Any company can use innovative technology, but different companies tend to look very much the same unless they also come up with new ideas that can help people live happier lives, and maybe create technology to support that.

11: Tell stories

This sounds a little homespun, but the truth is that people's distrust of media manipulation – certainly the manipulation of symbols on advertisements – will soon undermine any long-term messages you want to get across. If your products are rooted in specific geographical communities, if your company is rooted in unusually powerful principles or ethical standards, then there are stories you can tell about them. And stories can get across complex truths in a memorable way better than almost anything else. People want to hear about real people living real lives in real places. And if you would prefer the stories behind your products not to be told, because they make you feel uncomfortable, that's a sign you need to think about New Realism a little harder.

12: Experiment with new kinds of money

The advent of the internet means that almost anything can be abstracted, turned into electronic pulses and exchanged over the internet as if it was money – whether e-gold.com, permits to burn carbon, or the greenness of green electricity. That sounds unreal, but then money never was very real – it represents wealth rather than being the wealth itself. The arrival of local currencies in particular provides the chance for communities to keep money, ideas, resources and skills circulating locally. The highly innovative printed currency, Ithaca *hours* in upstate New York, has had an enormous impact on local habits – underpinning the local agricultural economy and putting a premium on healthy food. The Japanese Slow Food magazine *Sotomoto* calls it 'slow money', because it stays put. Real money recognizes and gives value to local assets we think are important – real shops or real views. It doesn't just recognize what Wall Street wants.

13: Don't dispense with people's dreams

New Realism has little in common with a puritanical commitment to rooting out dreams and imagination – quite the reverse. People's dreams have become so impoverished because they are so packaged. But they still need them, as the Chilean writer Ariel Dorfman discovered after he co-wrote a diatribe against Disney called *How to Read Donald Duck*: 'Don't take my dreams away from me,' one slum dweller pleaded. The challenge is to provide people with stories that touch real human dilemmas and emotions – real mythic stories that satisfy human needs.

14: Respect people's need for continuity

They need change as well, of course, but the present nostalgia wave is a reminder that people desperately need some things to stay the same. It helps them navigate through the modern world, and we shouldn't be berating them for clinging to the past – as architects and planners did during the 1960s and 70s when communities objected to the disappearance of their entire streetscapes. The passionate reaction from the public against New Coke in 1985 was among the first glimmerings of New Realism.

15: Don't look back

This may seem to contradict the last point. But there need not be any problem about simultaneously protecting what we have, yet refraining from looking back too dangerously to a golden age that never existed. We need to make our cities human and good to live in, instead of the choking rubbish-strewn places they have become. That can't mean going back to the past when they were often dirty, diseased and crime-ridden. Real cities mean Slow Cities, electric buses and sweet-smelling plants in gardens – as well as the bright lights of virtual life. And we don't get there by going backwards.

16: Commit to culture

As art and music are slowly being removed from curricula on both sides of the Atlantic, it's time to remember the crucial role the arts play in New Realism – and how integral they are to our economy. In the UK, music now outstrips nearly all manufacturing industries in earning power. The enormous popularity of galleries like the Tate Modern is a sign that people regard high culture as real, and they want to be surrounded by it. When the BBC European Service broadcast to occupied Europe during the Second World War, they chose music and poetry because it was more real, answered a more basic need than propaganda ever could. It's the same today.

17: Commit to real news

Telling real from fake real depends to some extent on accurate news, and I write this at a time when television news organizations are failing to provide it. A succession of respected BBC reporters have queued up to condemn current news values as patronizing: Martin Bell was goaded into print when a threatened footballer's strike was chosen for coverage over the fall of a critical town in Afghanistan. 'ITN set the trend by its decision, early in the 1990s, to promote an agenda of crime, celebrity and miracle cures – and to downgrade foreign news to a couple of slots a week on Tuesdays and Thursdays,' he said. But the real problem is the way the US model of TV has been designed to deliver audiences to advertisers rather than programming to audiences – even sometimes tailoring the news to suit the advertisers. It's the same with newspapers. Real local newspapers are rooted in their communities: they are not knitted together in central offices miles away by journalists who never leave the office.

18: Respect the sophistication of consumers

Modern audiences are enormously sophisticated in their ability to understand a range of messages and references. They know they are being taken for a ride by advertisers, and they take revenge for it. And when advertising is effective, they don't see themselves as taken in either – they just choose to accept the message. Not only do the public hate spin, they are also now largely unspinnable – certainly consistently. Unfortunately, government advisers have been slow to realize that. Gladstone was able to keep audiences at public meetings spellbound for two hours at a time, in the drizzle, because – according to Roy Jenkins – he talked 'up' to them and increased their self-esteem.

19: Whatever you may have been told, do sweat the small stuff

Little things make a difference. This isn't just about butterflies flapping and weather patterns in China, it's simply day-to-day reality. The vital importance to people's lives of making the walk to the shops feel a little safer, the sense you get from your doctor that you can tackle your problems yourself, a moment with your local headmaster – even the litter in your street – all may fly below the radar of the technocrats. But if you want to make a difference to real life, it's the little things that matter – in people's experience of companies or public services. It is becoming increasingly apparent that big plans at national level don't work – however much money you may pour into the National Health Service. If you want to make a difference you have to deal directly with real people in real places.

20: Recognize that people have a spiritual side that needs feeding

Most people can't bear to devote their lives to companies whose only purpose is to make a profit. They need a sense of higher purpose. And even then, they have creative and spiritual needs that most companies wouldn't have dreamed of in the old world. Meeting these employees' needs is risky. Finding ways that employees can become the people they want to be is a dangerous business – they may leave. But if they stay, their ability to come up with solutions, work loyally and with enthusiasm will be out of all proportion to what it was before. Nobody wants to work for a machine. Social scientists have been predicting the demise of religion for three centuries now, but the truth is that people need a sense of something beyond them.

The political scientist Benjamin Barber provided the accepted interpretation of our times in his 1995 book *Jihad versus McWorld*. And although Barber described both as threats to democracy, since the collapse of the World Trade Center people tend to forget that, and just remember the bogeyman of nationalist fundamentalism summed up in the word 'jihad'. 'Jihad may be the last deep sigh before the eternal yawn of McWorld,' he wrote.

But that's not the choice before us. Barber was right that both ends of his spectrum are pretty unpalatable: I don't want to live in a world run by vindictive fundamentalists, but I also don't want my life reduced to small automated chunks where image and reality have blurred into one. Few would embrace either, but they are part of a much wider struggle and one that involves us closely every day. 'The majority of our political analysts have a bipolar vision of the world,' says Marc Luyckx of the

European Commission's Forward Studies Unit. 'They consider the existence of only two visions of the world, a good one and a bad one. The good one is the "modern" one. To be modern is to accept the rule of Western law and the superiority of rational and linear thinking over intuition, poetry or spirituality.'

The rise of the New Realists is part of a much more fundamental clash that is beginning to emerge between opposing world views, one that you might characterize as being between modernism and spirituality. Those are the alternatives and Jihad and McWorld are caricatures of them. Put like that, nobody is going to want to cluster round McWorld for fear of its alternative. This isn't so much a clash between atheism and religion as a battle between what the alternative economist James Robertson, Harold Macmillan's former speechwriter, described in the 1970s as HE versus SHE ('hyper-expansion' versus 'sane, humane and ecological').

In the blue corner we have the moderns and postmoderns, thrilled by technological advance and extrapolating it as the key driver of humanity's future. They are excited by the possibilities of understanding all branches of human knowledge in terms of information. For the moderns, human intelligence is just a complex manipulation of information, and genetic code just a version of digital code. They are sophisticated people, who understand the layers of meaning behind any human conversation or media broadcast, and the layers of cultural differences that make meaningful communication practically impossible. They can't pin down any fundamental difference between real and virtual, between authentic and fake. And thus, authenticity for them is an almost meaningless term – certainly a relative term (as in 'Is this authentic artificial intelligence?').

For the spirituals and creatives in the red corner, the next stage of human evolution isn't primarily technological – it's rather to do with the human mind and its limitless potential. Suspicious of the calamities that technology seems constantly on the verge of visiting on the planet, they are nostalgic for the mythical time when people interacted successfully in communities, and with the environment – believing that the natural world holds within it its own kind of wisdom. Uncomfortable about the attempt to redefine human beings as machines, they feel strongly that the real problems of hunger and disease are unlikely to be solved by technology alone – let alone by GM food or the Human Genome Project.

This is the great divide that will shape the next century, between those who want to entrust humanity to technology alone and those who want to embrace something inside people and planet that takes us beyond ourselves. This is an old struggle – between classical and romantic, between Aristotle and Plato – but it is bursting out again in a new definition of authenticity, and between two different interpretations of human potential.

McWorld is technology taken to an extreme, just as Jihad is religion taken to an extreme. The real division is between those who think the twenty-first century is going to be like the twentieth, except more so, and those who want to push forward into a new frontier of the human spirit. Or between those who believe that a 'new post-human history will begin', in Francis Fukuyama's phrase, and those who believe that humanity is actually the new yardstick for success.

And behind that, it's a battle for the meaning of progress – the word that bamboozled the twentieth century. 'You can't stand in the way of progress,' said the technocrats, even though high-rise flats, nuclear weapons and poison gas didn't look much like progress when you got too close to them. For the New Realists, 'progress' is something that goes beyond just 'new' – and it's an idea that badly needs reclaiming. Is it 'real progress' or is it just more second-rate rubbish that will impoverish more people than it enriches?

Neither side is anti-technology. It's true that the creatives and New Realists fear that too great a focus on technology has made us myopic. But I don't believe the creative side are Unabombers. They merely want to keep technology in its proper place. They believe that, just as the internet emerged out of the California counter-culture of the 1970s, so the next counter-culture is going to be of the mind.

Moderns believe that the twentieth century was a period of unprecedented change – and if you just look at the technology that's probably true. But in another sense, we have just closed the door on a century where remarkably little real progress was made. In my own city of London in 1900, it's true that only 100,000 people had telephones. But still we have the same street names, use many of the same corridors of the same buildings, we live at the same addresses, work similar hours, commute similar journeys as they did a century ago. Even the bus routes have the same numbers. The 1900 FA Cup Final took place in Crystal Palace where I live and attracted a crowd of 100,000 – in 2001 it took place in Cardiff. Big deal.

Looking at the gigantic changes in the eighteenth century – the shift from a rural agricultural economy to an urban industrial one – there's really no comparison. But we still imagine, just like the Victorians, that our technology is something quite unprecedented and will mean enormous changes in the way people live.

I wouldn't be writing this book if I didn't have considerable sympathy with the spiritual, but I was born at the end of the 1950s – so it's hard to escape the mechanistic thinking associated with modernism. But then again this clash of world views isn't necessarily something that goes on between two opposing camps. For one thing, as the drive towards authenticity gets played out, it's going to fracture. Does authenticity mean ethical, or does it mean traditional, or does it mean personal? Or sustainable, or genuinely emotional, or unadulterated, or fulfilling? Does it mean a Catholic emphasis on deeper truth or a Protestant suspicion of empty ritual? In practice it will mean all those things and more, but these are different interpretations, and some conflict. This is especially so for business, which is faced increasingly with an audience only too happy to leap on perceived hypocrisy and failure to keep to the spirit of authenticity.

For another thing, it's a battle going on inside us at the same time. Most of us have a foot in both camps, and sometimes lean in different directions at different stages in our lives – or even different moods. And if you think that's crazy, think of all those Canadian advertising executives who work on campaigns in the daylight – whilst in the dark they work for *Adbusters*.

Our demand for authenticity is partly a response to living in a fake, constructed world, to being manipulated over the airwaves at every moment of the day, to the way virtual communication is cutting out human contact. It is partly a simple reaction against modernity. But it is also something else: it's a demand for a different kind of life in the century ahead when, for the first time since the industrial revolution, questions about how we are intended to live – and how we should live – become central again.

Somewhere in the back streets of Rotterdam in 1466, a boy was born with no surname – the illegitimate offspring of a priest – who was to grow up to be the central pillar of a new intellectual movement devoted to learning, truth and honesty. For nearly forty years, Desiderius Erasmus wandered around Europe as a tutor and lecturer, seeking out old manuscripts of the classics, campaigning against corruption by princes and prelates alike.

Erasmus's *In Praise of Folly* was a sarcastic diatribe about the way the rulers of Medieval Europe behaved. It went through seven editions in a few months. But, most important of all, he was the best-known 'humanist' of his day – the central figure of an enormously influential movement that underpinned the Renaissance and gave birth to some of the greatest paintings and sculptures in history.

Humanism meant something different then. It didn't imply the atheism it does today – in fact Erasmus was a priest himself, with a papal dispensation to work as a scholar. Renaissance humanism was a determination to discover the original wisdom of the ancient world – going back to what they saw as the pure source of truth, pulling together all knowledge into one whole. It was a revolution in learning and civilization just as artists like Michelangelo and Leonardo da Vinci were engaged in a parallel quest – to make mankind and the human form the measure of all things. Their choice was tolerance, understanding, kindness and peace, in the face of the political insanity that threatened to overwhelm Europe.

The Renaissance shifted God from the centre of the universe and put mankind there instead. The vision of the dignified human form is still there to see in Michelangelo's David or his ceiling in the Sistine Chapel. But it unravelled when Erasmus' contemporary Nicolaus Copernicus decided – freed from his fear of retribution by his rapidly approaching death – to publish the discovery that man wasn't at the centre of the universe after all.

What does all this have to do with authenticity? It's that the same idea – of humanity as a measure of reality – turns up again and again throughout this book and the search for authenticity.

Erasmus Prize winner Vaclav Havel – for whom Erasmus has been a key inspiration for 'living in truth' – urged us to use a deeper understanding of ourselves as the basis of reality. 'The more thoroughly all our organs and their functions, their internal structure, and the biochemical reactions that take place within them are described, the more we seem to fail to grasp the spirit, purpose, and meaning of the system that they create together and that we experience as our unique "self",' he said in his Independence Hall speech in 1994.

There was Rabbi Michael Lerner talking about humanity being the essence of the 'new bottom line' by which all endeavours should be judged. There was Jaron Lanier using human contact as the measure of whether artificial intelligence was beneficial or malign, or Robert McKee using human reality as the measure of whether a Hollywood story would hold our attention.

We seem on the threshold of a new kind of humanism, that again judges the authenticity of things and ideas by whether or not they are human-scale, or enhance direct contact between humans, or are made by fallible humans for fallible humans – rather than trying to squeeze us into whatever shape is most convenient for the factory, machine or computer. It's a humanism that respects irregularities because they are a sign of human manufacture, and respects the energy that comes from artefacts made by hand.

The highest wisdom is to know yourself, said Erasmus. For new humanists and old, that's the key – to go beyond virtual systems that can't recreate the complexity of the human spirit. 'Abandon then those collections of formulae and calculations, slovenly and muddy,' he wrote in his *Method of True Theology*. He might just as well have written it today.

It's a new attitude that's discernible behind all this demand for authenticity – a new way of approaching business or culture or politics that's rooted in a very old way – one that is tolerant of human failings. This isn't a humanism that puts mankind on a pedestal that people can never live up to, or which believes that humanity's shining light is so thrilling that no other species on the planet counts. It sees people as rooted in tradition and community and nature, as part of our humanity. That's the great truth at the heart of New Realism.

So authenticity may mean natural or beautiful, it may mean rooted geographically or morally, but behind all that it means human. It means that the full complexity of people is recognized, that their need for human contact, their uniqueness and individuality are recognized too. And that seems to me to be an exciting prospect, not least because the old medieval humanism led to an explosion of art and understanding that levered civilization out of medieval brutality. We need a similar Renaissance today.

It never happened

'Religious believers are likely to be found only in small sects, huddled together to resist a worldwide secular culture.'

Peter Berger, *New York Times*, 1968

12

The New Renaissance

'I think there are good reasons for suggesting that the modern age has ended. Today, many things indicate that we are going through a transitional period, when it seems that something is on the way out and something else is painfully being born. It is as if something were crumbling, decaying, and exhausting itself, while something else, still indistinct, were arising from the rubble.'

Vaclav Havel, speech in Independence Hall, Philadelphia, 1994

'I am not yet born; O fill me
With strength against those who would freeze my humanity,
Would dragoon me into a lethal automaton.'

Louis MacNeice, 'Prayer Before Birth', 1944

When Erasmus was fifty-six, and at the height of his fame, the great Japanese Tea Master Sen no Rikyu was born – many thousands of miles away in a country the humanist had barely dreamed about. When his teacher told Sen no Rikyu to tidy the garden as a test before accepting him as a pupil, he worked until it was absolutely perfect. Then before finishing he had another look, and thought again. Then he shook the cherry tree so that a few flowers fell on the ground, and by doing so passed the test.

Rikyu's final touch with the tree was the essence of the concept of which he became the leading advocate: known for the past five centuries as *wabi-sabi*. It emerged originally as a reaction against lavish ornamentation in sixteenth-century Japan, but it has survived there as an elusive concept and is now being embraced for much the same reason in modern California.

The Tea Ceremony that he did so much to develop also remains an integral part of Japanese culture. There is even going to be a traditional tea-ceremony room in the Japanese section of the International Space Station currently being built in space. And it contains within it something of the same simplicity: *wabi* means the beauty of simple things. *Sabi* is the beauty of things that are worn by their use over time. The combination comes very close to the definition of authenticity as understood by the New Realists. It means natural, human and decaying. It means the power of overlooked details. It means the bitter-sweet awareness of the briefness of life. It means unprocessed food and frayed cuffs.

I started this book in Japan, so it makes sense to go back there at the end – though if you wandered down today's average neon-lit Tokyo shopping street, you don't find much sign of *wabi-sabi*. Japanese youth culture, especially, has developed an energetic virtual cartoon culture, steeped in technology. Everyone under twenty seems to be clutching small silver devices like the ones used by Captain Kirk to beam himself up to the *Starship Enterprise*. Every river or stream seems to have rational concrete walls. Not forgetting, of course, that fatal attraction for theme parks like Ocean Dome.

The Japanese have become amazingly adept at assimilating other cultures, and at tearing down and rapidly rebuilding whole stretches of cities. This is the nation where Tokyo's lowest paid rent small boxes – more like filing cabinets – in which to live, and where married couples slope off to Love Hotels, rented by the hour, to snatch a few moments away from the kids. It doesn't seem exactly real.

But it's more complicated than that. For one thing the Japanese are subject to the same marketing pressures as everyone else. The most extreme I saw was on a Tokyo subway advert for Virginia Slims cigarettes, with the slogan 'Be You'. This is the modern call to self-determination adopted by advertising everywhere over the past decade. But in this case, not only was the slogan in English, but the two girls in the picture were obviously American. How should the locals read that kind of complex demand? Be you, but also be us?

For another, the *wabi-sabi* tradition and the breathtaking simplicity of traditional Japanese homes – open spaces divided by sliding paper walls – have probably enabled them to adopt virtual living more easily than those of us who are used to cluttered permanent homes made of bricks.

Even so, modern Japanese consumers have clung tightly to their commitment to real food. It has to be pure and it has to be grown somewhere specific for it to be trustworthy. The Japanese agriculture minister recently announced his strong interest in Petrini's Slow Food campaign. They have stepped back from the high-pressure schooling by numbers that Western nations believe somehow makes education 'real', and are shortening the school week, and emphasizing creativity and respect for individual differences. And there is evidence that many Japanese people have been rearranging their priorities, aware of the negative impact rapid economic growth has had on what's really important. They also seem now to be turning their backs on all those theme parks, except for Disneyland Tokyo and the highly successful Universal Studios (not so real that they actually make films there).

The economy still hasn't recovered from the bizarre flights

of fantasy in the 1980s, when the price of Tokyo land inflated itself to such heights that it could provide collateral to fund the massive worldwide buying spree by Japanese business. The result has been deflation and a dangerous debt carried by the Japanese banking system, which continues to threaten world financial stability.

The conventional explanation for the failure of Japanese consumers to spend their way out of their recession is fear of the future. I heard a range of other explanations when I was there – anything from not wanting to use credit to not wanting to spend conspicuously when others might be out of work. But perhaps they are also able to live without lavish spending because of the continuing *wabi-sabi* tradition that still survives in Japanese culture.

I'm not suggesting somehow that *wabi-sabi* actually *prevents* them from going out and buying shiny new goods. That's clearly not the case, just that they can live without them better. But if that's true, it emphasizes the economic challenge that New Realism brings with it. The engine which has driven Western economics since the start of mass production may not be reliable any more. The New Realists have consumed and, while they're not quite sated, they don't require quite the flurry of newness that they did before.

If that's so, we will need to find better ways of funding the services and the pensions we need, because the economic growth won't be there to provide it. But since green economists have been working on this very issue for the last twenty-five years, there are at least some alternatives available.

Part of the solution is going back to the local to find the very real resources that we tend to ignore there, while continuing to hold on to a global vision of the world. 'Ideas, knowledge, art, hospitality, travel – these are things which should of their nature be international,' said Keynes in 1933, urging the Irish government to minimize economic entanglement with other nations. 'But let goods be homespun whenever it is reasonably and conveniently possible; and, above all, let finance be primarily national.' That is good advice for the future.

Like authenticity, *wabi-sabi* can't be reduced to simple formulas. It embraces not just what's real, worn and human, but also what is somehow deformed or outcast. *Wabi-sabi* is imperfect, and glorying in what are sometimes very small signs of human diversity and activity. It is human in the same way that Christianity expresses it, as the normal, slick rules of human life turned upside down so that the last shall be first and the first shall be last.

But like the Christian spirit, it's elusive. If you try to define it too closely, it slips through your fingers. You can't pay a consultant to *wabi-sabi* your home, as you can with Feng Shui. You can't open a *wabi-sabi* shop. You certainly can't advertise it. It is the precise opposite of the shiny perfection of the market economy, and – let's be honest – the precise opposite of much of modern Japan.

It's peculiar that *wabi-sabi* should be an honoured concept in the country where authenticity most seems under threat – wired-up, shiny, virtual Japan. Kalle Lasn, the man behind *Adbusters*, is married to a Japanese woman and claims his determination to battle corporate mind control was inspired partly watching the disintegration of Japanese culture while he lived there.

But then California is just the same, as the very centre of the 'extreme reality', the 'virtual perfection' that the French philosopher Jean Baudrillard says we are powerless against. Driving through California in the early 1980s, the novelist Umberto Eco came across seven three-dimensional wax tableaux of Leonardo's painting *The Last Supper* between Los Angeles and San Francisco. All were in full Technicolor and complete with a taped monologue informing the viewer that they are having the most profound spiritual experience of their life.

Eco describes his encounters with these versions of one of the most famous *wabi-sabi* paintings in the world – the original is in very poor condition – in his essay *Travels in Hyper-Reality*. Each tableau is described by their creators as 'more real' than the real thing. But, like Ocean Dome, they don't let you take too close a look at the real picture – any more than they let you look at the real beach: the original for comparison was usually a poor black and white reproduction.

Wabi-sabi is the very opposite of hyper-real – yet it has emerged as a trendy concept in the very same place. California is now hosting a small industry of books, and exhibitions have been devoted to the idea that maybe there is something good about the weather-beaten, the worn and the human after all. And when I look in the mirror in the morning, and see the *wabi-sabi* looking back, I'm inclined to agree.

Postmodernism died in New York City on 11 September 2002 at 8.48 a.m. (or thereabouts). Or, if it didn't actually expire, it certainly began feeling a little under the weather.

Other writers have pinpointed the moment as early as the explosion of the Space Shuttle *Challenger* in 1986 – before post-modern thinking, in which everything is relative and ironic and authenticity is impossible, had really got a comfortable hold.

But, despite that, I imagine generations to come will also look back on the events in New York and Washington as the moment the world woke up from the bizarre excesses of the dot.com explosion – where tiny websites suddenly became as valuable as long-established major companies. Actually, of course, the dot.com boom was well on the way out when the hijacked planes hit the World Trade Center, but 9/11 meant more than that. There was suddenly a collective concentration on what was really important, particularly in the financial markets. 'I don't know about you, but I kind of like being awake,' wrote Geoffrey Colvin in *Fortune* magazine.

I started this book well before 9/11, but afterwards I found people seemed to understand what I was talking about when I explained my project, whereas they had just furrowed their brows before. Whether they would have agreed with me that New Realism is more than just the next big consumer trend is another matter. We have lived with postmodernism for so long now that it's hard to imagine any other attitude to the world beyond the clever, cynical, flip way we see it these days – where everything from history to physics is relative, where everything gives rise at best to a world-weary smirk. Yet I believe the New Realists and their demand for authenticity are the first glimpse of what comes after the demise of postmodernism, and how the next generations will live their lives.

We are deep inside the postmodern age now. It's hard to imagine a style that will be different from the Art Deco, mock-Tudor, neo-Georgian pastiches going up in concrete all around us. Or the theme pubs everywhere, or the layer upon layer of cultural reference that lies behind adverts or films, or the disapproval heaped on anyone who dares to make a statement of belief. Or the infuriating inability of politicians or academics to adopt any idea as true until they have exchanged a great deal of money to measure it.

The remains of the previous 'modern' age are all around us, in those glass towers, those white neat lines, that fanatical obsession with honesty, the belief that form should follow function. The idea that individuality must make way for the Age of Factories. That houses were, as the architect Le Corbusier put it, 'machines for living in'. For the modernists gathering round the new Bauhaus School under Walter Gropius in 1919, the pretence, bluff and deceit of the old world had simply led to the horrors of the trenches. But what began with such high ideals led to high-rise flats, arrogant officials who knew best how everyone should live, and International Style hotels which are the same from Rio to Reykjavik.

New Realism is partly a response to the way that modern architects disconnected building from their history and traditional meanings. But it is also a response to what has followed – the ironic, postmodern products of the social construction of reality, the followers of Derrida and Foucault, the mixture of world-weariness and exhausted acceptance that men, women, people of different races or different classes, really can't understand or communicate with each other at all. If modernism was a deeply-held belief in the perfectibility of mankind by honest lines, post-modernism rejected belief of any kind.

I suppose I've had the same kind of journey as everyone else. More than a decade ago, when writing a book about the future of cities, I was more than happy to embrace postmodern pastiche. It was fun, after all. It was everything those po-faced, puritanical modernists were not – with the brutal concrete structures they expected everyone else to live in. If the truth was so awful that it led to buildings like that, then let's bury it, I thought. 'Less is a bore,' said the postmodern architect Robert Venturi, paraphrasing Mies van der Rohe, and I absolutely agreed.

A decade later, I see it differently. I can see the attractions of not believing in anything, giving up the struggle to know anything for certain. That is tolerance of a kind. But equally, it provides no signposts to the future, and no hope – and hope, says Theodore Zeldin, is the essence of humanity.

New Realism is a challenge to our contemporary conviction that nothing is true and everything is relative. It doesn't pretend it's possible after all to work out unambiguously what's true in this world. It doesn't turn its back on the understanding and tolerance we have generated with the social construction of knowledge. But it isn't stuck there either. It moves on, looking around for something we *can* be sure of – something we can use to measure everything else against – and finds it in ourselves.

Humanity never goes back: we simply stop worrying about the issues that so concerned us before. The New Realists are pioneering a way out of the paralysis of postmodernism. And they are doing so by finding that all those different points of view that so obsess us are all rooted in a larger reality, of humanity rooted in nature. It's a spiritual insight because it finally understands just how interconnected life is.

We're not there yet. We're still fascinated by fake, and I'm sure we always will be – even when the issue of what's real and what's not sinks down into its proper place eventually. I'm sure that fast food will continue to proliferate, and that plastic surgery will continue to expand – maybe even by the 50 per cent every five years that it's expanding at the moment. I'm sure people will still want Botox injected into their foreheads to get rid of the lines. I'm sure there will be new versions of the dot.com bubble where people give tiny start-ups the same value as nations in their excitement. But the demand for the survival of the opposite will continue to grow at the same rate – if not more so.

It's a new kind of humanism that defends human choice against the giant corporations and the technocrats who would find it cheaper just to use machines or computers to interact with us. Or the biotech companies that are happy to release GM organisms into the environment, because they know they'll breed and then that's all we'll have left. It's an attitude that doesn't condemn extra thick-skinned tomatoes, extra ripe bananas, decaffeinated coffee beans – but does condemn the economic processes which mean they drive out the real stuff.

This new Renaissance isn't post-human – it isn't post-anything. It puts humanity first, and finally gets to grips with those old industrial attitudes that people are controllable cogs in machines that our business and political leaders cling to. And gives humanity back some dignity, rejecting Richard Dawkins's view that we are no more than 'bytes and bytes and bytes of digital information'.

In a mild way, we already live in a version of Aldous Huxley's *Brave New World*, where drugs, conditioning and eugenics combine to produce a nightmarish and inhuman existence. In a commentary on his book written three decades later, Huxley felt much less hopeful that we could avoid that fate than he had when he wrote it. The combination of pharmacology, brainwashing and 'scientific' education would be too much for the human spirit to resist. 'Under a scientific dictator, education will really work,' he wrote. 'With the result that most men and women will grow up to live their servitude and will never dream of revolution.'

But Huxley was wrong. The new authenticity may be dangerous, it may sometimes be snobbish or puritanical, but it is at heart a dream of exactly that revolution against propaganda for the status quo that Huxley believed was impossible. We will use the technology, but we will cling to the human touch to make sure it survives.

In the meantime, perhaps we should follow the advice of C. S. Lewis in *The Lion, the Witch and the Wardrobe*: 'If you meet anything that's going to be human and isn't yet, or used to be human once and isn't now, or ought to be human and isn't, keep your eyes on it and feel for your hatchet.'

INDEX

Abbott Mead Vickers 32
ABC Television 19
Absolut 27
Absolutely Fabulous 168
accountancy 218–19
accuracy 143–4
Adbusters 24, 27–8, 105, 123, 263, 282, 290
adventure holidays 48, 162–3
advertising
  children and young people 26–7, 30–2, 43, 80–1, 106–12, 114, 116–22, 125, 264
  films and 132
  mass 36, 121
  political 104–5
  reaction against 27–9, 70, 105, 263, 264, 274, 277, 282
  in UK 42, 130, 228
  in USA 19, 130, 276–7
  use of word 'authentic' xvii
  virtual 24
  volume of 19, 228
  see also branding *and* marketing
Advertising Regulation Bureau 105
Aga 45, 58
Age of Spiritual Machines, The 159, 186, 198
agriculture
  city farms 97–8
  local 98–9
  organic 90–1, 170
  intensive 81–3, 92, 93–4, 99
  small-scale 169–70
  see also food
Agricultural Testament, An 90
AIDS 109
Airport 133
Albrecht, Jurgen 20
Alcoholics Anonymous 250
All Hail the New Puritans 140–2
Allen, Paul 126
Allen, Woody 254
Alpert, David 5
Al-Qaeda 250
alternative health 8, 17, 60, 181, 261, 272
Amazon 34, 67, 192, 193
American Airlines 18, 33, 292
American Beauty 169
American Liveable Cities 273
Amis, Martin 140, 149
Andersen, Hans Christian xiv
Anderson, Gerry 260
Anheuser-Busch 90
Andrews, Julie 66
Anguilla 242
anti-establishmentism 105, 107, 108–9
Anyon, James 219
AOL/Time Warner 125, 192, 193
Apollo space program 4, 74, 78, 96, 260
Apple 8, 111, 174, 190
Archers, The 194
architecture 20, 61–4, 293
Argentina 247–8, 249
Aristotle 151, 280
Ark Royal 133
Armani 102
Armitage, Simon 143, 148
Armstrong, Neil 74
Aroma 13
Around the World in 80 Days 184

art 128–9, 130–1, 177, 276
Arthur Andersen 218
artificial intelligence (AI) 6, 177–8, 197–202, 220, 284
Arts Council 147
Asimo (Advanced Steps in Innovative Mobility) 196, 294
'Assassin' 110
Associazione Riccccreativa Culturale Italiana 95
Astaire, Fred 49
AT&T 6, 8, 190
Atlantic Monthly 245
atheism 279, 283
attention deficit disorder 30, 187
attention span 30, 124–5
Australia 51
authenticity
  demand for xviii, 3–4, 8, 12–13, 15, 37, 43, 121, 124, 262, 292
  elements of 15–21
  history of 13–14
  language of 268, 272
  mass market and 59–66, 71, 87
  meaning of xvii, xviii, 14–15, 53, 287
  twenty guidelines for 269–78
Autumn Journal 1

Babbit, Joel 30
back-shifting 21
'bad', concept of 105–8, 116
Bad as I Wanna Be 106
Baird, John Logie 259
Balance: Get it Right, The 80
Bangladesh 18, 47
Bank of England 33, 215, 247
banks
  community 49
  local 49, 50, 193
  time- 56–8, 67, 71
  virtual 48–9
Barber, Benjamin 278
Barbie doll 36
Barings Bank 33
Barnes & Noble 59
Batman 32
Baudrillard, Jean 7, 290
Bauhaus 293
Baxter, Raymond 75, 153, 176
Bazalgette, Peter 136
BBC 1, 2, 4, 35, 75, 134, 135, 160, 229, 276
BCCI 218
Beach, The 140
Beardsley, Aubrey 113
Beatty, Jennifer 31
beauty 20
Beckham, Victoria 24
being yourself 271–2, 273
Bell, Martin 276
Ben & Jerry's 13, 84
Benecol 67, 83
Benetton 109, 111
Bentham, Jeremy 208, 209, 239–40
Bentley, David 29
Berardino, Joseph 218
Berger, Peter 285
Berlin Wall 172
Berman, Ed 97
Berthillon 45
Betjeman, John 1, 78
Bevan, Aneurin 240
Bible, the 262
Big Brother 60–1, 67, 71, 134–8, 150, 263
Bill, The 205
bin Laden, Osama 50
Black and White 156
Black Hawk, Colorado xiii
black street culture 107, 110, 118
Blair, Tony 72, 183, 194, 207, 216, 228, 239, 249
Blair Witch Project, The 144–5
Blincoe, Nicholas 140
Blind Date 136
Bloomberg, Michael 227
Bly, Robert 104, 121
Boddingtons 90
Body and Self-Esteem 36
Body Shop 24, 36–8, 47, 109
bohemia 113, 115, 116
Bohr, Niels 224
Boizot, Peter 64

Bolivia 23
Borsook, Paulina 8, 126
Bosnia 250
botox 295
Bové, José 51, 93–4
Bowling Alone 5
Bradley, Bill 235
branding 11–12, 13
  anti-brands 47–8
  authentic 12, 28–30, 59
  craft 58
  defence of 265–7
  internal 173
  loyalty to 42, 49
  as new tradition 35, 39, 46–7, 53, 267
  see also marketing
Branson, Richard 108, 163, 223
Brave New World 295–6
Breakdown of Nations, The 242
brewing industry 48, 84, 89–90, 91–2, 107
Brief History of Time, A 43
British Airways 108
British Association for the Advancement of Science 294
British Gas 179
'Broken Windows' 245
Brotman, Juliano 89
Brown, Gordon 210
Brown, James 49
Bruce, Robert 270
Brummel, Beau 131
BSE (mad cow disease) 18, 76, 93, 96
BT (British Telecom) 6, 47, 159, 198
Buber, Martin 146
Burger King 10, 31, 80–1, 82
Burke, James 75, 153, 176
Burkittsville, USA 144–5
Burnett, Mark 136
Bush, President George 191–2
Bush, President George W. 5, 209, 214, 229, 234–5
Business @the speed of thought 184
Business as Unusual 38
Business Week 13
Business 2.0 173
Buy Nothing Day 28
Byron, Lord 112–13, 116, 121

Cahn, Edgar 182–3
Caine, Michael 124
California 51, 264, 287, 290–1
call centre 3, 204–6, 223
Camberwick Green 139
Cameron, Mike 31
Campaign for Real Ale (CAMRA) 18, 76, 89, 91
Campaign for Real Labour 250
Campbell, Alastair 234
Campbell, Joseph 150, 163
Campbell's Soup 11, 84, 207
Canada 27–8, 30, 105
capitalism 120
Capone, Al 117
Carmageddon 7
carnival 132, 145
Carr, Simon 229
Carrey, Jim 9
Cascadian 91
Castaway 134, 136–7
Castronova, Edward 155
CBC 28, 105
CBS 85, 136
Celebration, Florida 8–11, 157, 171
Celente, Gerald 167
Central Electricity Generating Board 42
Centreparcs xiv , 67
Chadlington, Lord 50
Challenge of Leisure, The 160
Challenger space shuttle 291
Chaney, Liza 78
change 275, 281
Changing Rooms 67, 134, 263
Channel One (USA) 11, 30, 231
Channel 4, 130, 249
Charles, Prince of Wales 194
Charlie's Garden Army 134
Charter 77 236, 256–7
Chatterton, Thomas 113, 115
cheese-making industry 83, 94, 96
Chicago Bulls 105
Chicago, University of 88
chickens 81–2

children and young people
advertising and marketing to 26–7, 30–2, 43, 80–1, 106–12, 114, 116–22, 125, 264
attention span 30, 125
education 30–1, 161, 185–6
food 80–1
games 7, 69–70, 116–18, 154–7
microchipping 263
names 26–7
television 125, 126–7
youth culture 107–12, 116–22
China 57, 85, 241
chocolate, organic 66–7, 71
choice 272
Chomsky, Noam 254
Christian Aid 104
Christianity 290
Churchill, Winston 103
CIA 192
cinema 131–2, 141–4, 150–1, 171–2
Citizen Organisation Foundation Institute 246
Citizens Committee of New York City 244–6
Clark, Michael 243–6
Clarke, Arthur C. 160, 161
Clinton, President Bill 243
Administration 185, 235
Clinton, Hilary 251–3
Club 18–30 107
Cobain, Kurt 116
Coca-Cola (Coke) 29, 160
brand name 11, 13, 14, 26, 107
design 49, 143
'internet police' 265
loss of market share 17
New Coke 275
in schools 31
Cochrane, Peter 6, 159
Coen Brothers 132
coffee 64
Cold War 3, 258
Colegrave, Stephen 35
Coleridge, Samuel Taylor 113, 199
Colombia 98
Columbine High School, Denver 116
Colvin, Geoffrey 49, 192, 292
communities
agriculture and 97
fake 5, 8–11
geographical 180–3, 193, 202, 274
local 52–3, 56–8, 193–4, 244–7, 285
politics in 236–7
television and 190
virtual 9, 180–3
computers
dating 60, 67, 185
future of 6–8
games 7, 69–70, 116–18, 154–7
intelligence *see* artificial intelligence
medicine and 179–80, 186, 222–3
schools and 30, 185–6
Confédération Paysanne 93
Connery, Sean xiii
Conran, Terence 77
consensus 237
consistency 272
Consolations of Philosophy, The 43
'consumenism' 43
consumerism 112–14, 131
consumers
categorisation of 41–4
respect for 277
technology 12
continuity 275
contradiction 272
conversation 248–9
cafés 181, 249
cookery 76–9
'Cool Britannia' 72, 115–16
'cool', concept of 115–19, 121, 127, 128–9
Cool Rules 115
Cooper, Aaron 118
Copenhagen 224
Copernicus, Nicolaus 283
corporate
mergers 50
sponsorship 11–12, 30–1, 80–1
cosmetic surgery 23
cost-benefit analysis 210
counter-culture 111–12, 121–2, 128–9, 281

'Couple Fucking Dead (Twice)' 128
Courage 90
Cowley, Malcolm 113
craft 45–6, 48, 58
creativity 223, 278
credit union 49
Crick Crack Club, London 145
cryogenics 6
Cultural Creatives 15, 42–3
culture, real 123–53, 276
culture-jamming 27–8, 120, 263
currency, local 274–5
customer
  loyalty 192–3, 206
  relations 204–6, 263, 272, 273
cyberanalysis.com 180
Cybernetic Poet 148
cybernetic totalism 7, 198
cyborg 6, 201–2, 263

Dacyczyn, Amy 169, 170
Daily Express 13
Daily Telegraph 128
Dalai Lama 177
Dammers, Horace 169
Dangerous Sports Club 163
Dare to Connect 194
Darwin, Charles 4
David Copperfield 226
David, Elizabeth 77–9, 100, 101
Dawkins, Richard 295
de Botton, Alain 43
debt
  national 33
  personal 157–8
  third-world 104–5
DeGrandpre, Richard 7, 123
Deliverance 162
democracy 10–11, 255–8, 278
Democratic Party (USA) 231, 260
Denmark 243
depression 7, 19, 158, 188–91
Derrida 293
Descartes, René 113
Diana, Princess of Wales 227
Dickens, Charles 226
DigitalAngel 263
Dion, Mark 129
DiSabatino, Richard 191
Disney Corporation 18, 48, 81, 131, 132, 275
  town of Celebration 8–11, 157, 171
Disney World, Florida 8, 10, 267
Disneyland Europe 51
Disneyland Tokyo 288
Disruption 110
Dixons 39
DKNY 44
doctors *see* medicine
Dogme 95 141–2, 146, 150
Dole, Bob 243–4
Dominguez, Joe 169
Dorfman, Ariel 275
dot.com businesses 34, 192, 198, 291–2, 295
downshifting 41, 164–71, 174–5
Dr Pepper 81
Dream of John Ball, A 251
dreams, honouring 275
Droog 47
Dru, Jean-Marie 110
Drucker, Peter 210–11
drugs 116, 131, 187–9, 245
Dubin, Tiffany 44
Duck, Mandarina 47
Dunkin' Donuts 75, 80

Eagles, The 142
earthquakes 19–20
EastEnders 3, 193, 205
eBay 155
Eberstadt, Mary 188
eclipse of the sun (1999) 1–2
Eco, Umberto 31, 290–1
e-commerce 121, 179, 193
economics
  green 289
  teaching of 212–14
Ecstasy 168
'Edge City' 138–9
Educating Rita 123–4
education
  computers and 30, 185–6
  online 180

self- 43, 49
school league tables 214, 215, 217, 221
truancy 216–17
Educational Testing Service 185
Einstein, Albert 224
Eisner, Michael 9
electronic intelligence 191–2
Elgin, Duane 166, 169
Eliot, T.S. 175, 199
Ellul, Jacques 127
email, volume of 16–17
Emerson, Ralph Waldo 204
Emin, Tracey 129
Emmerdale Farm 205
emotional literacy 237
Empire State Building, New York 164
End of History, The 6
English Bread and Yeast Cookery 79
Enjoy 91
Eno, Brian 132, 145
Enron 34, 210, 218, 264
environment 37, 40, 95, 239, 280
Environment Agency 217
Erasmus, Desiderius 283, 284, 286
Erasmus Prize 284
Estonia 28
ethical
business 36–40, 47, 70, 261, 270
food 87, 88–9
investment 16, 48, 67, 263
production 21, 37, 66
spending 43
E*Trade 12, 33, 48
Etzioni, Amitai 183–4
European Commission 99, 207
Forward Studies Unit 279
European Union (EU) 91, 96, 217, 240, 243
Everest, Mount 23, 164
EverQuest 154–5, 156
experience 2–3, 47

FA Cup Final 281
fabric technology 264
Fair Trade 48, 88
fake
businesses 54
communities 5, 8–11
food 4, 23, 24, 75–80, 82, 85, 87–8, 93–4, 100
places 5, 8–11
politicians 5, 70, 238
public obsession with 23–4, 264–8, 294
rejection of 4–5
relationships 5
smells 5
'fake real' 67, 71
Falkland Islands 242
Fall, The 141
Family, The 133
Fans for Fairer Football 266
fantasy 151–2
farmers' markets 48, 60, 76, 97
fashion 44
Fast Food Nation 82
Fein, Ellen 194
Feng Shui 290
Feuerbach, Ludwig 102
Fever Pitch 143
Fifth Generation, The 203
'Fifty Years Hence' 103
Financial Services Agency 247
financial systems, global 33–5
Financial Times 85
Fitch 267
Fitoussi, Jean-Paul 213, 214
Flynn, Errol 144
food
'analogue' 76, 80, 90
English 78–9
ethical 87, 88–9
fake 4, 23, 24, 75–80, 82, 85, 87–8, 93–4, 100
fast 75–6, 80–2, 264, 294
future of 75, 96–7, 261, 263
GM 17, 24, 67, 83, 84, 87–8, 90, 249, 266, 280, 295
local 48, 60, 76, 89, 92–4, 97–102, 262
Mediterranean 77
organic 4, 18, 48, 66–7, 71, 76, 87, 89, 90–1, 261, 262

processed 82–4
raw 89
real 4, 45, 48, 74–103, 264
slow 94–6, 101–2
foot and mouth disease 76, 92, 93, 238
Ford 160
Forests Forever 28
Fortune 49, 86, 177, 192, 196, 204, 223, 292
Foucault 293
Four Arguments for the Elimination of Television 126, 138–9
Frames of Mind 220
France
American culture and 51, 93–4
eating habits 85, 93–4
economics teaching 212–14
government 243
shops 44–5, 51
Frank, Thomas 111–12, 114, 120
Franks, Lynne 168
Frayn, Michael 224
Freedom Foods 48, 88
Freeze exhibition 128
French Connection 107
French Revolution 95, 104, 112
Freud, Sigmund 14, 175
Friedman, Thomas 22
Friends of the Earth 90
Friends Reunited 67
Frostrup, Mariella 188
Fuji 108, 109
Fukuyama, Francis 6, 280
fundamentalism 262, 278
future
computers and 6–7, 8
virtual xvi-xvii, xviii, 3–4, 7–8, 177–81, 198, 261
Future Foundation 42
Futurist, The 197
Futurological Congress, The 131

Gandhi, Mohandas 79, 168, 182, 241
Gap 107, 120, 265
Gardner, Howard 220
Garland, Alex 140
Garreau, Joel 138
Garth, David 227
Gates, Bill 184–5
Gemini space program 4
General Accepted Accounting Principles (GAAP) 218
General Election (2001) 226–7, 229, 234
General Electric (GE) 12, 174, 192, 222, 243
General Mills Corporation 74
General Motors 160
General Strike (1926) 160
genetic engineering 6, 83
genetically-modified (GM) food 17, 24, 67, 83, 84, 87–8, 90, 249, 266, 280, 295
Gerrie, Andrew 37–8
Getting a Life 166
Ghazi, Polly 166
Ghetto Boys 110
Gho, Paola 101–2
Gibson, William 68
Gifford, Kathie Lee 267
Gitlin, Todd 158
Giuliani, Rudolph 245
Gladstone, W.E. 231, 277
globalisation 4, 12–13, 239
future of 3, 22–3, 261
reaction against 50–3, 93–4, 107, 111, 120, 269
symbols of 64, 65
glossophobia 71
Gluckman, Ron xix
Godin, Seth 56
Godzilla 150, 151
Good Life, The 165, 166
Goodhart's Law 215
Google 224
Gore, Al 214, 234–5
Gorillaz 67, 132
Gould, Stephen Jay 69, 220
Grainer 83
Grand, John 195
Grand Auto Theft III 156
Grant, John 26, 35, 46, 53, 65, 89, 108

Gray, Jim 198
Green & Black 67
Greenhalgh, Dr Trisha 222
Greenpeace 249
Grimm, Rod 183–4, 187, 190
Grolsch 90
Gropius 293
Guardian 149, 178, 181, 205
G8 summit (2000) xv, 105

Häagen-Daz 47
Hagen, Gunther von 129
Hall, Sir Peter 102
Haller, DR G.L. 222
Hammerstein, Oscar xvi
Handy, Charles 41
Hansard Society 229
Haraway, Donna 201
Harland & Wolff 268
Harley-Davidson 267
Harper's Bazaar 77
Harry Potter 145, 151
Hasbro 116–17, 119
Hattersley, Roy 250
Havel, Vaclav 256–8, 284, 286
Hawking, Stephen 43
Hayward, Martin 13
Hearst, Patty 165
Heart Aroused: Poetry and the Preservation of the Soul in Corporate America 172
Heim, Prof. Michael 70
Heineken, Freddie 242
Hello Kitty xiv
Helstein, Richard 49
Hemingway, Ernest 113
Hendrix, Jimmy 107
Henley Centre for Forecasting 13, 29, 271
Henry V 172
Hercules 32
Hewitt, Patricia 234
Hewlett Packard 190
Heyer, Steve 265
hierarchy 271
High-Tech/High-Touch 7–8, 168
Hilfiger, Tommy 122
Hillis, Daniel 20, 22
hip-hop 110, 118
Hirst, Damien 128–9, 144, 177
Hock, See 204
Hoffmann LaRoche 12
Hoggart, Simon 181
Hokkaido, Japan xiv
holidays 160–4
  adventure 48, 162–3
  'real' 159, 162–3
  virtual 159
Holzer, Jenny 47
Homebase 92
Homes and Gardens 62
Honda 196, 294
honesty 17–18, 270, 272
Horizon 91
Hornby, Nick 143
hospital waiting lists 214–15, 217
Hotel 132–3
House of Commons 237, 238 *see also* General Election
How to be a Domestic Goddess 79
How to Read Donald Duck 275
Howard, Sir Albert 90, 170
Howell Henry Chaldecott Lury (HHCL) 108, 109
Hoyt, Dan 89
human contact 17, 270–1
Human Genome Project 280
human-scale 21
humanism 283–5, 295
humanity
  definition of 6, 294
  demand for real 12, 21, 279–80, 284, 295–6
Husak, Gustav 257
Huxley, Aldous 295–6
Huxley, Julian 160, 161
hyperactivity 7, 263
hyper-real 31

IBM 6, 29, 146, 197
  Big Blue 199
Iceland 90
i-Cybie 196
Ideal Home 62

Ideal Home Exhibition 179
IKEA 267
IMAX cinemas 69
Immelt, Jeff 174
Impressionism 130
Inca-Cola 48
independence 40, 41, 42, 106–9
Independent, the 51
India
  agriculture 90, 170
  call centres 3, 204–5
individuality 42
Indonesia 249
infantilism 121
inner-directedess 15, 40–4
innovation 273–4
Institute for Local Self-Reliance 246
Institute for Social and Economic Research 190
Institute of Contemporary Arts (ICA) 177
Institute of Radio Engineers 55
Institute of Noetic Sciences 42
Intel 16–17, 190
Intellectual Capital 223
intelligence
  artificial (AI) 6, 177–8, 197–202, 220, 284
  electronic 191–2, 198–9
  'gene' 220–1
  human 191–2, 197–202
  IQ tests 220
Intelligence Revolution, The 192
Intelligence Support Group 191
International Coalition to Protect the Polish Countryside 99
International Economics Association 214
International Flavours and Fragrances (IFF) 83
International Forum on Globalisation 126
International Space Station 287
internet 9, 12, 125
  beginnings of 281
  campaigns 266
  chat rooms 59
  depression and 190
  medicine 179–80
  'police' 265
  relationships 67, 179–80, 195
  revolution 3, 34, 178
  shopping 192–4
Internet Underground Music Archive (IUMA) 26
interview testing 219
intuition 199, 200, 208, 279
Ireland 51, 250
Irish Republican Army (IRA) 165, 250
irradiation 93
i-Society 42
Israel 254 254
Israel, Dorman D. 55
ITN 276
It's a Wonderful Life 9, 221
ITV 259
Iuma 26–7
Jack, Fiona 29
Jackson, Michael 106
James, Clive 130
Japan
  advertising 288
  agriculture 97
  commerical success 192
  communities 57
  eating habits 85, 288
  economy 288–9
  education 288
  housing 287–8
  robots 196
  Tea Ceremony 286–7
  theme parks xiii-xvi, 287, 288
  wabi-sabi 287–90
  youth culture 287
Jell-O 11
Jenkins, Roy 277
Jenkins, Simon 147, 240
Jihad 278, 280
Jihad versus McWorld 278
Jones, Judy 166
Joseph, Jenny 147
Joseph, Sir Keith 230
Jowell, Tessa 210

Joy, Bill 6–7
Jung, Carl 219

Kahn, Hermmann 258
karaoke 71–2
Kasparov, Gary 199
Kaveney, Roz 153
Keats, John 112
Kelleher, Herb 174
Kelling, George 245
Kelloggs 80
Kennedy, Charles 234
Kentucky Fried Chicken (KFC) 80, 81, 82, 85
Kerouac, Jack 107
Keynes, John Maynard 33, 160, 161, 199, 206, 289
Kinsman, Francis 42
Kipling, Rudyard 124
Klein, Calvin 122
Klein, Naomi 31, 120, 259, 267
Kohr, Leopold 242
Koolhaas, Rem 47
Koran, the 262
Korean Airlines xix
Kosovo 242, 250
Kostyra, Martha *see* Stewart, Martha
KPMG 50
Kramer, Peter 191
Kroc, Ray 85
Krueger, Myron 186
Krugman, Paul 53, 213
'Kubla Khan' 199
Kubler-Ross, Elisabeth 32
Kumar, Satish 79
Kundera, Milan 256
Kurzweil, Ray 159, 186, 198
Kuwait 242

Lamb Weston and Simplot 88
Lang, Helmut 47
Lang, Jack 213
Lanier, Jaron 7, 68, 178, 185, 198, 220, 284
Lasn, Kalle 27–8, 32, 105, 290
Last Supper, The 290–1
Lauren, Ralph 23, 44, 46
Lautrec, Toulouse 113
Lawrence, D.H. 148
Lawrence, T.E. 13–14
Lawson, Nigella 79, 87, 261
Le Corbusier 293
Le Pen, Jean-Marie 229, 237, 269
Leavis, F.R. 78
Lebow, Victor 114
Leeson, Nick 33
Lefebvre, Henri 183–4
Lehmann, John 77, 255
leisure 160–4, 181
Lem, Stanislaw 131
Leonardo Da Vinci 283, 290–1
Lerner, Rabbi Michael 252–5, 257, 258, 284
Letchworth, Hertfordshire 62
Levi's 115
Lewinsky, Monica 18
Lewis, C.S. 296
Lewis, David 42
Lewis, Michael 129, 269
Lexus and the Olive Tree, The 22
Liberal Democrats 41, 227, 234, 236
Liberty Orchard 30
Life computer game 159
Life magazine 25
Life Style Movement 166, 169
Lilly, Eli 188
Limbaugh, Rush 253
Lincoln, Abraham 224
linear thinking 279
Lion, the Witch and the Wardrobe, The 296
Lippert, Barbara 87
Listening to Prozac 191
literature manifesto 140–1, 149
Lithium 189
living
  real 154–76
  simplifying 18–19, 165–71, 270
  video record of 198
  virtual 154–9
Living Weekdays 85
LLadro porcelain 58
local 4, 21, 289–90

action 50–1
businesses and 37–8, 51–3
communities 52–3, 56–8, 193–4, 244–7, 285
economies 52, 12
shops 48, 51, 92, 93
Lockheed Martin 33, 292
loft living 115–16
Loft Story 135
Logical Positivism 209
logophilia 19
London
Blitz (1940) 255
changes 281
streets 152
suburban semis 61–3
London Independent Online 242
London Re-building Society 49
London Underground 5, 146–7
Lonely Crowd, The 41
Lonely Planet series 270
Long Now Foundation 20
Long-Term Asset Management 218
looking back 275–6
Lord of the Rings 151, 152–3
Lovegrove, Nick 210
Lowry Gallery, Manchester 128
Loy, David 54
Lubars, David 70
Lucas, George 150
Luddites 7, 17
Lumière Brothers 70
Lush 37–8, 47
Luyckx, Marc 279

McAllan's sausages 265
McCain Foods 88
McCain, John 235
McCartney, Stella 15, 44
Macauley, Thomas 26
McCoffee shop, San Francisco 265
McCorduck, Pamela 197, 203
McDonald, Ronald 265
McDonald's xvii, 10, 11, 67, 267
brand name 26, 80, 265
GM foods 88
hotels 22
loss of share value 13
marketing of 12
reaction against 51, 88, 93, 94, 269
service 85
size of 82
in schools 31, 80–1
sponsorship of sports stars 106
McDonald's Family Restaurant, Illinois 265
McEwan, Ian 140, 149
McGuinness, Martin 217
Machiavelli, Niccolo 240
Machines That Think 197
McKee, Robert 123, 150, 151, 284
McKinsey 210
McLaren, Michael 71
Macmillan, Harold 260, 279
MacNeice, Louis 1, 286
McQuaid, Brad 154
MacRae, Hamish 51
'McWorld' 278–80
mad cow disease 18, 76, 93, 96
Madonna 111
Malevich, Kasimir 130
management
face-to-face 17, 181
gurus 210–11
personnel 164
public 208
virtual 17
Management by Walking Around (MBWA) 17, 50, 223
Mander, Jerry 126, 138
Manhunt 136
'Manifesto for Cyborgs' 201–2
Marco, Noemi de 248
Marinescu, Ioana 212
marketing
children and young people 26–7, 30–2, 43, 80–1, 106–12, 114 116–22, 125, 264
mass 13, 36, 59–66, 71, 87
'new' 35–6, 46, 53
suspicion of 41
triumph of 28
see also advertising *and* branding

Marketing of Cool, The 117, 119–20
Marks & Spencer 90, 148
Mars 59, 91, 264
Marx, Karl 14, 175
mass media 59, 102
Massachusetts Institute of Technology *see* MIT
mathematics, use of 212–14 *see also* numbers
Matrix, The 12, 265
Matsushita 180
Mattel 36
Maxwell, Robert 38, 218
Mayle, Peter 100
Mead, Margaret 127
Mead, Peter 32
meaning, politics of 251–3
meaninglessness 252–3, 257
measurement culture 206–25, 239–40
meat production 82
Mechanics Illustrated 103
media
  manipulation 274
  mass 59, 102
  ownership 125
Media Foundation 27, 28
Media Unlimited 158
medicine
  alternative 8, 17, 60, 181, 261, 272
  computer diagnosis 179–80, 186, 222–3
  drug treatment 187–9, 191
  high-tech 8, 181
  narrative-based 146, 222
  online 179–80
  'time-banks' and 56–7
Mediterranean Food 77
Meeker, Mary 34
Men are from Mars, Women are from Venus 194
mental health 168, 180
Merchant of Venice, The 56
Method of True Theology 284
Michelangelo 199, 283
Michener, James xvi
micro-breweries 48, 84, 90, 91, 107
microchipping 263
Microsoft xvii, 11, 126, 170, 184
  Powerpoint 146, 204, 223–4, 225
  Research 198
Mies van der Rohe, Ludwig 293
Milburn, Alan 217
Milken, Michael 49
Millennium Dome, London 128
Miller 90, 120
Milli Vanilli 143
Mills, Jeremy 133–4, 136
mind control 173
Mind Gym 49
Minsky, Marvin 6, 25, 197, 198
MIT 6, 35, 125, 213
Miyares, Ana 57
modernism 279–82, 292–3
Moet and Chandon 58
Monde, Le 212
money, new kinds of 274–5
Monopolies and Mergers Commission 89
Monopoly 155
Monsanto 24
Monty Python's Flying Circus 125
Moore, Charles 128
Moore, Henry 176
Morecambe and Wise 125
Morgan 45, 58
Morgan Stanley 34
Morning Calm xix
Morris, David 246
Morris, Phillip 11
Morris, William 251
Morvan, Fan 143
MTV 4, 48, 108, 132, 134
Muji (Mujirushi Ryohuin) 47
Mummy Returns, The 32
Murdoch, Rupert 48
museums 128–9
music, traditional 129
Myers-Briggs personality test 219
Myst 156
Mystical Forests 27–8

Nader, Ralph 266
Naisbitt, John 7, 12, 70, 85, 119, 168, 181

nanotechnology 6
Napoleon I 238
NASA (National Aeronautics and Space Administration) 96, 264
National Commission on Testing and Public Policy (USA) 215
National Health Service (NHS) 208, 214, 238, 240, 277–8
  Direct 5, 59, 67, 179
National Institute for Mental Health (USA) 252
National Museum of Pop, Sheffield 128
National Portrait Gallery, London 216
National Science Foundation (USA) 68
nationalism 250, 262, 278
NBC 23, 130
Negativland 28, 120
Negroponte, Nicholas 35, 125–6, 132
Nestlé 64
Netherlands 41, 85
Netscape 190
networking 271
Nevermind 116
Neville, Richard 122
New Civics 273
New Consumers 42, 44
New Economics Foundation 237
New Economy 18
New Generation poets 148
New Leaf 88
New Left Review 181
New Marketing Manifesto, The 26, 35, 65
New Mexico State University 68
New Realism 100, 171, 225, 262–4, 267, 281, 287, 292–4
  charactistics of 43, 71, 181, 285, 289
  elements of 15–21
New Road Map Foundation 169
New Statesman 153
New York 244–5, 227
  9/11 attacks *see* September 11 attacks (2002)
New York Mercantile Exchange 33
New York Stock Exchange 196, 294
New York Times 22, 88, 127, 129, 187, 190, 237, 242, 248, 285
  Magazine 10
New Yorker 170
news, real 276–7
Newsnight 127
Newspad 242
Newsweek 122
NHS Direct *see* National Health Service
Nigeria 38, 39, 109
night clubs 163, 168
Nike 11, 13, 29, 106, 110, 118, 265–6
Nintendo 30, 70
Nirvana 107, 116, 189
No Logo 31, 120, 259
non-governmental organisations (NGOs) 249–50
Norrath 154–5, 156
North Face 163
Norvig, Peter 224
nostalgia 49, 142–3
Nothing 29
Nozick, Robert 7, 262
numbers 206–25, 238–40

O Brother Where Art Thou? 132
Ocean Beach, California 264
Ocean Dome, Japan xiii-xvii, xix, 287, 291
'Ode to a Nightingale' 116
Odell, A.D. 74
Ogilvy, David 259
Ogilvy and Mather 259
Ogoni people, Nigeria 39
O'Hagan's Sausages 18
OK 67
Oki-ni 47
Old Navy 107
Olivier, Richard 173
Omnicom 70
One-2-One 47
Opportunity Knocks 136
'Ordinary evening in New Haven, An' xiii
Organica 89

Organisational Storytelling Conference (2001) 146
organisations, small-scale 219–20
Orwell, George 226
Osterie d'Italia 101
outer-directedness 41
Overworked American, The 161
Oxfam 249
Oz 122

Pace Foods 84
Pack, Arthur 160
Packer, Tina 172, 173
Paddington Green 133
Paine, Tom 113
Paris 44–5, 95
Parker, Barry 62
Parliamentary Standards Committee 237
Parris, Matthew 228
PATER (Passion, Authenticity, Truth, Enthusiasm and Respect) 49–50
Paterson, Don 127
Patterson, Christine 148
Patterson, Jeff 26
PBS 117
Pearl Harbour 143–4
Pearl Jam 107
Pepper, John 49
Pepsi-Cola 17, 29, 31, 81, 107
Peretti, Jonah 266
Permission Marketing 56
'personal' products 270
personality classification 219–20
Peters, Tom 17, 223
Petrini, Carlo 94–5, 102, 273, 288
pharmaceutical industry 83–4
Phoenix Resorts xiv
Pietmontese cows 96
Pilatus, Rob 143
Pittman, Sandy 164
Pizza Express 64–5
Pizza Hut 80, 82
places
  fake 5, 8–11
  real 273
  virtual 138–9
plastic surgery 294
Plath, Sylvia 130–1
Plato 280
Poems on the Underground 147
poetry 127–8, 147–9, 279
Poetry Society 147–8
Poland 99
police 215, 245
politicians
  emotions and 226–7, 233
  fake 5, 70, 238
  honesty 17–18
  language 228–9, 256–7
  power 230, 232–3, 243, 246, 250–1, 253
  public image 70, 226–31
politics
  centralism 240–3, 250
  community 236–7
  local 241–7
  of meaning 251–3
  'by numbers' 238–40
  real 226–58
  spin doctors 227–8, 234
  spiritual 253, 255, 258
Politics of Meaning, The 252–3
polling, telephone 59, 199–200
Pop Idol 229
Popcorn, Faith 170
pornography 61
Portinari, Folco 95
Post-Autistic Economics 212–14
'post-human' debate 201
post-modernism 291–4
Pot Noodle 5, 59, 67, 75, 266
Pountain, Dick 115
Power, Michael 208, 218
'Power of Powerlessness, The' 258
'Pox' 116–17
Prada 47, 122
Praise of Folly 283
Prayer Before Birth 286
Prelude, The 104
Prince, The 240
Procter & Gamble 13, 49, 64
progress 280–1

Prozac 59, 188, 189
Prozac Nation 189
public houses 67, 91–2
punk 110
Putnam, Robert 5, 52, 183

quantum mechanics 224
Quintessence 89
Quitting Time at the Lumière Factory 70
Rand Corporation 261
rap 110
Raveaud, Giles 212
Raw Experience 89
Ray, Paul 42–3
reading 168
  groups 60, 67, 128
Ready Steady Cook 79, 134
Reagan, President Ronald 126, 252
real, meaning of xvii
Real Simple 270
Real World, The 134
realism 13–14, 254
reality movement 149
rebellion 106–14, 119–20, 122
Reebok 111
regeneration 169–70
Regeneration newsletter 170
regionalism 250
Reich, Robert 235
Reichl, Ruth 89
Reid, Richard 262
relationships
  customer 192–3, 204–6, 263, 272, 273
  fake 5
  with machines 195–202
  online 67, 179–80, 195
  real 59, 177–202
remote control 5–6
Renaissance 283, 285, 295
Replay TV 129, 269
Republican Party (USA) 231
Resurgence 79
Rheingold, Howard 185
Riesman, David 41
Rikyu, Sen no 286–7
Ritalin 23, 30, 67, 187, 188, 189
Ritzer, George 88, 269
Robertson, James 279
Robins, David 115
robots 177–8, 195–7
Rocky IV 265
Rodale, Robert 169–70
Roddick, Anita 37, 38, 43, 54, 109
Rodman, Dennis 105–6, 116
Rogers, Richard 20, 139
Romantic poets 112–13
Romsey by-election (2000) 230
Rose, Sir Julian 98–9
Roszak, Theodore 6, 7, 185–6
Rousseau, Jean-Jacques 113
Royal Academy, London 129
Royal Free Hospital, London 222
Royal Navy 223
Rúa, President Fernando de la 248
Rubin, Vicki 169, 247
Rules, The 194–5
Rushdie, Salman 140
Russell, Bertrand 209
Russell, Willy 123–4
Russia 155
Rutgers University 245

Saatchi and Saatchi 35
Saatchi, Charles 128
Sailor 133
Sainsbury's 92
Saint-Exupèry, Antoine de 201
St Luke's 35, 108
St Simon Stylites 166
Sale, Kirkpatrick 7
Saro-Wiwa, Ken 38
Saumarez Smith, Charles 216
Saunders, Harland 81
Schama, Simon 137
Schlosser, Eric 81, 82, 83
Schmalz, Bill 27
Schneider, Sherrie 194
schools *see* education
Schor, Juliet 161, 162
Schultz, Howard 64, 65
Schumacher, E.F. 79, 154
Sculley, John 174
Seattle, Washington 181, 249

Securities and Exchange Commssion (USA) 218
See, I Told You So 253
self-actualisation 41, 113, 114
self-employment 41
self-esteem 237
self-expression 40, 42
self-improvement 43, 49
self-sufficiency 165–6
Selosse, Anselme 46
September 11 attacks (2002) 33, 50, 149, 191–2, 249, 253–5, 278, 291–2
sex 158, 186–7
Sex Pistols 71
Shadbolt, Blanden 63
Shakespeare in Love 172
Shakespeare Inc. 172
Shakespeare, William 56, 172–3, 222
Shakespeare's Lessons in Leadership and Management 172–3
Shandwick 50
Shays-Meehan Bill (USA) 237
Shell 31, 38, 109
Shelley, Percy Bysshe 112
shopping malls xiii, 51, 67, 138
shops
  local 48, 51, 92, 93
  real 44–8, 51
  virtual 192–4
Shrek 8
Sibling Society, The 104, 121
Simms, Andrew 104–5
simplicity 18–19, 165–71, 270
Sims, The 157
Singing Ringing Tree, The 143
Slater, Nigel 77
Slough 1
Slovakia 233, 258
Slow Cities Movement 102, 273, 276
Slow Food Movement 18, 94–6, 101–2, 273, 274, 288
slow money 274
Small is Beautiful 79, 154
small stuff 277–8
Smash 76–7
Smith, Tom 88
Smythe Dorward Lambert 39, 40, 146
Smythe, John 39
Sobrino, Renzo 96
social innovation 273–4
social transformation 255–6
Soggy Bottom Boys 132
Sol 90
Sony
  Everquest 154–5
  Playstation 7, 59, 67, 263
  robot cat 177–8, 195
Sorbonne University, Paris 212
Sotheby's 44
Sotomoto 270, 274
Sound of Music, The 66
South Africa 256
South Korea 156
Southwest Airlines 174
Soviet Union 28, 215, 258
Spencer, Earl 239
Spice Girls 24, 67
Spielberg, Steven 66
spin 19, 227–8, 234, 277
spirituality 167–8, 253, 255, 258, 278–81
Spretnak, Charlene 233, 250, 258
Springer, Jerry 23
Stallabrass, Julian 181
Stallone, Sylvester 265
Star Trek xvii, 287
Star TV 48
Star Wars 32, 150
Starbucks 12, 64–5, 66, 67, 272
Starkey, David 137
Starski, Lovebug 110
statistics *see* numbers
Stein, Gertrude 113, 152
Stevens, Wallace xiii
Stewart, Martha 85–7, 94
Stewart, Thomas 204, 223–4
Story 123, 150
story-telling 145–6, 149, 151, 274, 275
stress 252
Stussy 122
sugar 80, 84
Suharto, President 249

Sun Microsystems 6, 8
supermarkets 45, 48, 51, 87, 90, 92, 98–9, 100
Survivor 23, 67, 136, 272
sustainability 19–20, 179, 270
sustenance-driven people 41
Sutherland, Ivan 67
sweatshops 266, 267
Sweden 243
Symbionese Liberation Army 165
'symbolic reality' 130

Taco Bell 80, 82
Tales of the South Pacific xvi
Tamagochi toys 196
Tango 108
target setting 207, 214–17, 225
Tate Britain 239
Tate Modern 67, 128, 276
Taylor, Frederick Winslow 210–11
Taylor, Matthew 230
Taylor, Nicholas 240
technology
  obsession with 259–62, 279–81
  importance of 296
  innovation in 273–4
teenagers *see* youth culture
TELCO 246
telephone, mobile 161–2, 166, 183, 185
television
  advertising on *see* advertising
  'authentic' 132–7
  children 125, 126–7
  community involvement and 190
  criticism of 126, 172
  docu-soap 134, 137
  fly-on-the-wall documentary 132–3
  food shows 76, 79, 85–7
  future of 125–6
  news 276–7
  'reality' 60–1, 134–7, 263
  rejection of 168
Temptation Island 135
terrorism 239
Tesco 92
test-tube babies 60, 71
Thailand 83
Thatcher, Margaret 41, 230
theme
  park xiii-xvi, 47, 287, 288
  pub 67
  restaurant 47
theory and practice 212–14
Theresa, Mother 167
'Third Way' 183
Thomas, Dylan 269
Thoreau, Henry David 166, 167
Thorne, Matt 140
Tiger Electronics 196
Tightwad Gazette, The 169
Tikkun magazine 253
Tikkun movement 253
time 161–2
Time 23, 45, 58
time and motion study 210–11
'time-bank' 56–8, 67, 71
Times, The 147, 228, 270
Titanic 267–8
TiVo 129, 269
Tochigi-ken, Japan xiv
Toffler, Alvin 168
Tolkien, J.R.R. 152–3, 154
Tomorrow's World 75, 76, 131, 153, 176
Toyota 170
Trading Places 134
tradition 20–1, 35, 43–4, 101–2, 261, 285, 293
Trafford Centre, Manchester 48
tranquillization 131
Travels in Hyper-Reality 291
Tree and Leaf 152
Trier, Lars von 141
Trench, The 134, 135
Tricon Global Restaurants 82
Truman Show, The 9, 171–2, 175, 265
Trumpton 139
Turing, Alan 197–8
Turing Test 197–8
Turn Off TV Week 28, 105
Turner, Lynn 218
Turner, Ted 177

Turning the Tables 134
TV21 259–60
Tyranny of Numbers, The 208
Tyson's Corner, Washington DC 138

Unabomber 281
Uncertainty Theorem 224
Uncommercial 105
underground 105, 112
Unilever 13
Uniqlo 47
United Kingdom (UK)
  advertising 42, 228
  agriculture 83, 90–1, 92, 93, 97–9
  alternative health 17
  debt 158
  depression 158
  devolution 243
  eating habits 76–9, 85, 88–90
  government targets 207–8, 214–16, 239–40
  inner-directed people 40, 41–2, 43
  schools 31, 214, 215, 217, 221
  shops 51, 92
  towns 139
  work 158, 161
United States of America (USA)
  advertising 11, 19, 28, 276–7
  agriculture 81–4, 88, 91, 94, 97, 98
  alternative health 17
  budget deficit 33
  children 30
  community associations 244–5
  consumer categories 42–3
  cosmetic surgery 23
  crime 182, 245
  debt 158
  eating habits 80–2, 88–9, 91
  Moral Majority 250
  politics 214, 231, 237, 241
  presidential elections 214, 234–5, 260
  schools 30–1, 80–1, 185, 217, 231
  shopping malls xiii, 51
  television 276–7
  towns 138
  work 158
Universal Studios 32, 288
Unplugged 109
Unwin, Raymond 62
Urban Task Force 20
Utilitarianism 209, 239
utopia 171
U-571 144

Vaury, Olivier 212
Velvet Revolution (1989) 256
Viagra 60, 67
Venturi, Robert 293
Vicious, Sid 108
Videocarte 30
video-conferencing 185
Vietnam War (1954–75) 215
Viewpoint 43
Vines, Rose 195
Vinterberg, Thomas 141
violence 7, 110, 116, 129, 158
Virgin 108, 163
Virginia Slims 288
virtual
  adverts 24
  banks 48–9
  communities 9, 180–3
  dating 185
  future xvi-xvii, xviii, 3–4, 7–8, 177–81, 198, 261
  holidays 159
  living 154–9
  management 17
  places 138–9
  shops 192–4
'virtual real' 59–72, 138, 139, 263
virtual reality 7, 67–72, 159
Vivendi 32
Vogel, Bobbi 10
Vogue 160
Voluntary Simplicity 166
voluntary simplicity 168–9
volunteering 57–8, 244–5
VPL Research 68
wabi-sabi tradition 287–91
Wailing Wall (Jerusalem) 3, 261
Wall Street Journal 225
Walmart 10, 51

Walters, Julie 123
Walz of Saxony 46
'War on Terrorism' 50
Washington Post 73, 138
Waterford Crystal 45
Waterford, Virginia 168
Watson, Paul 133
wealth 58, 274
Weir, Peter 171
Welch, Jack 12, 174, 192, 243
Welwyn Garden City, Hertfordshire 62
Whigs 167
Whitechapel Art Gallery 246
Whitney, John 172, 173
Whyte, David 172, 174
Wiener, Anthony J. 258
Wilde, Oscar 113
Wilkinson, Denny 24
Williams, Robbie 205
Wilson, Harold 260
Winfrey, Oprah 84, 270
Wired 4
women's movement 254
Woodstock II 107
Woodward, Helen 259
Wordsworth, William 104, 112, 113
work 158, 160–4, 171–5
  creativity at 172–4
working hours 158, 160, 161
World Bank 146
World Trade Centre, attack on (2002) *see* September 11 attacks
world views, clash of 278–82
Worldcom 264
Wu Wei Wu 154
Wurtzel, Elizabeth 189

Yahoo 18, 192
Year in Provence, A 100
Year 2000, The 258
You Only Live Twice xiii
Young & Rubicam 35, 267
Young Men's Hebrew Association, New York 160
Your Money or Your Life 169
youth culture 107–12, 116–22

Zeldin, Theodore 249, 294
zero tolerance 245
Ziegler 170
Zionism 254

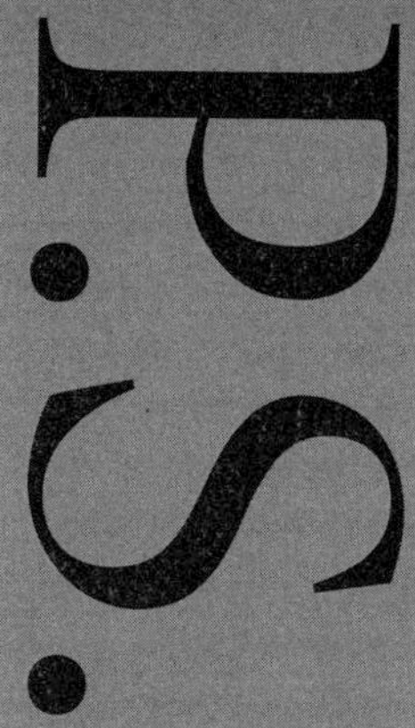

Ideas, interviews & features . . .

About the author

2 Meet the Author: Travis Elborough talks to David Boyle

4 Life at a Glance

7 Favourite Books/Writers

About the book

8 Ffff Fake

Read on

13 Have You Read?

15 If You Loved This, You Might Like . . .

16 Find Out More

Meet the Author

Travis Elborough talks to David Boyle

'THE WORD STALIN came up in one review,' says David Boyle, sounding genuinely, and understandably, perturbed. Boyle, bespectacled, softly spoken, founder of the London Time Bank, looks as unlikely an agent of totalitarianism as you could meet (but then, sadly, history confirms not dissimilar things were said about Uncle Joe). In the interests of authenticity this interview is being conducted face-to-face, though the background – the concrete South Bank Centre – is possibly a mite incongruous and the elderly no-brand-you've-ever-ever-heard-of tape recorder I've brought along does not entirely cut the mustard with Boyle. 'Shouldn't you be using shorthand?' he jokes as I set up the microphone and he loosens his yellow tie – Boyle is a Liberal Democrat, after all. A fact that a couple of critics tossed pejoratively into their reviews as if it were the journalistic equivalent of slamming down four aces. Stalin, though, does seem a little harsh. 'There was an interesting division about the reviews of this book: business magazines tended to like it, broadsheets were, to be honest, less favourable. Which wasn't the way round I'd expected. But I think for broadsheet book reviewers, steeped in the postmodern thing, any appeal to authenticity is seen as null and void. By appealing to it, some felt I was intending to impose it on other people. Whereas what I was trying to do was to track those saying we really want something else, or, at least, another option because we can see it disappearing.'

Boyle initially broached the topic of this 'something else', the real or the authentic, in the final chapter of his previous book, *The Tyranny of Numbers*. In the face of officialdom's mindless dedication to number crunching, he perceived 'a new longing for significance and complex truth, for poetry', and in response called for a 'Campaign for Real Wisdom'. When he began writing *Authenticity*, the discussions about the future and virtuality were raging with greater potency than now; the whole dotcom thing was then, along with microscooters and getting smashed on alcopops, still a newish phenomenon and not an embarrassing and best-forgotten memory. 'A lot of the virtual reality people I was attacking seem to have gone! Not that I had anything to do with it,' he laughs. In any case, the hobgoblin of globalization, the subsequent expansion of reality TV and the plague of celebrityitus only heightened the book's relevance. Equally significant, however, to its actual plane and germination was Matt Thorne and Nicholas Blincoe's iconoclastic literary anthology *All Hail the New Puritans*, of which Boyle speaks effusively. 'It was amazingly successful and it set me thinking about why we were constantly discussing what was real and what was not.' He doesn't see what he calls his New Realists, with their fondness for the organic and the unspun, as puritanical. 'That's a bit of a misnomer; I think it's about depth, I think it's about fun, I think it's about life in all its dimensions. What I didn't say in the book, and I should have done, was that ▶

'Authenticity is really all about being 3-D.'

BORN

1958, Paddington, London.

EDUCATION

Attended Clifton College, Bristol and read philosophy and theology at Trinity College, Oxford.

CAREER

After graduating became a reporter on a local newspaper in Oxford.
Editor of *Town & Country Planning* magazine.

***from* 1985**
First book published: *Building Futures*, about inner cities.
Worked for Rapide Productions making TV documentaries.

***from* 1991**
Went to New Zealand and discovered local currencies: completely inspired.
Self-employed writer: work included editing weekly newspaper, *Liberal Democrat News.*

Meet the Author *(continued)*

◀ authenticity is really all about being 3-D. It's about having real human experiences which are more than just surface. Real life is three-dimensional, McDonald's is not.'

Neither, obviously, are Pot Noodles, which came in for rather a drubbing throughout. 'Sorry, I just think they are disgusting. You can't say it's a meal, can you?' One of the criticisms levelled at Boyle has been that the authentic and the inauthentic simply boiled down to whatever it was he himself happened to like or dislike. 'I think there has to be an element of truth about that. If you get away from measurement you do end up with a very subjective view. That's the whole paradox of the book, because I am trying to get away from subjectivity and I think – this is a glimpse of what comes after postmodernism – find a way of holding on to something which is ourselves, measuring things by what is human. So I am aware that's a bit of a contradiction.'

That human reality is the only measure is, ostensibly, the book's mantra. But aren't technological advances essentially human – products of our imaginations and, therefore, part of human experience? 'That's a valid point, human beings invented them after all, but the problem is that the way we are confronted with technology, or marketing, means that it often only speaks to us and wants to engage with us as if there was just one little aspect, one dimension. I accept that they are human, in that they are human artefacts, but I mean "human" and "real" in very specific senses. And, I believe, we can recognize what's human and authentic in an instant. Take, for example, my friend with the flat in Paris that I wrote about. As soon as he said the shops were still real there, we all knew – immediately – what he meant, we didn't have to discuss it or measure it. And yet he was using "real" in a very specific way – ethical, local, etc. – that, probably, twenty years ago wouldn't have been understood.'

Chain stores and multinationals were, or certainly appeared, less pervasive then, but isn't there something snobbish about wanting these little shops, real food and hand-crafted goods? A whiff of the 'I'm more authentic than thou', an inner-directed version of keeping up with the Joneses? The New Realists seem slightly reminiscent of what Michael Thompson in *Rubbish Theory* referred to as the 'Knockers-Through', the gentrifying middle classes of the 1970s who set about gaily installing old fireplaces in their homes. 'There definitely can be an element of that. It's hard to unpack,' Boyle admits. 'I want to be pretty forgiving about it. People doing that kind of thing to their homes were trying to make something that was really theirs, and that seems authentic to me. What I would say against the keeping-up-with-the-Joneses idea is this: often when you talk to people who are clearly into this sort of thing, they believe – and Paul Ray in the book *Cultural Creatives* found this too – that they alone have such concerns. A lot of these people feel quite lonely – that the world is going the other way.'

Such reactions to the modern world could easily be dismissed as reactionary or nostalgic, but Boyle believes there's far ▶

LIFE *at a Glance*
(continued)

***from* 1996**
Winston Churchill scholarship to study local currencies in the USA.
Helped launch the time banks movement in the UK.
Became senior associate at the think tank, the New Economics Foundation – where he has been since, editing newspaper *Radical Economics.*
Funny Money published.

2001
Launched the London Time Bank network.
The Tyranny of Numbers published (*The Sum of our Discontent* in the US).
Stood in general election for Regent's Park and Kensington North (came third).

2003
Authenticity published

Currently working on a history book about Richard the Lionheart and his ransom.

FAMILY

Married to Sarah.
Son Robin born, July 2004.

Meet the Author *(continued)*

◀ more to this than sauntering down memory lane. 'I suppose it could be characterized as harking back to old-fashioned roots and communities, but I don't think this is a conservative book. I think it's simply looking for the real, looking to a future that's rooted in tradition and not floating in the way postmodern life can be.'

Of big business and marketing's attempts to meet, or co-opt, what he obviously sees as a growing demand for the 'real', Boyle is apologetically ambivalent. 'I do keep changing my mind on this. I think on one level it's definitely sinister and on another it means that we are winning, because it shows they are trying to meet what people want. Sometimes of course it's totally meaningless, like "the World's Local Bank" [the HSBC slogan]; sometimes they are genuinely trying to get close to what a real human experience might be. This is where I think the virtual real comes in. It's using virtual systems to deliver something that smacks of real experience.' Pressed on what has been dubbed the '*No Logo* logo' issue, multinational wolves hiding in ethical and indigenous sheep's clothing, he says it is 'completely invidious' but doubts in the end 'that people are fooled. You see, the big question for me is whether business as it's currently constituted can deliver anything authentic at all; I suspect it can't.'

Despite this scepticism, he remains fundamentally optimistic. 'You see, if there are enough people who feel this way – and there are – then business will fall into line. Because ultimately people get what they want in a market economy – OK, they don't get

‘Boyle believes there's far more to this than sauntering down memory lane.’

quite what they want – but they get close enough.' Boyle concedes, 'I am making predictions. I may be wrong. When it came to virtual reality, I found myself arguing with both ends of the spectrum. My gut feeling is that we very much want reality in the end. We may spend time in these virtual worlds but somehow reality keeps us sane.'

He seriously doubts that these distinctions will diminish even for a younger generation for whom virtual reality might, very possibly, be less troubling. 'When I wrote this, I did worry: is this just a middle-aged person's book? Maybe it is, but I actually think a yearning for the real is shared by people far younger than me, because they don't like to be taken for a ride – like the boy in the section on "cool". I don't think because they are familiar with "virtual reality" they will lose touch with reality, and in fact, they'll cling on to it all the more. They'll go and explore these virtual worlds – like this new one, Second Life, that people are apparently spending hours in – sure, but they'll know where home is.' ■

Favourite *Books/Writers*

1. **The New Confessions**
   William Boyd
2. **Possession**
   A. S. Byatt
3. **The Chymical Wedding**
   Lindsay Clarke
4. *James Hillman*
5. *Richard Holmes*
6. **Love in the Time of Cholera**
   Gabriel García Márquez
7. **Ulverton**
   Adam Thorpe
8. *Anne Tyler*
9. **The Heart Aroused**
   David Whyte
10. *Henry Williamson*

Most Admire
Vaclav Havel
William Morris ■

About the book

Ffff Fake

by Travis Elborough

‘SHE’S A PHONEY, but she’s a real phoney.’ Martin Balsam’s line in the film of Capote’s *Breakfast at Tiffany’s* neatly distils many of our anxieties about sifting the fake from the real in our joyfully post-postmodern world. As Boyle’s examples of a lip-synching Posh Spice’s lip ring and a soap star commentator on *Survivor* illustrate, we live in rather unreal times.

Fakery itself is hardly a new thing: Jacob donned Esau’s clothes and animal furs to snaffle Isaac’s blessing and, closer to home, the medieval City of London had pretty rigid penalties for sellers of counterfeit goods and banned the wearing of false beards. The verb ‘to forge’ had already gained its pejorative sense (in addition to its literal – ‘to make’) by the 1300s. The word ‘fake’ took until the nineteenth century, the first age of mass production, to make the transition from general no-good skulduggery – ‘to fake a man out’, was, according to Vaux’s 1812 *Vocabulary of Flash Language*, cant for killing a man – to a specific term for counterfeiting. There’s a nice theory that ‘phoney’, the buzz-word of post-war adolescent existentialism (first recorded in 1900), had its origins in the way people instinctively felt that telephone conversations were somehow false or unreal. Sadly, its more likely root is a con scam – a brass ring or ‘fawney’ would be passed off as gold to some unsuspecting ‘bacon’ – but technology *has* consistently shifted our understanding of fakery, introducing whole new avenues and methods for fakers and, conversely, new ways of detection too.

‘The word ‘fake’ took until the nineteenth century to make the transition from general no-good skulduggery to a specific term for counterfeiting.’

Like nostalgia, there's a keen sense that, with reproduction techniques currently so advanced that they simultaneously enhance the desire for 'scarce' originals and yet call into question our very preferences for them, fakery isn't quite what it used to be.

On the cusp of the millennium, the heyday of the virtual real, San Francisco's Terrain Gallery held an exhibition of works by the master forger of modern art, Elmyr de Hory. His biographer, Clifford Irving (himself later imprisoned for faking an autobiography by Howard Hughes), described de Hory as having 'the air of a slightly wicked forest elf'.

A dispossessed Hungarian aristocrat, de Hory ambled into a career of fakery in 1946 when a visitor to his impoverished rue Jacob studio mistook one of his drawings for a Picasso. For the next twenty years, a stream of de Hory Picassos, Monets, Matisses, Dufys, Chagalls and Légers ('I never did Miro . . . even the real Miros look like fakes', he informed Irving) found their way to collectors and galleries across the globe. Algur Hurtle Meadows, the Texan oil magnet, bought, unwittingly, over forty de Hory fakes. Harvard's Fogg Museum and the Japanese National Museum of Western Art in Tokyo were also among the duped. De Hory claimed to have produced over a thousand fakes; only 300, so far, have been identified. He was finally exposed in 1968, briefly imprisoned, and eventually committed suicide in 1976. There are, unsurprisingly, those who believe he faked ▶

‘De Hory ambled into a career of fakery in 1946 when a visitor to his impoverished rue Jacob studio mistook one of his drawings for a Picasso.’

Ffff Fake *(continued)*

◀ his death. Such is his cachet (de Hory and Irving both starred in Orson Welles's late masterpiece, *F for Fake*) that genuine de Hory fakes – and he has numerous imitators – go for around $20,000. De Hory was a phoney, but a real phoney. Virtual real, maybe, to use Boyle's phrase.

Hand-crafted art forgery looks quaint, old-fashioned, dare I say, authentic. It still goes on, naturally; fakers, ever creatures of the market, have always sought to replicate what was 'authentic' in the traditional, exclusive sense. However, we usually seem to get the fakes we deserve (relics, old masters, Piltdown Man, new masters, Nessie, Hitler diaries, Paul Daniels's death . . . etc., etc.) and, in our brand-conscious society, commercial counterfeiting has increased exponentially since the 1990s. In February 2004, customs officers at the port of Felixstowe seized fake Louis Vuitton, Gucci and Prada goods of a retail value of more than £750,000. The Anti-Counterfeiting Group estimates that up to 11 per cent of clothing and footwear now in circulation could be fake. (The propensity to buy counterfeit clothing and footwear in the UK is, according to the ACG's 2003 survey, starkly regional. Forty per cent of people in the West Midlands would knowingly purchase fake clothing and footwear, compared to only 18 per cent of keeping-it-real Londoners.)

‘The Anti-Counterfeiting Group estimates that up to 11 per cent of clothing and footwear now in circulation could be fake.’

It's doubtful that anyone buying, say, a knock-off Louis Vuitton bag for ten quid from a 'stall' on Chapel Market or by the Bull Ring thinks they are buying the 'real thing', although technology makes such fakes increasingly convincing. A trading standards officer for Leicester City Council, interviewed about the phenomenon in the *Observer* in November 2000, confessed that the quality of embroidery and labelling on some fakes was so good they had to bring clothing experts along on raids to determine if they were real or not. In the same piece, an unnamed fashion editor swathed her own, fake, Louis Vuitton bag in a protective layer of knowing irony: 'It's fun carrying a fake bag. More fool the person who thinks it's a real label. I think there's a smugness about people who only want the real thing.' But, in any case, the fake still confers value on the real by acknowledging the original item as a powerful symbol of status, wealth and/or discernment. (A profusion of fakes can, of course, devalue the exclusivity of the original, causing the value of both real and copy to plummet. I suspect that it didn't take very long for the editor's 'Vuitton' bag to find a new home in the local Help the Aged shop.)

Brands arose as symbols of quality in the fallout from industrialization, when factory products squared up to local wares. Today, brands strive, through increasingly nefarious and successful means, to ensure that at least the illusion of quality is sustained. But, as Boyle has pointed out, if something like a Ralph Lauren polo shirt and a fake Ralph Lauren polo shirt are made in similar Bangladeshi garment factories, and to similar standards, then labels start to look, well, fake. As a consequence the urge to fake them could, arguably, also diminish. Not that this has followed for de Hory's paintings, ▶

'The fake still confers value on the real by acknowledging the original item as a powerful symbol of status, wealth and/or discernment.'

Ffff Fake *(continued)*

◀ and the sceptical (the unnamed fashion editor for one, perhaps) may be inclined toward Donald Barthelme's remark, 'all there is, is trash, we just learn how to dig it'. Yeah, baby.

Well, maybe not. Coca-Cola's recent fiasco over Dasani bottled water sold in the UK only serves to hint that Boyle's observation that 'authenticity is going to take an increasingly strong grip on the way we live our lives' is correct. The soft drinks giant has spent close to a century trading on the authenticity of its product. It is notoriously secretive about its recipes and protective of its trademarks. Consumers have been asked to '*Demand the genuine*' since 1912; the drink became *The Real Thing* in 1970. (Oh for 1886's pleasingly authoritarian '*Drink Coca-Cola*'.) And what could be better than The Real Thing? Certainly not *New Coke*, the company's disastrous foray into tampering with the 'original' formula, launched in 1985. Dasani, ironically like New Coke, was created in response to a perceived change in attitudes. In the mid-1980s the company was losing market share to the sweeter-tasting Pepsi. By 2004 the threat came from bottled water and 'healthier' fruit drinks, a symbol surely of a growing thirst for *the real* as Boyle defines it. But, as failures in authenticity go, selling treated Kent tap water containing illegal levels of bromate as 'pure' will take some beating. ■

‘Consumers have been asked to '*Demand the genuine*' since 1912; the drink became *The Real Thing* in 1970.’

Have You Read?

Other titles by David Boyle

The Tyranny of Numbers: Why Counting Can't Make Us Happy (2001)
Never before have we been so inundated with statistics, targets and league tables. This timely and passionately argued book examines our obsession with numbers. Are we drowning in numbers? Do our sums add up? And could we be in danger of neglecting the incalculable – creativity, intuition, imagination . . . happiness?

'A great antidote to cynicism, and a sharply witty reminder of what is important in life'
Independent

'I disagree with David Boyle's premise, deplored his conclusions, and enjoyed *The Tyranny of Numbers* immensely'
Management Today

Funny Money: In Search of Alternative Cash (1999)
Money is now just blips on computer screens: the days when you knew where you were with those chunky coins have gone for good. Its value can disappear overnight; it pops up unexpectedly in the form of credit or pseudo-money like Air Miles or supermarket affinity cards. In *Funny Money* Boyle journeys to discover the people who are creating an alternative to bank-based cash and turning all our ideas about money upside-down. ▶

Have You Read? *(continued)*

◀ ***The Little Money Book*** (2003)
Ever thought about what happens to bank notes after they've left circulation? How the IMF works? Or simply why we conjured up the damned enslaving stuff in the first place? This svelte, easy-to-read guide illuminates things fiscal.

Edited by David Boyle

The Money Changers: Currency Reform from Aristotle to E-cash (2003)
A fascinating and wide-ranging collection of historical and contemporary pieces all about the nature of money, ranging from the likes of Marco Polo, Francis Bacon, Daniel Defoe and Abraham Lincoln to Henry Ford, John Maynard Keynes and George Soros.

'Boyle's fascinating book collates a range of key economic thinkers' arguments, from the historical to the present day, and analyses their work in a unique discourse' *Ecologist*

'Lively and illuminating' *Future Survey*

Also by DAVID BOYLE

Alternative Identities, Alternative Currencies (1999)

World War II: A photographic history (1997)

What is New Economics? (1993)

Building Futures: A layman's guide to the inner-city debate (1989) ■

If You Loved This, You Might Like . . .

No Logo
Naomi Klein
Klein's dissection of the invidious power of brands needs little by way of introduction – quite simply the bible of the anti-corporate movement and a notable influence on Boyle too.

Jihad vs. McWorld: How Globalism and Tribalism Are Reshaping the World
Benjamin Barber
In the face of the twin forces of consumerist capitalism and religious fundamentalism, Barber's book makes a spirited case for reclaiming democracy by reviving local, voluntary institutions.

Authentic: How to Make a Living by Being Yourself
Neil Crofts
A life-laundry guide for those striving to find a way to square that work/personal balance and reach a more authentic existence.

Fast Food Nation
Eric Schlosser
This shocking exposé of the fast-food industry is enough to make even ravenous carnivores think twice before ordering a hamburger.

The Politics of Meaning
Michael Lerner
A thoughtful examination of discontent in American politics. Lerner calls for a ▶

FIND OUT MORE

www.david-boyle.co.uk
The author's site, with information on his books, articles, speeches and poems.

www. cyborgmanifesto.org
Man and machine in perfect harmony? On this site the Cyborg Manifesto spells out a vision of a post-human world.

www.adbusters.org
Adbusters' site offers plenty of information about their subversive Culture Jamming campaigns.

www.advanced.org/jaron/
Virtual reality guru Jaron Lanier's homepage

www.authenticbusiness.co.uk
A website devoted to 'authenticity' in business

www.farmersmarkets.net
National Association of Farmers' Markets

www.ilsr.org
Institute for Local Self-Reliance

www.neweconomics.org
New Economics Foundation site, of which Boyle is a senior associate

www.paecon.net
Post-Autistic Economics webpage

www.slowfood.com
The Slow Food movement's website

If You Loved This *(continued)*

◄ 'politics of meaning' in which faith is restored through decentralization, and democratic grassroots institutions are explored in the chapter on Real Politics.

The Cultural Creatives: How 50 million People Are Changing the World
Paul H. Ray and Sherry Ruth Anderson
Ray and Anderson's study, cited by Boyle, looks at a growing social group in American society – the Cultural Creatives. Like the New Realists, they value social justice and personal fulfilment over material wealth and traditional social status.

High Tech/High Touch: Technology and Our Accelerated Search for Meaning
John Naisbitt
Naisbitt, author of the groundbreaking 1980s social analysis *Megatrends*, turns to the wired world and prescribes a return to the human and the simple to escape what he sees as an intoxication with dehumanizing technology – all themes germane to Boyle.

The Resurgence of the Real
Charlene Spretnak
Spretnak, a postmodern ecologist, argues it's high time we gave up unquestioning scientism and recognized the human connection to nature and the environment.

In Praise of Slow: How a Worldwide Movement is Challenging the Cult of Speed
Carl Honore
Don't hurry, be happy. ■